1992

Children at Risk in America

SUNY Series, Youth Social Services,
Schooling, and Public Policy
Barry M. Franklin and José R. Rosario, Editors

Children at Risk in America

History, Concepts, and Public Policy

Roberta Wollons,
Editor

STATE UNIVERSITY OF NEW YORK PRESS

Published by
State University of New York Press, Albany

For information, address State University of New York
Press, State University Plaza, Albany, N.Y., 12246

Production by E. Moore
Marketing by Fran Keneston

Library of Congress Cataloging-in-Publication Data

Children at risk in America : history, concepts, and public policy /
    Roberta Wollons, editor.
        p.   cm. — (SUNY series, youth social services, schooling, and
    public policy)
        Includes bibliographical references and index.
        ISBN 0-7914-1197-4. — ISBN 0-7914-1198-2 (pbk.)
        1. Child welfare—United States. 2. Children—Government policy-
    -United States. 3. Public schools—United States. I. Wollons,
    Roberta Lyn, 1947-   . II. Series.
    HV741.C536138 1993
    362.7'0973—dc20   91-38871
                                                                      CIP

10 9 8 7 6 5 4 3 2 1

Contents

Part III
Contemporary Public Discourse

Acknowledgments

This volume of essays began as a private three-day conference on public policy and child risk, developed at the request of Darwin Stapleton, director of the Rockefeller Archive Center in Tarrytown, New York, in May 1988. Combining his interest in the philanthropic work of the Rockefeller foundations and my interest in the history of ideas about childhood, we organized the conference as an opportunity for scholars and practitioners who work with children considered to be "at risk." The purpose was to present new research and discuss the problems associated with developing cohesive national child-care policies. The outcome of that conference is represented in the twelve essays that appear in this volume.

My deep appreciation goes to the staff of the Rockefeller Archive Center, especially Darwin Stapleton and Ken Rose, who coordinated the conference and created an environment conducive to serious and pleasurable dialogue at The Rockefeller University Center at Seven Springs, New York. I would also like to thank the seventeen presenters and the eight commentators who participated in that conference. Fourteen of the presenters are represented in this volume and have since given patiently of their time in revising their essays and preparing for the publication of the volume. Each lent his or her expertise in the form of the original research presented here and to rich discussions of historical and current child-care policies. The other participants included Steve Antler, Ira Burnim, Robert Cairns, Barbara Finkelstein, Elizabeth Lomax, Mary Mahowald, Margaret McHugh, Jonathan Moreno, Mike Piraino, Barbara Starfield, and Ruth Striegel-Moore. They too brought to the conference discussions a wealth of insightful critiques and intense concern for the well-being of children in the United States.

Funding for the conference came from the generous support of the Rockefeller Archive Center, the Rockefeller Family Foundation, the Brothers Fund, and the Hazen Foundation. Further support for editing the volume came from the Charles Reilley Armington Foundation at Case Western Reserve University.

I want to thank Priscilla Ross, the editor at SUNY Press who has given her unfailing support and patience to the development of the volume, and to Barry Franklin and Jose Rosario, the series editors, who enthusiastically chose this volume to introduce a new series, "Youth, Social Services, Schooling, and Public Policy." Finally, Michelle Fine, Barbara Finkelstein, and Maris Vinovskis contributed invaluable assistance in the planning of the volume.

The people associated with this volume deserve credit and appreciation for the contributions they have made to furthering our understanding of the status of children and our abilities to assist them. However, full responsibility for any errors or inadequacies in the volume is mine.

ROBERTA WOLLONS

Introduction

When journalist Ellen Key declared this to be the "Century of the Child" in 1909, she was hopeful that by the end of the century we would no longer have to fear for the well-being of America's children.[1] Recognition of the problems, cooperative efforts, and understanding of children's special needs, she believed, would certainly lead to solutions. Today, however, at the close of the century, contemporary journalists join with educators, health care professionals, psychologists, government officials, and researchers in a charged language that defines our children as still being "at risk." The term itself declares urgency, demands action, and signals failure. Moreover, the risks implied are not only to the children, but to the future of a healthy, competitive society. Unlike times past, the language of risk today is an indictment not of children's moral failure, but rather of the social institutions that fail children: the family, the schools, and the government.

The intention of this collection of essays is to address twentieth-century historical and contemporary issues regarding children who are considered to be at risk. The essays explore the language of risk as it is used by the courts, the schools, governmental agencies, and child advocates, those who discover risks and create correctives for children who both need protection and threaten to disturb the social order. To do so requires an exploration of differing, often contradictory, concepts of the child and society that are embedded in public policy debates. Deepening the complexity of the problems, institutions to which we look for solutions are too often faced with conflicts that arise when the needs of the child are at variance with the needs of the institutions themselves. These dilemmas are central to this volume and to understanding our failure to achieve adequate public policy solutions for children at risk.

Conceptions of childhood throughout American history have conformed to a matrix of interconnected goals, values, and institutions that form society.[2] Although the use of the concept of risk to define children's status is a twentieth-century practice, nonetheless fears for children's well-being, and efforts to save children when parents have failed or are absent, are evident in past centuries. Moreover, the notions of what dangers might compromise a child's well-being have changed dramatically over time.

In the colonial period, the task of society regarding children was to insure their salvation, usually through baptism or conversion.[3] Puritans considered children to be depraved from birth, and the child at risk was one who might not ultimately find a home with God. While risks to children's health were high, control over a child's health was minimal, making salvation an even greater imperative.[4] Insuring salvation was the responsibility of the parents; fathers, as a matter of law and custom, had absolute authority over the child and were responsible for instilling discipline, obedience, and self-denial in the child, all essential to a child's ultimate salvation. Reinforced in the tracts and sermons of religious leaders, the authority for childrearing practices and definitions of social and religious goals came from the church, and responsibility lay squarely with the parents. However, when parents failed, the consequences were both religious and civil.[5] As early as 1648, according to historian Ross Beales, heads of New England families were required by law to catechize their children once a week.[6] In the 1670s, the Massachusetts General Court appointed "tithingmen," each overseeing ten or twelve households, whose duty it was to ensure domestic harmony and be sure that parents properly disciplined unruly children.

Beyond parental training, children were expected to learn and obey a host of moral lessons. When discipline failed, children became responsible for their own behavior. Although "stubborn child" laws, enacted in Massachusetts in 1646, threatened disobedient children with the death penalty, in fact willful children were bound out as apprentices, and parents of boys over sixteen could turn to the courts to compel obedience in their children.[7]

In the Chesapeake, where the parental mortality rate was

higher than in New England, children who were orphaned became members of extended or step families, "rooting the parentless child within the society."[8] Moreover, the fear of early death often prompted fathers to ensure their son's well-being by deeding cattle and appointing trustees to oversee that the sons received the cattle at marriage or majority.[9] Legal mechanisms protected these children and their property, and, signaling consensus about the need for children's financial protection, historians Darrett and Anita Rutman found relatively few unscrupulous guardians or stepparents.[10]

In the tightly woven New England communities, the family was the basic political, economic, and religious unit, with the family deeply embedded in public life. Moreover, family responsibilities extended to the care of orphans, invalids, and the elderly. The family and the church, the principal institutions taking formal responsibility for children, shared a common set of values regarding social order and religious salvation and a common language for defining and controlling deviance.

Still, the greatest risks to children in the seventeenth and eighteenth centuries were childbirth and disease. Historian John Demos estimates that 25 percent of all children born in seventeenth-century Plymouth died during the first decade of life; and epidemics of smallpox, diphtheria, whooping cough, measles, and mumps that swept North America in the first half of the eighteenth century "doubled and tripled" the normal average of thirty deaths per one thousand born in Boston during those years.[11]

By the middle of the eighteenth century, a variety of public charitable institutions began to reproduce traditional family responsibilities. Most visible in the complex commercial centers of the Atlantic seaboard, cities built almshouses to offset the cost of caring for widows, orphans, and the poor and mentally ill. Free schools and common pay schools began to replace the educational function of families, and workshops increasingly substituted for families in the apprenticeship of youth. Among civic leaders, revolutionary ideas about individualism and secularism permeated the language of public policy discourse over expectations for the youth, and therein the future, of the nation. For adolescents, the end of the century witnessed an upsurge in premarital pregnancy and weakening of the traditional parental control over young men and women. Moreover, rising educational standards coincided with an expansion of choices available to youths, prolonging economic dependency.

Slave children were of course threatened by the risks attendant upon their status. In this period, the slave trade was at its peak. According to historian Alan Kulikoff, of the 550,00 Africans forcibly brought into the colonies, 60 percent arrived between 1720 and 1780.[12] Malnutrition, poorer health, separation from parents, and demands for work contributed to higher death rates and less protection for these children.

By the end of the eighteenth century, attitudes about strict discipline were softening, less punitive, and more nurturing. Concepts of individual rights that permeated the political landscape were reflected in greater respect for the individuality of the child and in the language of childrearing. Even before the revolution, the language of family governance changed from that of discipline and authority to that of government and laws.[13] The goals for children were shifting from salvation to citizenship, and concern for children's religious life expanded to include education and health.[14] Family law, however, did not change much during this century. The father retained absolute authority over the person and property of the child, with the exception of the poor laws.[15] For example, following the Act of 1735 until the end of the century, half of Boston's eleven hundred poor children between the ages of five and nine were "bound out," boys to learn a trade and girls to domestic service. During this period, too, children could be separated from their parents and forced to work, or grandparents could be compelled to support them when their parents were incapable of doing so.[16]

In the case of orphans, a "reasonably effective mechanism" developed from Orphans Court to protect property and create a method of adoption, even though no common or statute law provided for the assignment of parents.[17] Through the practice of apprenticeship or indenture, parents could petition the General Court for permission to change a child's name and transfer inheritance to a child "created" in this way.

At the opening of the nineteenth century, goals for the child came to reflect the goals of the new nation: republican citizenship, secular governance, and work.[18] Although Christian moral goals continued to form the basis of children's education, social control and secular order were taking on equivalent importance. A growing number of larger, less intimate towns were straining to accommodate rapid population growth from increasing numbers of foreign immigrants and domestic southern and rural migrants. The exigencies of industrial labor and poverty shifted responsibility for orphaned or delinquent children away from families with inadequate resources to public and private institutions, to schools, and to courts. Illegitimate births, for example, led mothers in increasing numbers to abandon their infants to the care of private almshouses, churches, and convents rather than to relatives. Public discourse increased to define and ameliorate problems and to find the means to intervene on behalf of other people's children.

The Civil War, an unfortunate watershed for children, left thousands of children with one or no parents, in numbers that almshouses could not accommodate. Public outcry against incarcerating children in public poorhouses with the adult insane, vagrants, drunks, and prostitutes led, albeit slowly, to an increase in orphanages and to policies of fostering out children to families. This recognition of the special needs of children was accompanied by experiments with industrial schools, lodging homes for working youth, and foundling hospitals for abandoned infants. Attempting to house child criminals orphaned and impoverished by the loss of parents, reformatories became vastly overcrowded. Postwar inflation added to the stress on these publicly funded institutions, making contract labor inside the reformatories appealing to hard-pressed directors. These practices continued into the 1890s, when child labor laws led to their abolition.

The Civil War also created new classes of black and female juvenile delinquents. Reformatories during this period were segregated both by sex and by race. Girls were customarily incarcerated in single-sex institutions not for the petty larcenies usually associated with boys, but for precocious sexual behavior, a crime with which boys were virtually never charged.[19] Moreover, few institutions admitted newly emancipated black youths at all, and those that did kept them strictly segregated. Nineteenth-century reformers expressed little concern with preventing the exposure of black children to the influences of adult criminals. Most black youths charged with crimes were locked up with adult criminals.

Linking juvenile crime with immigration, heredity, poverty, and urbanization, late-nineteenth-century reformers began to distinguish between the dependent and the delinquent. These distinctions were, however, often based more on ethnicity and class than on children's behavior. Urban reformers feared the congestion and urban disorder associated with rapid migrations to the cities of blacks from the South and poor Catholic and Jewish immigrants from Europe, and sought to control rather than assist those groups of children born of 'inferior" stock. Social Darwinists and hereditarians linked crime and school failure with the foreign born and black and turned to local governments for the solutions that would shield the community against their disruptive and unsavory influences. By the end of the century, juvenile crime was considered to be the concern of the government, with most reformatories supported by public funds. Child poverty, however, an idea more sympathetically applied to white native-born children and to children within ethnic groups, required protection from the impersonal and dangerous cities. Organized assistance remained outside the public sphere, with most orphanages supported by private charitable organizations or religious groups taking care of their own.[20] The Children's Aid Society, for example, proved to be a model of such child welfare efforts. Founded in 1853 by Yale-trained minister Charles Loring Brace, the Children's Aid Society sought to save the needy homeless children of New York by placing them in foster care, lodging houses, and industrial schools.[21] Others followed this pioneering agency in efforts to protect the child from impersonal and crowded institutions, negligent parents, and urban dangers.

Often linked with the decline in rural craft and farming culture and the rise of commercial life, responsibility for children in the nineteenth century shifted from the father to the mother, both legally and in terms of education and socialization. Child custody laws came to favor the mother during a child's "tender years," and courts took on parental responsibilities when both parents failed their children.[22] In addition, the complex process associated with the rise of common schooling increased the participation of women both as educators in the homes and as teachers. The idea of mother as nurturer both elevated the responsibilities of women in the home and increased their culpability for children's failures.

By the end of the nineteenth century, several dramatic shifts had occurred to reorient children's place in society. Fundamental in its significance, the school became the most pervasive public institution for socialization and control over the lives of children. An almost universal institution, reinforced by restrictive child labor laws, schools constituted irrevocably and increasingly a substitution for former environments of work. Thus, as the primary workplace for children, schools became entrenched as the common mediators through which the problems of risk were negotiated. Although the local authorities of family and church did not disappear, control became a shared and often contested enterprise with the schools.[23]

Further, in the eyes of child advocates, children's moral failures shifted from an emphasis on personal character flaws to being the result of negative environmental and genetic influences. Moralistic children's literature of the nineteenth century gave way to social scientists' analyses of parental, neighborhood, and socioeconomic factors, thereby shifting responsibility away from the child and onto the community and its institutions.[24]

Finally, by the end of the nineteenth century, the categories of risk were elaborated in conformity with new theories of child development.[25] Moreover, laws such as those limiting child labor, establishing compulsory schooling, and defining juvenile crimes combined to segregate children as a unique class of people with special needs for protection and guidance.

Broadly drawn, the goals for American children have changed from the intense colonial religious need for salvation, with the church in authority, to the nineteenth-century need for order and citizenship, controlled by private philanthropy in local communities, to the twentieth-century belief in individual development, with law, science, and government as the arbiters.

Along with these differences, the twentieth century brought new language and nuance to older, well-established concepts of the child. Armed with the new vocabulary of science and psychology, and the weight of truth associated with scientific research, reformers joined with social scientists to reinforce the values of social order, Christian morality, nativism, and racism in defining which children were at risk and which children were causing risk to society. In all times, protective policies toward children, whether private or public, have been heartfelt attempts to reconcile the conflicting values of parental responsibility and authority, the well-being of children, and the preservation of social order defined by the institutions designed to promote that order.

This volume surveys twentieth-century public policy toward children at risk as revealed in the language of public policy debates waged within the schools, the courts, and private agencies in their efforts to define which children need protection and which children threaten the unspoken but powerful matrix of established social goals. The three sections review the conceptualization of children historically, analyze the nature of dialogue among interested parties, and present a selection of contemporary public issues. Taken together, the essays look at a cross-section of risks, the institutions and authorities who take on the responsibilities for intervention, the language used to define risk, and mechanisms, objects, and goals of intervention. Although the essays do not address all risks associated with all children, they do offer ways for the reader to analyze public debate and the frequently contested goals of public policy decisions.

The first part of this volume, "Historical Public Discourse," reviews the development of public policies toward children as conceived by twentieth-century reformers, by the courts, and by the schools. The essays provide an overview of child-saving patterns in the twentieth century; a review of the history of the juvenile court system's definitions of offenders; and the history of public school policy in the service of classroom order. In each case, definitions of risk were as important as the solutions themselves, and each author explores how language and labeling were used to identify treatment while only selectively affecting the behavior or circumstances of the child.

Hamilton Cravens, in his paper "Child Saving in Modern America 1870s-1990s," presents three broad eras that have framed notions of the child in the twentieth century, showing how the social construction of the child has been malleable over time. His work suggests that there has been a change from an emphasis on conformity and adjustment, witnessed by the building of child-saving institutions in the early part of the century, to the rise of individual child rights, accompanied by the deinstitutionalization of children.[26] For Cravens, these changes have influenced not only how the child is viewed in society, but also the goals and methods of reform.

Using the example of Los Angeles, Steven Schlossman and Susan Turner, in chapter 2, "Status Offenders, Criminal Offenders, and Children 'at Risk' in Early Twentieth-Century Juvenile Court," examine the juvenile court, one of the primary twentieth-century institutions developed to address the needs of children classified as delinquent. These included both criminals and blameless "status offenders," children whose behavior is criminal only by virtue of their age. They chronicle the rise of the juvenile court at the turn of the century as a child-saving institution and the later movement to decriminalize status offenses in the 1970s. Schlossman and Turner's data suggest a shift from the ideal of trusting institutions to protect society from the deviant child, to protecting the child from oppressive institutions. The process was achieved by relabeling the offense rather than changing the behavior of the child. Supporting Cravens's categories, Schlossman and Turner's study finds that in the 1930s the court sought the adjustment of the child to a standard for the normal. Moreover, they reveal court bias in terms of gender-appropriate behavior, and the gender division of crime and punishment.

In "Structuring Risks: The Making of Urban School Order," Joseph Tropea shows how compulsory schooling laws brought children into the schools, saving them from child labor and the streets. Underlying schools' undisputed educative purposes was the development of schools' role as the major agencies of social reform. At the turn of the century, schools began practices whose purpose was to preserve order within the institution rather than provide direct aid or assistance to "problem" children. As were the courts, the schools were little concerned with ameliorating the cause of the problems, nor was a distinction made between behavioral and learning problems. In a highly textured array of data, Tropea probes beyond school policy and rhetoric to find the underlying attitudes toward children at risk for failure within the school system. Also supporting Cravens's periodization of the years 1920-40 as one of adjustment, Tropea argues that schools used adjustment language to segregate and control the school population during the depression. Even when the rhetoric changed in the 1960s to support policies of meeting the individual needs of students, relabeling the problem child served the interests of school order rather than offered individual assistance. The rhetoric changed, but the practices remained effectively the same. Interrelating schooling, work, delinquency, and the need for school order, Tropea spans the century to argue that order has been the primary goal of schools, taking precedence over pedagogical integrity or the needs of the individual child.

The second part of this volume, "Reconceptualizing Children at Risk," directly addresses the complex conceptualizations of risk in three areas: in the schools, in the courts, and among social scientists. Public discourse, in Cravens's terms, represents the collectively agreed-upon ideas that can be found in every historical era. While debates may surface over solutions, the conception of the child is often an agreed-upon idea. Nevertheless, by looking closely at the debates over the definitions of the problem, we see how competing social goals and attitudes are translated into conflicted policy rhetoric.

Following upon Tropea's analysis of dropouts, Michelle Fine in "Making Controversy: Who's 'At Risk'?" looks at the ideological debates that surround children at risk in the schools, focusing again on the language of the debates and the policies that flow, and do not flow, from the definitions of both the problem and a narrow range of solutions. Fine analyzes the dropout problem as it is manifest in public discourse, forcing out of the debates the issues that are controversial and those that remain subjugated by exclusion from the discourse. She looks at the complexities of measurement, intervention, promotion, and retention, and discipline. Reflecting on the recent deinstitutionalization movement and the history of schools' conflicts over dropouts, Fine analyzes the current debate, suggesting that the language of students' rights to drop out recasts the issue as a benefit, rather than a detriment, to the child, thereby relieving the institution of responsibility. She also points out the conflict between the policymakers and the child advocates.

Michael Grossberg, in his essay "Children's Legal Rights: A Historical Look at a Legal Paradox," looks also at the language of rights that has obscured the role of the courts and confused questions of social responsibility. As with Fine's and Tropea's papers, Grossberg, too, looks beyond empirical studies to find the meanings in language and definitions that result in public policy toward children. The language of children's rights has dominated this decade's discourse regarding many social ills, particularly with regard to education, poverty, and protection, but it is especially apparent in the law. As Grossberg points out, children are dependent both on their parents and on the state; however, says Grossberg, "rights have become so wedded to our notions of individual entitlement and protection that denying children rights has also seemed to make them even more defenseless," thus creating the paradox of children's rights. Moreover, the nineteenth-century ideological commitment to the private/public distinction clouded direct discussion of children's policies behind the rhetoric of the proper role of the state in family life. The law created a dual system of family law, one for middle-class families and another for lower-class families and racial and ethnic groups.

The Progressive Era, roughly the 1880s to 1920s, produced a host of new regulations, each adding to the definitions of risk and, according to Grossberg, "premised on the assumption that public regulation of childrearing had to be expanded." The law mandated cultural homogeneity in the home. As Tropea looks at the impact of compulsory schooling laws on the schools, Grossberg looks at the intersection among the courts, the prohibition of child labor, and compulsory school laws. Each act expressed the assumption that childhood should be prolonged by keeping children within their families. The result was to lengthen and strengthen children's dependence on adults and to legally remove the young from the marketplace. Grossberg emphasizes the change from custody in the Progressive period to liberty in the last few decades.

Margo Horn, in "Inventing the Problem Child: 'At Risk' Children in the Child Guidance Movement of the 1920s and 1930s," focusing on private philanthropic efforts, uses definitions of risk to see how some children were included, and others excluded, from institutional help. She turns her attention to the efforts of private-sector professionals in identifying and formulating services for children at risk. Horn's research directly addresses the period Cravens describes as one of "adjustment." Looking at the programs initiated by the Commonwealth Fund in the 1920s and 1930s, Horn argues that the designers of the child guidance movement began with the expectation of solving the delinquency problems of poor youth living in urban slums but soon redefined the at-risk population so as to serve native-born middle-class children with "mild behavioral and emotional problems, within the confines of clinic offices." By focusing attention on middle-class families, Horn suggests that the child guidance practitioners neglected the children whose needs seemed intractable, preferring the children of the middle class with whom they could show success. Redefining risk in this way both created professional opportunities and increased the legitimacy of the newly developing fields of psychology, psychiatry, and social work.

The third part of this volume, "Contemporary Public Discourse," addresses six public environments in which conflicts over policies are debated. In the first paper, "Children at Risk: Students in Special Education," Alan Gartner and Dorothy Kerzner Lipsky look at the educational effects of labeling and relabeling students and the laws and fiscal constraints that burden the schools. As do the essays that follow theirs in this part, Gartner and Lipsky introduce specific policy recommendations.

Patricia Gandara's "Language and Ethnicity as Factors in School Failure: The Case of Mexican-Americans" is a study of the multiple factors that contribute to school failure for these children. Identifying poor language abilities as the problem, she argues, obscures the more difficult issues that have to do with discrimination, strong Hispanic family and community culture, and confinement to marginal economic opportunities. Moreover, Hispanics, because of their long existence in the United States, cannot escape a history of stereotyping and negative associations.

P. Lindsay Chase-Lansdale and Maris A. Vinovskis, "Adolescent Pregnancy and Child Support," along with Robert T. Lerman, "Reversing the Poverty Cycle with Job-Based Education," address the question of children in poverty, the group who are currently at the heart of public concern. Chase-Lansdale and Vinovskis's paper extends the analysis of public policy discussions in the area of teen pregnancy. Arguing that seemingly separate policy issues are in fact closely linked, they suggest that paternal involvement in teen parenthood should be encouraged, to relieve the rise in child poverty and increase the emotional health of the child.

Building on the idea of more effective enforcement of paternal support, Lerman suggests ways to improve the employment chances of young men in poverty categories. In Lerman's view, apprenticeships are comparable to internships in the academic professions, such as medicine, law, and management, and should be an integral step in job training. Related to the father's side of Chase-Lansdale and Vinovskis's advocacy of paternal support for out-of-wedlock children, Lerman advances an analysis of the fear held by young black women that they will not be able to find employable black men and that of young black men who have little hope that they will rise out of poverty.

Presenting another important aspect of the question of

parental responsibility and the risks to children of working parents, Judy Auerbach, in her essay "Public Policy and Child Care: The Question of Quality," carefully analyzes the various sides of the debate over federal child-care policy and the concerns that underlie each position. In the 1990s, Auerbach suggests, consensus has come to favor federal support of child care. As the female labor force has increased to include most mothers with preschool-age children, child care has come to be a public, rather than purely private, concern. Auerbach cautions, however, that the rationale favoring public support is based on the uncomfortable argument that children represent the economic future of the nation, rather than on their immediate needs as children.

The last essay, "Public Policy and Child Protection," is a contribution by James Garbarino, longtime child advocate in the field of child neglect and abuse. Garbarino also approaches the discourse over children from the point of view of policy. He points out the practical difficulties of reconciling policy with practice, and the conflicting underlying assumptions that inform both. Raising minimal standards of risk, he suggests, creates a gap in compliance and exaggerates the dilemmas of individual liberty versus social responsibility.

The essays as a whole intend to focus attention on how language has been used in the formation of public policy, as an historical as well as a contemporary process; the importance of understanding underlying attitudes toward the place of the child in society and the distribution of responsibility for child welfare; and the tension between fears and expectations for the society as a whole and support for the individuality and protection of the child. *Risk* as a generic term both raises the anxiety of the nation and masks the complexities that impede the formation of a national consensus and viable public policy solutions. The papers that follow explore the subjective meanings of *risk* and the debates and policies that have resulted from them. Over time, the process of discovering new problems has resulted in a patchwork of often conflicting institutional responses to child risk. Most significantly, the essays suggest that the concept of risk is a social construct that has changed over time, at various times including some children while ignoring others, always reflecting our nation's level of tolerance for criminal deviance, school failure, parental neglect, and the effects of poverty on children.

NOTES

1. Ellen Key, *The Century of the Child* (New York: G. P.Putnam, 1909).

2. Philippe Aries, *Centuries of Childhood: A Social History of Family Life*, trans. Robert Baldick (New York: Vintage Books, 1962). Aries was the first modern historian of childhood to recognize the conception of the child as a social construction.

3. Works for seventeenth-century history of childhood include: Edmond S. Morgan, *The Puritan Family: Religion and Domestic Relations in Seventeenth-Century New England*, rev. ed. (New York: Harper & Row, 1966); John Demos, *A Little Commonwealth: Family Life in Plymouth Colony* (New York: Oxford University Press, 1970); Philip J. Greven, Jr., *Four Generations: Population, Land, and Family in Colonial Andover, Massachusetts* (Ithaca, N.Y.: Cornell University Press, 1970); Kenneth Lockridge, *A New England Town, The First Hundred Years: Dedham, Massachusetts, 1636-1736* (New York: Psychohistory Press, 1974); Thad W. Tate and David I. Ammerman, eds., *The Chesapeake in the Seventeenth Century: Essays on Anglo-American Society* (Chapel Hill: University of North Carolina Press, 1979).

4. Health risks varied between the New England and the Chesapeake colonies. For detailed histories of both, see Peter G. Slater, "'From the Cradle to the Coffin': Parental Bereavement and the Shadow of Infant Damnation in Puritan Society," in N. Ray Hiner and Joseph M. Hawes, eds., *Growing Up in America* (Urbana: University of Illinois Press, 1985); David E. Stannard, *The Puritan Way of Death: A Study in Religion, Culture,* and *Social Change* (New York: Oxford University Press, 1977); John Duffy, *Epidemics in Colonial America* (Baton Rouge: Louisiana State University Press, 1953); and Ross W. Beales, Jr., "The Child in Seventeenth-Century America," in Joseph M. Hawes and N. Ray Hiner, eds., *American Childhood: A Research Guide and Historical Handbook* (Westport, Conn.: Greenwood Press, 1985).

5. Philip J. Greven, *Child Rearing Concepts, 1628-1861* (Itasca, Ill.: F. E. Peacock, 1973).

6. Ross W. Beales, "The Child in Seventeenth-Century America," 32.

7. John R. Sutton, "Stubborn Children: Law and the Socialization of Deviance in the Puritan Colonies," *Family Law Quarterly* 15 (1981): 31-64.

8. Darrett B. Rutman and Anita H. Rutman, "'Now-Wives and Sons-in-Law': Parental Death in a Seventeenth-Century Virginia County," in

Thad W. Tate and David L. Ammerman, eds., *The Chesapeake in the Seventeenth Century: Essays on Anglo-American Society* (Chapel Hill: University of North Carolina Press, 1979), 153-82.

9. Lois Green Carr, "The Development of the Maryland Orphan's Court, 1654-1715," in Aubrey C. Land, Lois Green Carr, and Edward C. Papenfuse, eds., *Law, Society, and Politics in Early Maryland: Proceedings of the First Conference on Maryland History, June 14-15, 1974* (Baltimore: Johns Hopkins University Press, 1977).

10. Darrett B. Rutman and Anita H. Rutman. Op. cit. "Now-Wives and Sons-in-Law."

11. John Demos, *A Little Commonwealth: Family Life in Plymouth Colony* (New York: Oxford University Press, 1970); and John Duffy, *Epidemics in Colonial America*, 33-37.

12. Alan Kulikoff, "A 'Prolific' People: Black Population Growth in the Chesapeake Colonies, 1700-1790," *Southern Studies* 16 (1977): 391-428.

13. See, for example, James Axtell's *The School Upon a Hill: Education and Society in Colonial New England* (New Haven: Yale University Press, 1974).

14. See, for example, Lawrence Cremin, *American Education: The Colonial Experience, 1607-1783* (New York: Harper & Row, 1970); Barbara Finkelstein, *Regulated Children/Liberated Children: Education in Psychohistorical Perspective* (New York: Psychohistory Press, 1979).

15. Jamil S. Zainaldin, *Law in Antebellum Society: Legal Change and Economic Expansion* (New York: Random House, 1983).

16. Constance B. Schulz, "Children and Childhood in the Eighteenth Century," in Joseph M. Hawes and N. Ray Hiner, eds., *American Childhood* (Westport, Conn.: Greenwood Press, 1985).

17. Joseph Ben-Or, "The Law of Adoption in the United States: Its Massachusetts Origins and the Statute of 1851," *New England Historical and Genealogical Register* 130 (1976): 259-72.

18. Barbara Finkelstein, "Casting Networks of Good Influence: The Reconstruction of Childhood in the United States, 1790-1870," in Hawes and Hiner, *American Childhood* (Westport, Conn.: Greenwood Press, 1985).

19. Barbara Brenzel, *Daughters of the State: A Social Portrait of the First Reform School for Girls in North America, 1856-1905* (Cambridge: MIT Press, 1983), 120-23.

20. Gary Polster, *Inside Looking Out: The Cleveland Jewish Orphan Asylum, 1868-1924* (Kent, Ohio: Kent State University Press, 1990); John O'Grady, *Catholic Charities in the United States* (New York: Arno Press, 1971); Priscilla Ferguson Clement, "Families and Foster Care: Philadelphia in the Late Nineteenth Century," in Hiner and Hawes, *Growing Up in America* (Urbana: University of Illinois Press, 1985).

21. Thomas Bender, *Toward an Urban Vision: Ideas and Institutions in Nineteenth Century America* (Lexington: University Press of Kentucky, 1975).

22. Michael Grossberg, *Governing the Hearth: Law and the Family in Nineteenth Century America* (Chapel Hill: University of North Carolina Press, 1985).

23. Barbara Finkelstein, "Casting Networks of Good Influence."

24. For analyses of nineteenth-century children's moralistic literature, see Bernard Wishy, *The Child and the Republic: The Dawn of Modern American Children* (Philadelphia: University of Pennsylvania Press, 1968); Elizabeth Francis, "American Children's Literature, 1646-1880," and Sally Allen McNall, "American Children's Literature, 1880-Present," in Hiner and Hawes, *American Childhood*. On the shift to children as needing the help of others, see, for example, Anthony Platt, *The Child Savers: The Invention of Delinquency* (Chicago: University of Chicago Press, 1969); Ellen Ryerson, *The Best Laid Plans: America's Juvenile Court Experiment* (New York: Hill & Wang, 1978); Steven Schlossman, *Love and the American Delinquent: The Theory and Practice of "Progressive" Juvenile Justice, 1825-1920* (Chicago: University of Chicago Press, 1977).

25. The literature on child development and efforts to address stages of mental, moral, and physical development in children is extensive, represented throughout the historical literature in the fields of psychology, education, social welfare, and sociology. In psychology, see, for example, Dorothy Ross, *G. Stanley Hall: The Psychologist as Prophet* (Chicago: University of Chicago Press, 1972); in education, Lawrence Cremin, *The Transformation of the School: Progressivism in American Education, 1876-1957* (New York: Alfred A. Knopf, 1961); in social welfare and sociology, Robert Bremner, *From the Depths: The Discovery of Poverty in the United States* (New York: New York University Press, 1956), Walter Trattner, *From Poor Law to Welfare State: A History of Social Welfare in America* (New York: Free Press, 1974), and Roy Lubov, *The Professional Altruist: The Emergence of Social Work as a Career* (Cambridge: Harvard University Press, 1965).

26. This shift is symbolized by Emma Octavia Lundberg's 1947

work, *Unto the Least of These: Social Services for Children* (New York: D. Appleton-Century Co., 1947), and W. Norton Grubb and Marvin Lazerson's 1982 work *Broken Promises: How Americans Fail Their Children* (New York: Basic Books, 1982).

Part I

Historical Public Discourse

1

Child Saving in Modern
America 1870s-1990s

I.

In 1899 the young University of Chicago philosopher John Dewey published *The School and Society*. In its pages he outlined an ambitious program of public education for the new industrial age. Now and henceforth it was essential, he argued, for the state to undertake certain social functions that in earlier times private institutions such as the family or the church had assumed. Among those critical social functions were formal education and civic socialization, which, Dewey believed, were central to the new public school system that the newly expanded state would create. In these ways would public education insure a stable society and a healthy democracy.[1]

Dewey synthesized particular ideas current in American society since the 1870s into a useful, coherent ideology for the Progressive education movement. Progressive educators

believed that the schools should prepare students for the challenges of modern life. They believed that the most up-to-date
scientific knowledge about the child should be used to shape
both teaching methods and the curriculum. The curriculum
should focus on useful subjects that would make students think
critically and independently and include the study of history,
modern languages, and laboratory sciences. Progressive educators more conservative than Dewey—who dominated the movement's ranks—emphasized the individual's adjustment to society's norms.[2]

What Dewey said and wrote also influenced organized child
saving in modern American culture. Like all champions of organized child saving then, Dewey insisted that the child represented the nation's future, an optimistic message that resonated
through the nation at a time when most citizens believed in the
certainty of progress. Throughout America's past, Americans
cared for their own children's welfare. Since the 1870s, however, Americans have invented child saving as a closely related
series of public issues, thus creating an organized child-saving
movement in politics, society, and culture. Only in modern
times, then, have Americans asked public entities, whether governmental or not, to assume more and more responsibility for
various social goals. These concerns have gone beyond local
affairs of family, church, or community. As Barry Karl and Stanley Katz have remarked, the United States was the only major
nation in the industrialized world to create a national welfare
state without a national bureaucracy to administer it. As Americans used the State—meaning any level of government, but especially the states and the federal government—increasingly in
modern times to address social problems, it was always with an
eye to keeping state bureaucracy and machinery on as parsimo-
nious a level of functioning as possible.[3]

Organized child saving may be simply and abstractly
defined as institutionalized concern for children as members
of, and participants in, the social order, regardless of personal
relationships of one sort or another. Organized child saving has
involved multiple kinds of activities. These have included establishing institutions for the care of vulnerable children—the destitute, the delinquent, the mentally and emotionally disadvantaged—such as the regulation or elimination of child labor. They
have also meant working so that normal children grow up in
wholesome environments, by regulating the use of tobacco, alco-

holic beverages, and pornography, by expanding the curricula of the public schools, and by improving the delivery of health care to society's children. With differing emphases in various epochs, child savers have expressed their concerns about children at risk from disease, poverty, unwholesome living conditions, poor education, abuse, delinquency, discrimination, and the like, but also children not apparently at risk, most notably those of the middle and upper classes. Put more simply, the foci of organized child saving have included both remedies for problems and prevention thereof.

Champions of organized child saving have made three fundamental assumptions. They have defined the child as a completely natural being. The child was to be understood and explained from the standpoint of modern science and not, for example, from that of Christian supernaturalism or other antipositivistic systems of thought. They have also believed that the child represented the links between past, present, and future, not merely in the individual's life cycle but in that of the larger social order, a clear legacy from the nineteenth century's discovery of the multiple meanings of time—not simply as a regimen for work or other aspects of individual existence, but also as a blueprint of orderly change or evolution in nature and society. Finally, child savers have thought it appropriate for agencies outside the family, usually public or governmental agencies, to intervene in the family's affairs on behalf of children at risk.

There have been discontinuities in child savers' notions as well. Organized child saving marched to a different beat in each of the three distinct eras of modern American history. In the first age, lasting from the 1870s to the 1920s, child savers focused on what they dubbed the "subnormal" or "abnormal" groups of children, such as the dependent, the mentally defective, and the delinquent, insisting that there were as many such types or groups as there were social problems. In the main for child savers, normal, middle-class, white children of Anglo-Saxon Protestant background as a group exemplified the highest standards of modern culture, to which the subnormal and abnormal groups should be compared. The child savers, then, focused on the types of subnormal and abnormal children.

In the second period of modern American history, spanning the 1920s to the 1950s, child savers changed their tune. Now they focused on the normal child and the endless variations of normal children among the nation's many religious, nativity, and economic groups. Child savers emphasized devising ways and means to have all but the most difficult children learn to adapt to society's norms and to understand how normal children developed. In the last, or contemporary, era, starting in the 1950s, child savers abandoned the group determinism of the earlier epochs. They stressed that the individual child, with his or her difficulties with the system, was a child at risk, either potentially or in reality.

Put more abstractly, there were different notions of the order of things, as in the relations of the whole to the parts, in each era, which in turn spelled different notions of the meaning of group identity for the individual. In the first two eras, individuals could not exist apart from the group to which they belonged. In the third, individuals could, and did, exist apart from their group identities.[4]

II.

Notions of the child and of children were thus closely related to assumptions about groups in the larger population. From the 1870s to the 1920s, American society and culture seemed torn by endless binary conflicts of distinct groups, such as rich versus poor, Christian versus Jew, Protestant versus Catholic, urbanite versus country rube, white versus nonwhite, Easterner versus Westerner, Southerner versus Northerner, owners of enterprise and their employees, native-born versus immigrant, and the like. The middle-class white, Anglo-Saxon, Protestant elites that dominated American institutions then considered the national population divided into an apparently infinite number of racial, religious, economic, ethnic, and other kinds of groups.

Thus there was not one homogeneous population. There were many distinct types, or groups, within that population. Each was unique; none was equal. In a word, each group was different, or "other," to all, and "otherness" was an integral part of the American social credo. The discrete group, whose members retained their group identity from birth to death and had more in common with one another than with members of other groups, was understood as the stuff of social (and natural) reality. The notion of a freestanding, autonomous individual apart from her or his group was virtually unthinkable. From a horizontal perspective, the whole appeared to be a stew, constituted of many distinct, not to say indigestible, ingredients. From a vertical point of view, there was a hierarchy of different groups of unequal value. Put more schematically, it was a conception of the relations of the whole and the parts that was reductionistic, mechanistic, and deterministic, and it had numerous parallels throughout the culture in that era, as in notions of disease in medicine, thermodynamics in physics, inheritance in biology, and system in the social sciences.[5]

By the late 1890s and early 1900s the so-called Progressive reform movement was under way in American society and politics. As an integral element of that larger element, organized child saving crystallized into a sociopolitical movement as well. Child savers in the Progressive Era were largely responsible for the expansion or invention of institutions that would address the problems of the many dependent and abnormal groups of children in society. By "child savers," then, is meant precisely that interesting mixture of middle-class female activists, such as prominent clubwoman Hannah Schoff of Philadelphia, men who held public office, such as Judge Benjamin Lindsey of Colorado, or scientists such as psychologist Henry H. Goddard of the Vineland Training School, in New Jersey, all of whom had much to say when they addressed problems involving children—in the particular instance at hand, the problem of preventing juvenile delinquency through the new juvenile courts. And indeed, probably the most prominent of such child-saving institutions was the juvenile court, first created by the Illinois legislature in 1899.[6]

The fundamental notion of the juvenile court was easy enough to understand. According to the court's advocates, child offenders were not sufficiently developed, physically, emotionally, and spiritually, to be treated as adult offenders. Hence there should be special courts and special procedures just for them. The Illinois law defined a delinquent child as a child under sixteen years of age who had broken the law in a city or village. It created a special court in Chicago and provided further that any good citizen who knew of children that were neglected, dependent, or delinquent could complain to the court, which had authority to take children from their families and place them in institutions at the judge's will. The Chicago juvenile court began operations almost immediately.[7]

Within a few years the juvenile court idea had spread to

ten more states. By 1920 all but two states had a juvenile court law. Several distinguished scholars, including Steven Schlossman, one of the present volume's authors, have pointed out that the juvenile courts were less than ideal institutions. The judges had wide discretionary powers in determining what, if any, procedural rights the children had, what constituted admissible evidence, the nature and character of punishment, and so on. Only rarely could lawyers be effective in promoting the rights of child clients. If assessed according to the standards of traditional jurisprudence, the juvenile courts permitted improper questions, hearsay, and circumstantial evidence and often entangled their charges' relatives in their webs as well. Whether or not the courts were, in actuality, instruments of social control, as some historians would have it, some involved in their administration acted as if they were and deployed their powers within the system as if they were engaged in class warfare against the poor, the dependent, and the aberrant.[8]

Another kind of child-saving institution was the home for the "feebleminded" (as the mentally retarded were then called). Perhaps the most distinguished was the Vineland Training School, founded in 1890 and located in Vineland, New Jersey. Its trustees and chief administrator were enlightened for their day; they raised funds for a permanent research director, so that mental retardation could be understood scientifically. The man appointed was psychologist Henry H. Goddard. To about 1913 or so, Goddard approached the problem of feeblemindedness as a social evil, arguing that the affliction was innate and caused individuals to be criminals, paupers, dependents, and other bad sorts, as in such lurid monographs as *The Kallikak Family.*[9] Thereafter, as he attempted to work out practical solutions for retraining the higher-grade mental defectives, whom he dubbed "morons," he came to see that the mentally retarded were not necessarily bad people, merely afflicted and often poorly understood. By the 1920s he was arguing that most mental defectives were little or no threat to society and that juvenile delinquency could be cured through various social programs of reeducation and training, which experts would devise and administer, to be sure.[10]

Champions of organized child saving fought other battles to establish appropriate institutions. This was especially the case with the new hierarchical public school systems that the states were creating in this fifty-year time span. The new public school systems stretched from kindergarten to graduate and professional school, with the former at the pyramid's base, the latter at its apex. The new school systems were intended for all children— those who were white, native-born, middle-class, and Protestant as well as those who were nonwhite or of immigrant origins. The child savers completely reorganized existing educational institutions into the conceptual parameters of the new age.

Consider the kindergarten, once an exotic product of mid-nineteenth-century German Romanticism transplanted in New England soil. The child savers spiffed it up according to their own late-nineteenth-century notions. In so doing, they altered it from an institution with an individualistic, child-centered cur-riculum to encourage children to live to the utmost of their potentiality into an institution with a meritocratic and natural-scientific mandate to uplift society's distinct social groups to the American standard through scientific pedagogy. As early as the 1870s, school officials were developing charity kindergartens to help immigrant and poor families. The new progressive educa-tors of the early 1900s redefined the kindergarten as the place to start training minds, morals, and muscles for the uplift and improvement of the social order.

In the new elementary and high schools, the progressive educators and child savers established differential curricula for different groups of students, as well as other curricula to make children into responsible citizens, such as courses in American-ization, in English language and literature, in American history, and in the history of ancient Greece, Rome, the Protestant Refor-mation, and other Anglo-American cultural building blocks of what became "Western Civilization" courses in the interwar years. They also introduced the policy of formally segregated schools for nonwhites in all parts of the country. And the public schools provided a whole range of new services, including ele-mentary health care, athletics, guidance counseling, and achieve-ment testing. High schools grew enormously in these years and became the middle level between the public grammar school and the state university. The college-preparatory high school diploma became the admission ticket to the state university everywhere by 1900. Most states had also enacted compulsory attendance laws by then.

Progressive educators and child savers also engineered important organizational changes within the new pyramidal school systems in each state. The new systems vertically inte-grated all levels of education—the kindergarten, the elementary school, the high school, the vocational institute, the normal school, the technical college, the land-grant college of agriculture, engineering, and home economics, the special schools for special groups in the population, such as women or nonwhites, in most southern states, and, in all of the states, the state university with its arts and sciences programs, its professional schools, and its doctoral programs. Thus they reconstituted the schools along departmental lines that were relevant to the new unitary disciplines of the age, such as physics, chemistry, geology, history, economics, and the like. Students and subject matter alike were rearranged along strict vertical lines, in a manner strikingly similar to the organization of big business at roughly the same time in American culture and society. The level of education helped determine the degree of differentiation. Vertical integration, tracking different elements, centralization, efficiency, and standardization—these were the watchwords of the new state systems of public education no less than of American economic enterprise.[11]

Nor was this all. The federal government entered the playing field in the early 1900s. The champions of organized child saving won some battles and lost others in their attempts to enlist the federal government's aid. It was easier for the child savers and educators to prod the federal government to study a problem than to solve it. Thus it was not difficult for child savers to convince Theodore Roosevelt to sponsor the first White House Conference on Child Health and Protection, in 1909, just before he left office. At that conference, child savers, whether women's club activists, professors of pedagogy, or male officeholders, promoted a number of suggestions for the federal government's delectation in the child welfare area.

Perhaps the most important legacy of federal intervention in child welfare came with the Children's Bureau, established within the Department of Commerce and Labor in 1912. The bureau's budget was painfully small, barely enough for a chief and a miniscule staff. Its mandate was to collect information on the circumstances of child life and recommend legislation to Congress. If its enforcement abilities seemed weak, nevertheless the bureau's investigatory mandate was broad and included infant mortality, the birthrate, orphans, juvenile courts, desertion, dangerous occupations, accidents and diseases of children, employment, and laws affecting children in the states and territories—among other matters.

Hence the federal government inaugurated social investigation on behalf of child welfare as it had, for example, for farmers, agricultural scientists, food processors, and other interests through the various research programs of the Department of Agriculture. Child savers had fewer satisfactions when it came to winning the restriction of child labor. Congress actually enacted a child labor law in the fall of 1916, known as the Keating-Owen Act; the Children's Bureau won the right to enforce it. The next summer southern mill interests took the law to the United States Supreme Court, which in *Hammer v. Dagenhart* (1918) ruled the law unconstitutional because it arrogated to the federal government, in the name of interstate commerce, a power reserved to the states, that of regulating the hours of labor of children.

It remains easy, but monumentally erroneous, to overlook the great power and attraction that states' rights and its version of federalism had in these years as legal and political philosophies to millions of articulate Americans. More was involved than political conservatism in bench and bar. If states' rights provided mechanisms for such actions as the disfranchisement of black males in the southern states, not to mention the Supreme Court's tacit authorization of segregation throughout the federal union, it also was part and parcel of deeply held constitutional doctrine from the nineteenth century.

Since the 1870s, Americans had reorganized their notions of federalism so that now, in the new federalism's blueprint, the federal government stood at the apex of the governmental pyramid, above the states and localities, rather than as a specialized, weak entity juxtaposed cheek-by-jowl next to them, as prior doctrine had dictated. The reconstituted federal government could legislate and regulate certain issues of truly national concern— within sharply defined limits—through the commerce clause of the Fourteenth Amendment. But Americans would go no further toward the feared specter of Leviathan. In a society and an age in which most, if not all, denizens acted and responded as if each and every component of the larger whole was possessed of its own peculiar characteristics, it made sense to have a strong separation of powers and balance of the rights of the states as distinct from the national government. States' rights as constitutional law and ideology helped Americans tease out the implications and possibilities of enhancing the federal government's powers without yielding local or state control over many political, economic, and social issues. This was, after all, an age of enormous expansion of the powers and responsibilities of the states.

The progressive child savers created child-saving institutions and pushed local, state, and federal government to take more responsibility for the welfare of children, whether normal or not. They also established the role, so important ever since, for the scientific expert, whether in medicine, the social sciences, or education, to act as consultant and source of authority insofar as child behavior and development were concerned. Yet the balance of power within the ranks of the child savers still remained heavily in favor of the political activists, not the scientists and experts, for the former, not the latter, controlled most child-saving institutions outside the public schools themselves. And just as evidently, organized child saving was heavily imbued with the prejudices and values of the culture's dominant white, Anglo-Saxon, Protestant, middle-class population.

III.

From the 1920s to the 1950s, organized child saving was strikingly altered. The relations between the experts and the lay activists in organized child saving changed dramatically. The lay child savers no longer had the power they had enjoyed in the early 1900s. Much of the legitimacy in child saving had passed to the experts, the scientists and therapists concerned with the study of the circumstances of children and childhood, and the semiprofessionals these experts trained to take their places as functionaries in child-saving institutions. Yet more than a transfer of social and moral authority had taken place. Now the reformers were largely a cheering section, an audience, a mere constituency, for the experts. It was not a question of numbers; there were many more lay activists than experts. Why had this startling change occurred?[12]

Notions of natural and social reality had changed since the early 1900s and 1910s. The whole, or social system, was now understood as a system of systems, a holistic rather than a reductionist unity, a network of complex, interactive systems constituted by many distinct yet interrelated parts, a formulation that one finds in a variety of fields of knowledge, such as physiologists' theory of homeostasis, urban sociologists' definition of the city, biologists' notion of species as a population, chemists' ideas of polymer chemistry, physicists' articulation of quantum mechanics, or economists' discovery of the business cycle. No matter what the field of knowledge, the perspective was the same: Reality was highly complex. It was fluctuating, dynamic, and interactive. Only expert knowledge could guide change, for changes in such complex networks, or systems of systems, could have incalculable results. As before, there was the widespread notion that the individual could not shift membership from one group—meaning race, gender, class, or nativity group—to another. A rising tide carried all boats, but their relative positions did not change. This was hardly radical social dogma.[13]

And this sheds light on the new age's child-saving accomplishments. If, as historian LeRoy Ashby perceptively argues, the interwar year were largely ones of halting forward steps, the reasons are not so difficult to unearth.[14] Some relate, to be sure, to the persistently noisy din of conservative resentment and antagonism directed toward society's unfortunates as a staple element of public policy discourse in these years. Yet that hardly explains why what Ashby terms "half-measures" seemingly made so much sense to the child savers themselves.[15] There have always been conservative onslaughts in any age of history—and reformers' crusades as well. The more important point is that the reformers themselves had little faith in wholesale activism. Their ideology was fatalistic and deterministic, just like the models of wholes and parts in the natural and social sciences to which it was a parallel. Problems were complex, not simple. The experts knew best. In a dynamic, fluctuating world, the experts insisted, adjustment of the organism (or part) to the realities of the larger whole was crucial for survival; the whole was, finally, greater than, or different from, the sum of the parts. This was hardly a prescription for ambitious child saving through intervention.

And most Americans, child savers or not, applied this blueprint of natural and social reality to the national population itself. The implications for notions of group and individual were instructive indeed. All elements in the population were, from this perspective, equally valid and authentic components thereof—but manifestly not equal to one another in value and worth. The many different groups—races, classes, and nativity groups—were to be understood as distinct and legitimate members of the national population, for each element played its own particular role in the larger society, polity, and economy. All interacted with all others in many ways. So complex were these interactions that, as the University of Chicago urban sociologist Roderick McKenzie once put it, to change one part of the larger whole could have incalculable consequences for the whole. Drastic intervention seemed too risky; gradualism was obviously more prudent, the considered choice of the experts.[16]

This sense of disparate elements working together applied to public policy as well. In the interwar decades, large-scale foundations intervened as partners with local, state, and national governmental agencies to address, if not solve, particular social problems; oil and water could and did function together, so to speak. Here was the essence of Herbert Hoover as a reformer or Progressive. He wanted a partnership between government and voluntary institutions—meaning philanthropy, private associations, and local government in particular—to establish social and public policy on all manner of issues. In the administrations of Herbert Hoover and Franklin D. Roosevelt, the federal government was to be a broker among various interests or elements in society. The federal government could set policy and argue for it and come to the rescue in an emergency. But the other partners in the establishment of public policy, including the states, the experts, the specific popular constituencies (or audiences) for each issue, the interest groups, and others, all had their distinct yet interdependent roles to play in the larger implementation of policy. What Ashby calls "half-measures" made sense to contemporaries as parts of a larger holistic approach to, or method of, problem solving. In this way could national problems be addressed without creating a European-style Leviathan state bureaucracy.[17]

The federal government's involvement in organized child saving in these years underscores the point. In the 1920s, the federal government continued to maintain the Children's Bureau as a reporting agency to the Congress on matters of child health and protection. The federal government also provided matching funds to the states, through the Sheppard-Towner Act of 1921, to disseminate well-baby and other maternity information to mothers who could not otherwise afford to gain such information to care for their babies. Through its funding of home economics and agricultural extension programs in the land-grant colleges, the federal government subvened the dissemination of child-saving information derived from the experts, as in tips on how to discipline one's unruly adolescent or whether to use breast or bottle to nurse baby.[18]

Probably the capstone of federal involvement in this decade came with the 1930 White House Conference on Child Health and Protection that President Hoover convened. The 1930 conference was the most elaborate of the several White House conferences on child health and protection yet held. Certainly it had a very comprehensive agenda. Many important scientists and other experts cooperated. They wrote large and important studies in the field covering many diverse, yet interrelated, topics, themes, and problems. In its wake, groups of child savers held state versions of the 1930 conference, at which activists and experts reiterated many of the ideas that had first aired at the White House conference of 1930. Participants in the state conferences brought important findings to them and effectively disseminated the results thereafter. Yet new knowledge was the net result of the 1930 White House conference and its state versions. Even if the participants wished for follow-up to include implementing recommendations as programs, such was effectively precluded by the Great Depression's grim fiscal and budgetary realities.[19]

In 1929 Congress refused to renew the Sheppart-Towner Act, thus underlining the tenuousness of the federal government's commitment to organized child saving. Thereafter the federal government did more for child saving, chiefly because of the depression and World War II. Often this was accomplished through the back door or for purposes having little to do with child welfare. Franklin Roosevelt's New Deal programs contributed a good deal to child saving, and more than the efforts of Herbert Hoover's administration, but both operated from the same tacit assumptions about the taxonomy of natural and social reality. There was little precedent in the New Deal relief programs for a modern nationalized welfare state administered by federal apparatchiks. The Federal Emergency Relief Administration, for example, provided indirect assistance to impoverished children through the simple mechanism of providing jobs for their parents, hardly the stuff of continental social democracy. The overriding animus in every instance was economic recovery, not fancy socialistic social engineering. Often mere compassion, without grand ideological notions, was the thing. In many localities, welfare workers tried to keep members of poor families together as their first priority, regardless of particular regulations and realities. Such efforts strengthened child saving, but only on an emergency basis. The Works Progress Administration (WPA) promoted child saving, often by the simple means of hiring unemployed parents. The WPA pioneered federal hot-lunch programs in New York City schools in the early 1930s, not so much as a means of creating a new social program as to resolve the need to get rid of excess foodstuffs and feed the hungry. It also supported the building and staffing of thousands of playgrounds to help provide jobs for adults in need of work and, in the later 1930s, the support of day nurseries in many states. In each case, however, the WPA's administrator, Harry Hopkins, could get Congressional approval for such remedies only by promising to spend the appropriated funds for jobs for unemployed teachers, janitors, and other public school employees laid off during the economic emergency. In any event, Hopkins was no czar of an American welfare state, plotting to create a monster bureaucracy and plan for a welfare state. He was more a compassionate problem solver and professional welfare worker thoroughly respectful of local initiative for solutions to the problems of relief. In such ways would the various disparate parts work together for the greater good of all.[20]

Congress enacted several measures that fulfilled the goals of many child savers. Thus the Fair Labor Standards Act of 1938 partly limited child labor. Yet federal law did not cover such fields as agriculture, in which there was widespread use of children as laborers, and American entry into the war after Pearl Harbor led to much hiring of adolescents and winking at what child labor laws there were. Two pieces of federal legislation pointed the way toward federal day-care assistance and helping the preschool child. The Lanham Act of 1940 provided some funding to communities in which defense plants made day care a necessity. The other was the Emergency Maternal and Infant Care Act of 1943, which provided free hospital and medical care to the wives and children of servicemen in the lowest pay grades. These programs were neither lavishly nor cheerfully funded by the Congress. Support was miserly and grudging here as elsewhere for children.[21]

Probably the most important federal child welfare law of the 1930s was Social Security—especially the Aid to Dependent Children program (ADC). Here was the American welfare state—conceived of as a limited social insurance program hedged and circumscribed in a variety of ways. That program had its precedents in the mothers' pension programs that most states had enacted in the 1910s and 1920s. These programs provided direct payments to mothers so as to keep the children from being placed in institutions. Yet these programs provided only small amounts of money—and collapsed during the Great Depression. Moral rehabilitation, not economic assistance, was the main criterion of assistance in the mothers' pension programs. This was installed in ADC. Ultimately behavioral objectives, not economic remedies, were legitimated in the ADC program.[22]

The federal role thus because stretched and strained, during the emergency years of depression and war, far beyond what most politicians would have liked, liberals as well as conservatives, New Dealers as well as their opponents. Most special legislation enacted then was not intended to become permanent. To the extent that America was supposed to have a national welfare system, that was to be without the invention of a large national bureaucracy and national state, as had been the common experience in Europe.

Hence the strategy of "half-measures" made perfectly good sense to most who were involved in these matters in the interwar years. In this age's version of federalism and states' rights, as in that of the Progressive Era, the national government was strictly limited in its powers and responsibilities. There were intermediate structures of all shapes and sizes through which national issues were mediated; the federal government merely brokered them. In that regard, little had changed; whether the whole was reductionist or holistic, it still existed and defined the appropriateness of certain kinds of actions and made others inconceivable. The federal role was that of a partner, a cheerleader, a heuristic guide, not an Orwellian Big Brother intimidating atomistic mass humanity as an aggregate of individuals unconnected with one another. Other and different structures and relationships were deemed vital for the proper functioning of American democracy.

And what of the other partners in these oil-and-water childsaving consortiums? Consider the role of two New York foundations, the Laura Spelman Rockefeller Memorial and the Commonwealth Fund. Memorial program officer Lawrence K. Frank persuaded the memorial's trustees to spend about $5.5 million in the 1920s to create the entire apparatus for a professional subculture of the science of child development, including half a dozen research centers, a larger number of programs in early childhood education and parent education, a professional organization, several specialized journals, and even a postdoctoral program, all to train and situate professionals in this newest of the human sciences. Literally, Frank and the memorial provided the start-up costs for an entire academic subculture. Then they inserted it into selected colleges and universities, from which it spread to other academic institutions in the 1940s and 1950s with the return of prosperity. Soon results came from the research centers, which were located at a handful of leading universities, such as Iowa, Minnesota, Columbia, California, and Yale.

The paradigm for the field was group identity, not individual autonomy. Research flowed from that premise. Much focused on the behavior and development of the normal child, without concern for or interest in the specific experiences of individuals. Thus important longitudinal projects at Yale, Stanford, and Berkeley presented group averages on every conceivable type of biological or social measurement of the groups of children being so studied over a period of years, not tracking the measurements of particular individuals over time.[23]

Initially Commonwealth Fund officials wanted to create a program for the elimination and future prevention of juvenile delinquency through the ideas and methods of eugenics. The experts they invited to a key conference in 1921 persuaded them that prevention was better promoted through psychiatric intervention than through sterilization or other eugenics remedies, if only for reasons of good public relations. By the early 1930s the Commonwealth Fund had created institutional niches in a new system of private clinics for experts in the new field of child guidance, who were, in the main, child psychiatrists. The new ideas and institutional network enabled them to work on problems of child emotional disturbances while sidestepping the public hospitals, schools, and other facilities for delinquent children. The child psychiatrists sought to probe the causes of maladjustments and to recommend cures in which all members of the child's constellation of family, peers, and adult authority figures would be considered as a system of systems, a constellation of differing emotional interactions.

Not surprisingly, the child guidance movement's central credo was adjustment of the individual to the system. Thus there was no such thing as an individual apart from the group to which he or she "belonged." With child development, as with child guidance, the experts focused on the normal, middle-class child, either as the object of research in child development or as the focus of relatively minor behavior problems (e.g., bed wetting, petty stealing, masturbation, and the like). Within the limits of their mandates, the experts did a creditable job in contributing to knowledge about the circumstances of child life and of children. Above all, the experts believed that the key to human nature and conduct resided in the group, not the individual. Group identity defined and determined what the individual could do.[24]

And what of the schools? Notions of merit and expertise mattered here as well. The nation's elementary and secondary schools provided a more complex mixture of curricula. This certainly meant tracking, or discriminating among those who were deemed college material and those who were not. But it also meant a more varied mix of courses and even interdisciplinary work. The nation's schools also benefited, if benisons these were, from the ministrations of psychological testers, who devised batteries of tests to examine basal intelligence as well as academic achievements in various disciplines of knowledge. By the late 1940s the testers were creating admissions examinations, such as the Scholastic Aptitude Test (SAT), that would enable prestigious private and public universities and colleges to be more selective in recruitment and admissions of their entering classes.

The schools also expanded their mandates for the delivery of social services to their client populations. At the elementary and secondary levels, various kinds of counselors, including guidance counselors, came to advise children and parents; but the schools also promoted public health through physical and dental examinations and the employment of suitable personnel to attend to these expanded responsibilities. And central to the American educational experience also was sports, with teacher-coaches advising students on the importance of team spirit and group achievement.

Colleges and universities experienced, if anything, an intensification of these trends. Disciplinary lines remained the major justification for the organization of academic departments, for example, but interdisciplinary programs became entrenched in academe, either within larger entities, such as genetics in biological science departments or quantum mechanics in physical science departments, or as distinct entities themselves, as in child development, agricultural economics, religion, American studies, and journalism. Colleges and universities cultivated external constituencies, often through athletic programs, but also, at least in the case of universities, by inventing a new nexus of graduate degree programs and research capabilities for various consumers of their products, including private enterprise and the federal government, a development that the Cold War only accelerated. Horizontal expansion, however, did not come at the cost of vertical integration; the hierarchical pyramid as the model of natural and social reality remained intact.

In the years between the world wars, changes were made that were cautious and piecemeal—even in times of depression and war, which allegedly shook American society to its foundations. Reality was too complex to be trifled with. Organized child saving presented no revolutionary threat to established American institutions and folkways; it adapted to the complex realities of its own time.

IV.

What has defined the era since the 1950s is the overwhelming sense of the importance of the individual apart from the group, of the notion that the larger whole, or system, is or has been oppressing or in other ways hurting innocent individuals. Indeed, much of our public discourse since the 1950s has been a discourse of victimization, of oppression, of individuals being "at risk." Thus the liberalism and protest movements of the 1950s and 1960s have been of a piece with the "me-ism" and alleged narcissism of the 1970s and 1980s. All have added up to a taxonomy of natural and social reality—a sense of the order of things, in other words—in which there is no larger whole, but instead an infinity of dimensions, proportions, and elements in any situation. The dogma of individuation, like that of the larger whole or group, has had its good and bad sides from various points of view; thus the individualism of the New Left was the mirror image of the individualism of the New Right. Just as group determinism in the two previous ages had its good and bad sides, so has our post-1950 individualism and individuation.[25]

Organized child saving since the 1950s has been directed toward the unfortunate, the stigmatized, the poor, the oppressed youngsters within our midst. In a word, it has focused on individuals at risk. The most famous writers about children now are persons such as Robert Coles and Jonathan

Kozol, whose elegant works remind us that the system is oppressing individual children. Group analysis, and all that it implies, no longer drives the imagination of organized child saving. Thus the field of child development itself has undergone a theoretical about-face since 1950 or so. Before then, of course, most developmentalists insisted that there was something called "a normal child," that almost all children fell into that grouping, and that all individual children varied only around the mean for that category of children on any conceivable characteristic or trait. Since the 1950s the developmentalists have sung a dramatically different tune. They now speak of the rights of children as individuals, for instance, and, are much more splintered over research versus social activism than was the case before the 1950s.[26]

Representative of our contemporary individualized point of view is the work of such child development specialists as J. McVicker Hunt, who stressed the longitudinal development of the individual over time rather than the cross-sectional group portraits, so to speak, of children so fashionable in the prior era. Head Start clearly was premised on assumptions inconceivable in the period between the world wars, that the individual, if caught early enough in the life cycle, could be trained to "jump" from the norm of the group or subculture to which he or she was born, to that of an entirely different group. This sense of culture—and, for that matter, biology—being just like a suit of clothes, to be put on or taken off virtually at will, had few adherents before the 1950s. Now it appears to be a mainstream dogma.[27]

Yet there are other, and perhaps less salutary, implications of our age's fascination with the parts, not the whole, with the individual and individuation. It would be foolish to deny the positive gains from our individualistic ethos, whether they have been modest, as in race relations, or of greater reach, as in relations between the sexes. But often individualism, however expressed, whether as the rebellion against the conformity of the 1950s or against racism and the Vietnam War in the 1960s, or as the espousal of minimalism and "me-ism" of the 1970s, or 1980s-style hunger for shiny new possessions, has meant more than a rejection of a larger whole, a system, or a system of systems. It has also functioned as a denial of public responsibility for one's fellow citizen at some elementary level of civilized decency. This is quite evident in the so-called deinstitutionalization movement. That movement's champions insist that they only wish to emancipate victimized individuals from cruel and oppressive institutions. And that might well be the case. Some institutions, especially public institutions for the mentally impaired or for orphans, have not enjoyed an enviable reputation historically, and often for excellent reasons. Of course it might be remembered that an early and lurid example of the application of deinstitutionalization took place in the 1960s when the then governor of California, Ronald Reagan, purged that state's mental hospitals to balance the state budget, an act not usually interpreted as one of kindness or decency. What most advocates of deinstitutionalization have as their strongest argument is the past behavior of institutions. Obviously this is a complicated issue for all aspects of social policy, not merely for child saving.[28]

And we can easily recognize this individualistic perspective in organized child saving throughout the culture ever since the 1950s. Indeed, one can write the history of organized child saving in America, from the 1950s on, as the history of the invention of the idea that children have rights and of the various efforts to secure those rights. Historically speaking, this has been a novel perspective. But it has also been manifest.[29]

Consider, for example, the efforts of the federal government to guarantee children's rights to a decent education in elementary and secondary education since the early 1950s, with the creation of the Department of Health, Education, and Welfare as a cabinet department in 1950; the Supreme Court's 1954 epochal ruling on school desegregation, *Brown v. Board of Education*; and a multitude of federal programs to assist the schools, through programs for new buildings, school lunches, curriculum development, teacher training, and many other benefits. Even the Cold War emphases on education to meet the Communist peril, as in the National Defense Education Act (1958), in some sense benefited education by legitimating greater expenditures on schools than would otherwise have been the case. In the interwar era, the federal government had not become involved in funding, or even in directly recognizing, preschool education and only obliquely confronted the problem of day care. Through Head Start, begun in 1964 as a part of the Economic Opportunity Act, the federal government did begin to subvene early childhood education as a boost to children deemed to be at risk in society.[30]

Whether or not children have been better off since the inter-war years is difficult to say. Now there are many more programs to protect children than there were in the 1930s, for example; but our infant mortality statistics are more grim than ever. Hence not all children are equally at risk even today, but, to deploy an Orwellian paraphrase, if in some sense all children are equally at risk, nevertheless some are more at risk than others. If we cannot yet make any final judgments, nevertheless we may legitimately suspect that the condition of being at risk is directly related to such social constructs as social class and caste. And there has been a severe lessening of the reform idealism of the mid-century years.

There have been some startling changes, not all of them necessarily antagonistic to child saving. One of the most astonishing has been in the field of juvenile justice. This transformation began with federal involvement—the U.S. Senate Committee to Investigate Juvenile Delinquency, organized in 1953, came alive when Senator Estes Kefauver (D-Tennessee) became chair in 1955. In its nationally televised hearings, the committee pointed to the role of the mass media in fomenting juvenile delinquency. Frederick Wertham, a psychiatrist and extreme critic of pulpy comic books, insisted that violent comic books caused juvenile delinquency. In its deliberations and recommendations, the committee reached no firm conclusion, but it recommended further study. Thus the delinquency issue came again under the jurisdiction of experts in the social sciences and helping professions, and away from jurists, attorneys, and other functionaries in the criminal justice system. The experts' recommendations for juvenile justice would frame future debate and discussion. Within a decade, the states began to implement dramatic changes in juvenile jurisprudence, the most important of which was that children were to have rights in juvenile court, a complete reversal of prior practice. Also the concept of labeling children as "delinquents," and, therefore, presumably implying them to be incorrigible, came under determined attack. Thus in two famous rulings, *Kent v. United States* (1966) and *In re Gault* (1967), the United States Supreme Court overturned much of what had passed for juvenile jurisprudence, essentially by extending the federal Bill of Rights to that area of the law, in a manner thoroughly consistent with many other decisions by the Warren Court. By the early 1990s, a full-fledged children's rights movement existed, with two distinct and highly competitive wings, the one being those who believed in the liberation of the child and its identity with adults insofar as rights were concerned, the other being more paternalistic and traditional, concerned with a comprehensive program of adult protection for children.[31]

In the 1960s, in particular, entities and interests within the federal government promoted protection of children. In 1960, for example, the Children's Bureau and the Women's Bureau sponsored a joint conference on day care and endorsed it as a necessary aspect of the delivery of services to children at risk. The next year, the Congress overrode the "suitable home test" that eight southern states plus Michigan had constructed for the distribution of Aid to Dependent Children recipients, which effectively discriminated against nonwhite—and in particular black—mothers and children. In 1964, Congress passed the Economic Opportunity Act, which launched the much-heralded and much-criticized War on Poverty, including both funding for Head Start, which accommodated almost half a million young children that summer, and the Job Corps, a parallel of the Peace Corps for the inner cities, which did provide some funds for youths who needed jobs. Throughout the 1960s, Congress enacted other laws to provide, for example, for additional federal funding for school lunch programs and for more research on child development and the problem of being at risk, to provide funds to local and state governments to deal with the multiple aspects of juvenile delinquency, and to expand children's rights within the Social Security system. President Richard M. Nixon vetoed the Comprehensive Child Care Act (1971), which would have provided federal assistance for day care, thus demonstrating again, if further proof were needed, that this was (and remains) a remedy that conservatives in this country will not support.

The federal role in addressing child abuse has been less certain. By the early 1960s such physicians as C. Henry Kempe were popularizing the concept of the "battered child syndrome" as a genuine problem in family relations, and the Children's Bureau was contributing to public discourse on the problem, by, for example, holding conferences on child abuse. In the early 1970s a private organization, the Children's Defense Fund, was established and became an effective voice for abused children. In 1973 the Congress enacted the Child Abuse Prevention and Treatment Act, which required the states to meet federal standards on provisions for custody in cases of institutionalization and created a national center for the dissemination of information about the problem.[32]

Along with the enhanced federal role has come an important series of changes in what might be thought of as the balance of forces in organized child saving. One of the more important, yet more poorly understood, has been the evaporation—there is no better word for it—of traditional federalism and states' rights positions within constitutional law and political practice. As late as the 1930s, states' rights was still a virile, important ideology to millions of Americans and their political representatives. As comparatively long ago as the 1950s, however, it had become almost totally vitiated—no more than the transparent argument of southern white groups who organized so-called massive resistance to federal integration of the public schools in the wake of the Supreme Court's *Brown* case.

Why and how this stark alteration of Americans' notions of the relations between the states and the federal government, or, more abstractly, the parts and the whole, happened is too complex to discuss here. Apparently our notions of individuation and individualism reflect a deeper belief that there is no longer a battery of intermediate forces or structures between us as isolated individuals and what, for the lack of a better term, we commonly think of as "the system," whether we are discussing fellow citizens, the national government, the businesses for which we work, and so on. The parallels are obvious and do not require extensive comment.

We can note, however, that our notions of federalism, like those about ourselves and our fellow citizens, and, indeed, our changing sense of the appropriateness, and of the order, of things seems to have had a profound influence upon our sense of what is suitable as far as a whole range of activities is concerned, including, most emphatically, organized child saving. Perhaps it is part of the human condition to be locked into views of the world that circumscribe our notions of what we can do. But it is also clear that if we really want to change what happens to children in our society, we have to acquire at least a modest sense of historical perspective and begin to think of our children as subjects to be cared for instead of mere objects in a given historical and social situation. Whether we can do that or not is the challenge that faces us in public affairs today.

NOTES

Professor of history, Department of History, Iowa State University, Ames, Iowa, 50011-1202. I would like to thank Professor Alberta E. Siegel, of Stanford University, and Bernadine Barr, a doctoral candidate at Stanford, for many stimulating discussions of the scientific and professional issues surrounding this topic over a period of several years, and for helpful, constructive criticism and suggestions. I wrote the present version of this paper while a visiting scholar in the Department of History, University of California, Davis, in the 1990-91 academic year. I wish to thank Professor Roland Marchand, chairperson, and Professor Michael L. Smith for many kindnesses during my year, including—not incidentally—useful office space and stimulating conversations. My thanks also go to this volume's editor, Dr. Roberta Wollons, whose editorial suggestions were as superlative as they were thought provoking, and also to Maris Vinovskis, who offered constructive and stimulating comments as well.

Prior commentators and scholars have used the term "child saving" in ironic fashion, as if to take a cynical position on activities that could be classified as "child saving." In this essay, I hope to provide as objective and historicist a series of historical definitions to "child saving," "child savers," and similar notions as possible.

1. John Dewey, *The School and Society* (Chicago: University of Chicago Press, 1899).

2. The standard work on the progressive education movement is Lawrence A. Cremin, *The Transformation of the School: Progressivism in American Education, 1876-1955* (New York: Alfred A. Knopf, 1961).

3. Barry D. Karl and Stanley N. Katz, "The American Philanthropic Foundation and the Public Sphere," *Minerva* 19 (1981): 236-70. Many generalizations in this essay are based on my research over the last dozen years on the history of organized child saving (including the child sciences).

4. For a further elaboration of this point, see Hamilton Cravens, "History of the Social Sciences," in Sally G. Kohlstedt and Margaret Rossiter, eds., *Historical Writing on American Science: Perspectives and Prospects* (Baltimore: Johns Hopkins University Press, 1986), 183-207.

5. Good introductions to the social conflicts of the era include: John Higham, *Strangers in the Land: Patterns of American Nativism 1860-1925* (New Brunswick, N.J.: Rutgers University Press, 1955); C. Vann Woodward, *Origins of the New South, 1877-1913* (Baton Rouge: Louisiana State University Press, 1951); August Meier and Elliott Rudwick, *From Plantation to Ghetto*, 3d ed., rev., (New York: Hill & Wang, 1976). An

excellent discussion of notions of "otherness" in the era and what happened to them is Henry D. Shapiro, *Appalachia on Our Mind: The Southern Mountains and Mountaineers in the American Consciousness, 1870-1920* (Chapel Hill: University of North Carolina Press, 1978). Discussions of other conceptions of the relations of the parts to the whole in various fields of knowledge include Hamilton Cravens, *The Triumph of Evolution: The Heredity-Environment Controversy 1900-1941* (1978; reprint, Baltimore: Johns Hopkins University Press, 1988); Alan I. Marcus, *Agricultural Science and the Quest for Legitimacy: Farmers, Agricultural Colleges, and Experiment Stations, 1870-1890* (Ames: Iowa State University Press, 1985); Alan I. Marcus and Howard P. Segal, *American Technology: A Brief History* (San Diego: Harcourt Brace Jovanovich, 1988); Thomas L. Haskell, *The Emergence of Professional Social Science: The American Social Science Association and the Nineteenth-Century Crisis of Authority* (Urbana: University of Illinois Press, 1977); Mary O. Furner, *Advocacy and Objectivity: A Crisis in the Professionalization of American Social Science 1865-1905* (Lexington: University Press of Kentucky, 1975); George M. Fredrickson, *The Black Image in the White Mind: The Debate on Afro-American Character and Destiny, 1817-1914* (New York: Harper & Row, 1971).

6. On child saving, see Cravens, "Child-Saving in the Age of Professionalism, 1915-1930," and Ronald D. Cohen, "Child-Saving and Progressivism, 1885-1915," in Joseph M. Hawes and N. Ray Hiner, eds., *American Childhood* (Westport, Conn.: Greenwood Press), 272-309; Robert M. Mennel, *Thorns and Thistles: Juvenile Delinquency in the United States, 1825-1940* (Hanover, N.H.: University Press of New England, 1973); Susan Tiffin, *In Whose Best Interest? Child Welfare Reform in the Progressive Era* (Westport, Conn.: Greenwood Press, 1982). Less useful because of its relentless ahistoricity is David Rothman, *Conscience and Convenience; The Asylum and Its Alternatives in Progressive America* (Boston: Houghton Mifflin, 1980).

7. See Joseph M. Hawes, *Children in Urban Society: Juvenile Delinquency in the Nineteenth Century* (New York: Oxford University Press, 1971), 158-69. The Illinois statute is reprinted in Grace M. Abbott, ed., *The Child and the State*, 2 vols. (Chicago: University of Chicago Press, 1938), 2:392.

8. William Healy and Augusta F. Bronner, "The Child Guidance Clinic: Birth and Growth of an Idea," in Lawson G. Lowrey and Victoria Sloane, eds., *Orthopsychiatry, 1923-1948, Retrospect and Prospect* (New York: American Orthopsychiatric Association, 1948); Steven L. Schlossman, *Love and the American Delinquent: The Theory and Practice of "Progressive" Juvenile Justice, 1825-1920* (Chicago: University of Chicago Press, 1977); Ellen Ryerson, *The Best-Laid Plans: America's Juvenile Court Experiment* (New York: Hill & Wang, 1978); Anthony Platt, *The Child Savers: The Invention of Delinquency* (Chicago: University of Chicago Press, 1969).

9. Henry Herbert Goddard, *The Kallikak Family* (NY: MacMillan, 1912).

10. Hamilton Cravens, "Child-Saving in the Age of Professionalism, 1915-1930," 426-27; Cravens, "Applied Science and Public Policy: The Ohio Bureau of Juvenile Research and the Scientific Prevention of Juvenile Delinquency," in Michael M. Sokal, ed., *Psychological Testing in American Society, 1890-1930* (New Brunswick, N.J.: Rutgers University Press, 1987), 158-94.

11. Dominic Cavallo, "The Politics of Latency: Kindergarten Pedagogy, 1860-1930," in Barbara Finkelstein, ed., *Regulated Children/Liberated Children: Education in Psychohistorical Perspective* (New York: Psychohistory Press, 1979), 164-70 et seq.; Cremin, *The Transformation of the School*; Edward Krug, *The Shaping of the American High School, 1880-1920* (Madison: University of Wisconsin Press, 1964); Krug, *The Shaping of the American High School, Vol. 2: 1920-1940* (Madison: University of Wisconsin Press, 1972); Patricia A. Graham, *Community and Class in American Education, 1865-1918* (New York: Wiley, 1978); David B. Tyack, *The One Best System: A History of American Urban Education* (Cambridge: Harvard University Press, 1974); Marvin Lazerson, *Origins of the Urban School: Public Education in Massachusetts, 1870-1915* (Cambridge: Harvard University Press, 1971); Joel Spring, *Education and the Rise of the Corporate State* (Boston: Beacon Press, 1972); Paul Violas, *The Training of the Urban Working Class: A History of Twentieth-Century American Education* (Chicago: Rand McNally College Publishing, 1978). On business organization, see, for example, Alfred D. Chandler, Jr., *The Visible Hand* (Cambridge: Harvard University Press, 1977).

12. I have discussed this in my book-length manuscript *Before Head Start: The Iowa Child Welfare Research Station and America's Children*; see also Cravens, "Child-Saving in the Age of Professionalism, 1915-1930."

13. Among other works that delve into this transformation are Cravens, *The Triumph of Evolution*, Shapiro, *Appalachia on Our Mind*, Marcus and Segal, *American Technology: A Brief History*, and William S. Graebner, *The Age of Doubt* (Boston: Twyane, 1991).

14. LeRoy Ashby, "Partial Promises and Semi-Visible Youths: The Depression and World War II," in Hawes and Hiner, *American Childhood*, 489-531.

15. LeRoy Ashby, "Partial Promises," 489-531.

16. Robert E. Park, Ernest W. Burgess, and Roderick D. McKenzie, *The City* (Chicago: University of Chicago Press, 1925); McKenzie, *The Metropolitan Community* (Chicago: University of Chicago Press, 1933). Recent works on the Chicago school of sociology include: Stow Persons,

Ethnic Studies at Chicago, 1904-45 (Urbana: University of Illinois Press, 1987); Robert C. Bannister, *Sociology and Scientism: The American Quest for Objectivity, 1880-1940* (Chapel Hill: University of North Carolina Press, 1988). See also Alan I. Marcus, "The City as a Social System: The Importance of Ideas," *American Quarterly* 37 (1985): 332-45, an essay with far broader implications.

17. Karl and Katz, "The American Philanthropic Foundation," 236-70; Cravens, "Child-Saving in the Age of Professionalism, 1915-1930," 415-88.

18. See, for example, Dorothy E. Bradbury, *Five Decades of Action for Children: A History of the Children's Bureau* (Washington, D.C.: Government Printing Office, 1962); J. Stanley Lemons, "The Sheppard-Towner Act: Progressivism in the 1920s," *Journal of American History* 65 (1969): 776-86; Lemons, *The Woman Citizen: Social Feminism in the 1920s* (Urbana: University of Illinois Press, 1973), chap. 6.

19. The above is based on my research in the *Papers* of the White House Conferences on Child Health and Protection, 1909-1950 (chiefly the records of the 1930 conference and its follow-up conferences in the states), 143 1/2 boxes, Hanna Collection, the Hoover Institution, Stanford University, Stanford, California.

20. Stanley Lemons, *The Woman Citizen*, 153-80; Emma Octavia Lundberg, *Unto the Least of These; Social Services for Children* (New York: D. Appleton-Century Co., 1947); on FERA, for example, see "Rules and Regulations, no. 3, issued July 11, 1933, by the FERA," in Edith Abbott, ed., *Public Assistance: American Principles and Policies*, 2 vols., (Chicago: University of Chicago Press, 1940) 1:780; Dorothy Zeitz, *Child Welfare: Principles and Methods* (New York: Wiley, 1959) 155-58; Bradbury, *Five Decades of Action for Children*, 68 et seq.; W. Norton Grubb and Marvin Lazerson, *Broken Promises: How Americans Fail Their Children* (New York: Basic Books, 1982); Mary Irene Atkinson, "Child Welfare Work in Rural Communities," *Annals of the American Academy of Political and Social Science* 212 (1940): 209-15; Theodore L. Reller, "The School and Child Welfare," *Annals of the American Academy of Political and Social Science* 212 (1940): 51-58; Weaver W. Pangburn, "Play and Recreation," *Annals of the American Academy of Political and Social Science* 212 (1940): 121-29; Ruby Takanishi, "Federal Involvements in Early Education (1933-1973): The Need for Historical Perspectives," in Lillian G. Katz, ed., *Current Topics in Early Childhood Education* (Norwood, N.J.: Ablex, 1977), 1:139-63; Margaret O'Brien Steinfels, *Who's Minding the Children? The History and Politics of Day Care in America* (New York: Simon & Schuster, 1973); Mary Cable, *The Little Darlings: A History of Child Rearing in America* (New York: Scribner, 1975); Bernard Greenblatt, *Responsibility for Child Care: The Changing Role of Family and State in Child Development* (San Francisco: Josey-Bass, 1977).

21. Jeremy P. Felt, "The Child Labor Provisions of the Fair Labor Standards Act," *Labor History* 11 (1970): 467-81; Walter I. Trattner, *Crusade for the Children: A History of the National Child Labor Committee and Child Labor Reform in America* (Chicago: Quadrangle Books, 1970); Elizabeth S. Magee, "Impact of the War on Child Labor," *Annals of the American Academy of Political and Social Science* 236 (1944): 101-9; Gertrude F. Zimand, "The Changing Picture of Child Labor," *Annals of the American Academy of Political and Social Science* 236 (1944): 83-91; Beatrice McConnell, "Child Labor in Agriculture," *Annals of the American Academy of Political and Social Science* 236 (1944): 92-100; Nathan Sinai and Odin W. Anderson, *EMIC (Emergency Maternity and Infant Care): A Study of Administrative Experience* (Ann Arbor: University of Michigan Press, 1948); Charles P. Taft, "Public Health and the Family in World War II," *Annals of the American Academy of Political and Social Science* 229 (1943): 145-49.

22. On mothers' pensions, see Mark H. Leff, "Consensus for Reform: The Mothers'-Pension Movement in the Progressive Era," *Social Service Review* 47 (1973): 397-417; on social security, see, for example, Roy Lubove, *The Struggle for Social Security, 1900-1935* (Cambridge: Harvard University Press, 1968); Edward E. Witte, *The Development of the Social Security Act* (Madison: University of Wisconsin Press, 1962).

23. On the history of child development, see Steven L. Schlossman, "Philanthropy and the Gospel of Child Development," *History of Education Quarterly* 21 (1981): 275-99; Cravens, "Child-Saving in the Age of Professionalism, 1915-1930"; Robert R. Sears, *Your Ancients Revisited: A History of Child Development* (Chicago: University of Chicago Press, 1975). On the Stanford project, see, for example, Hamilton Cravens, "A Scientific Project Locked in Time: The Terman Genius Study," forthcoming, *The American Psychologist*, April 1992 issue.

24. On child guidance, see, Sears, *Your Ancients Revisited*; Cravens, "Child-Saving in the Age of Professionalism, 1915-1930"; Roy Lubove, *The Professional Altruist: The Emergence of Social Work as a Career* (Cambridge: Harvard University Press, 1965); Margo Horn, "The Moral Message of Child Guidance, 1925-1945," *Journal of Social History* 18 (1984): 25-36; Horn, *Before It's Too Late: The Child Guidance Movement in the United States, 1922-1945* (Philadelphia: Temple University Press, 1989).

25. Peter Clecak, *America's Quest for the Ideal Self: Dissent and Fulfillment in the 60's and 70's* (New York: Oxford University Press, 1983), presents much evidence for this argument. See also Marcus, "The City as a Social System."

26. Hamilton Cravens, "Recent Controversy in Human Development: A Historical View," *Human Development* 30 (1987): 325-35; see also

Cravens, "Preface," in *The Triumph of Evolution*, vi-xvi. Robert Coles, *Children of Crisis: A Study of Courage and Fear* (Boston: Houghton Mifflin, 1964); Jonathan Kozol, *Death at an Early Age: The Destruction of the Hearts and Minds of Negro Children in the Boston Public Schools* (Boston: Houghton Mifflin, 1967).

27. J. McVicker Hunt, *Intelligence and Experience* (New York: Ronald Press, 1961).

28. A sobering (and relevant) article on deinstitutionalization is Stephen A. Richardson, "Deinstitutionalization and Institutionalization of Children with Mental Retardation," in Harold W. Stevenson and Alberta E. Siegel, eds., *Child Development Research and Social Policy* (Chicago: University of Chicago Press, 1984), 318-66. The historical literature seeking to justify deinstitutionalization to date seems ahistorical; see Cravens, "History of the Social Sciences," 191-92, 201-2.

29. On children's rights, see the interesting and useful book by Joseph M. Hawes, *The Children's Rights Movement: A History of Advocacy and Protection* (Boston: Twyane Publishers, 1991).

30. See Charles E. Strickland and Andrew M. Ambrose, "The Baby Boom, Prosperity, and the Changing Worlds of Children, 1945-1963," 533-86, and Elizabeth Douvan, "The Age of Narcissism, 1963-1982," 587-618, in Hawes and Hiner, *American Childhood*, on the postwar era generally, especially for useful bibliographical assistance.

31. See, for example: James B. Gilbert, *A Cycle of Outrage: American Reaction to the Juvenile Delinquent in the 1950s* (New York: Oxford University Press, 1986); Elaine Tyler May, *Homeward Bound: American Families in the Cold War Era* (New York: Basic Books, 1988). On children's rights, see, for example, Beatrice Gross and Ronald Gross, eds., *The Children's Rights Movement: Overcoming the Oppression of Young People* (Garden City, N.Y.: Anchor Books, 1977), Kenneth Kenniston and the Carnegie Council on Children, *All Our Children: The American Family Under Pressure* (New York: Harcourt Brace Jovanovich, 1977). A representative text of the child liberationist point of view is John Holt, *Escape from Childhood* (New York: Ballantine Books, 1974), and an example of the critique of the child liberationist argument is Neal Postman, *The Disappearance of Childhood* (New York: Delacorte Press, 1982).

32. See, for example: Ray E. Helfer and C. Henry Kempe, eds., *The Battered Child* (Chicago: The University of Chicago Press, 1968); David C. Gil, *Violence Against Children: Physical Child Abuse in the United States* (Cambridge: Harvard University Press, 1970); Children's Defense Fund, *A Call for Action to Make Our Nation Safe for Children: A Briefing Book on the State of American Children in 1988* (Washington, D.C.: Children's Defense Fund, 1988).

STEVEN SCHLOSSMAN
SUSAN TURNER

2

Status Offenders, Criminal Offenders, and Children "At Risk" in Early Twentieth-Century Juvenile Court

The term *children at risk* may be modern, but there is little question that the concept underlying it has strong roots in the history of American child welfare and juvenile justice. Indeed, the term probably captures with greater precision the policy intent and prospective clientele of the early juvenile court than any term which the founders themselves used to describe the court's mission.

In order to win political approval from sometimes skeptical state legislatures, many juvenile courts began operations around the turn of the century under a rather narrow legal mandate. But as juvenile courts gained wide acceptance throughout the country in the 1910s, their legal prerogatives as multipurpose child welfare institutions were considerably expanded. By the

1920s, the great majority of juvenile courts (with New York City as a partial exception) were expected to deal regularly with many types of noncriminal as well as criminal children. We know the former group of children today as "status offenders."

In numerous books and articles, spokespersons for the court went out of their way to describe status offenders and criminal offenders in undifferentiated terms. By and large, they portrayed all children who were petitioned to court as blameless for their difficulties, malleable in their habits, and at risk of suffering irremediable harm without quick intervention by child welfare professionals. The court's founders stressed the commonalities, not the differences, in the backgrounds and behaviors of children in court. That one group of children was composed of lawbreakers, and the other was not, entirely missed the point, in their view. The children were, in a word, all "delinquents"; as such, they were equally at risk.[1]

During the 1970s, of course, it was precisely the undifferentiated clientele of the juvenile court that became a major source of concern to social workers and legal rights advocates. These critics insisted that, regardless of the court's benevolent intentions, it was not only unjust but harmful to brand status offenders as delinquents. Major reform efforts were undertaken to rewrite legal codes to eliminate status offenses—behaviors such as running away, disobeying parents, breaking curfew, being sexually promiscuous, playing truant—from court jurisdiction and to prohibit incarceration of status offenders in juvenile or adult jails, prisons, or training schools. Landmark legislation at the federal level, notably the Juvenile Justice and Delinquency Prevention Act of 1974, and in various states, such as AB 3121 in California in 1977, attested to the nationwide influence of the campaign to decriminalize status offenses.

Considerable controversy exists today about the extent to which status offenders have actually been removed from most courts and institutions. Clearly, the practice has not entirely stopped in many jurisdictions.[2] Moreover, recent scholarship has shown that the administrative relabeling of offenses can easily camouflage the presence of status offenders in courts and institutions.[3] Nonetheless, from a long-term perspective, the heyday of the status offender in American juvenile justice is clearly over. The political triumph and intellectual consensus that operationalized the expansive, Progressive Era definition of children at risk—a definition that the status offender quintessentially embodied—has largely passed into history.

The centrality of status offenses to the original mission of the juvenile court has been much remarked by historians—both those favorable to, and those opposed to, the court's broad discretionary powers over noncriminal children. Yet there has been surprisingly little historical inquiry regarding just who status offenders were; the nature of their objectionable behaviors; what fraction of the court's cases involved them; how the court disposed of their cases; and—perhaps least well understood—how status offenders compared to criminal offenders. This essay seeks to break new ground in interpreting the history of juvenile court by providing preliminary answers to these questions. Using case data, we seek to recall an era when saving children at risk was far more central to the mission of the juvenile justice system than it is today.

1. MALE VERSUS FEMALE STATUS OFFENDERS: PORTRAITS IN NUMBERS

Issues of Data and Method

We present information on children with filed delinquency petitions (both status and criminal offenders) from a single institution, the Los Angeles Juvenile Court. Our data derive from an unprecedentedly rich body of original case files. The data cover three broad categories of information concerning the children and their families: (1) background characteristics, such as age, race, occupation, and schooling; (2) offense characteristics, such as status versus criminal offense, use of weapons; and (3) legal processing, from initial petition to final dismissal, such as use of detention, probation, or custodial placement.

Our analysis draws from an ongoing, large-scale study of juvenile delinquency and its treatment in Los Angeles between 1900 and 1960. We focus in this essay on only a single data point, 1930, when the juvenile court was at the zenith of its popularity in the United States, and when it was also, we suspect, at its most aggressive in seeking to include status, as well as criminal, offenders within its jurisdiction.

We draw upon the records of 511 girls and boys who were petitioned to court for status and criminal offenses.[4] To simplify the presentation, we have included only descriptive statistics and have broken down the data under just two headings: offense (status versus criminal) and gender (male versus female).

Status Offenders in the Overall Caseload

Just how large a component were status offenders in the juvenile court's overall caseload? In Los Angeles, status offenders formed 36 percent (n = 184) of the delinquency petitions filed in 1930.[5] Thus, even in the early twentieth-century heyday of the status offender in juvenile court, the bulk (64 percent) of the children who were petitioned for delinquency were accused of criminal, rather than status, offenses.

Nonetheless, status offenders clearly did occupy a sizable share of the court's time and energy. Furthermore, from reading several thousand case files, it is our impression that children who were petitioned for status offenses generally took more of the court's time—both at initial processing and in repeat court appearances—than did children who were petitioned for criminal offenses.

To speak of status offenders as a single group of delinquents is more than a little misleading, for gender formed a major dividing line among them. Among delinquents as a whole, boys outnumbered girls 4 to 1 (407 boys to 104 girls); but among status offenders, boys and girls were almost equally represented (93 boys and 91 girls). The major gender differential occurred among the criminal offenders: 77 percent of the 407 boys were accused of criminal conduct versus 12.5 percent of the 104 girls. A delinquent girl was thus six times more likely to be charged with a status offense, even though the total numbers of boys and girls charged with status offenses were about the same.

Offense Characteristics of Status Offenders

The Los Angeles Juvenile Court may have dealt with boy and girl status offenders in equal numbers, but the particular kinds of status offenses for which they were brought to court differed.[6] The great majority of girl status offenders (81.3 percent) were charged with being "incorrigible."[7] Approximately 10 percent were charged with being runaways (from either home or a placement); 2.2 percent were charged with truancy; and another 6.6 percent were charged with sex offenses.[8] The alleged status offenses of boys, on the other hand, were more varied. A slight majority (51.6 percent) of the boys were charged with being incorrigible. Almost one-quarter (22.6 percent) of the boys were charged with being truant, and almost one-fifth (18.3 percent) were charged with being runaways. Slightly more than 5 percent of the boys were charged with a sex offense.

Background Characteristics

The background characteristics of the boys and girls petitioned for status offenses revealed some differences. Female status offenders were somewhat older than their male counterparts: 52.8 percent of the girls versus 33.4 percent of the boys were age sixteen or over.[9] More surprising was that female status offenders were more often racial minorities (Hispanics and blacks comprised 34.1 percent of the girls versus 19.3 percent of the boys),[10] and that females were more often referred to court by the police (43.2 percent of girls versus 25.8 percent of boys).[11] It may be that the police in Los Angeles—particularly the women officers who staffed the Crime Prevention Division and who regularly patrolled such popular teen hangouts as "the Pike" near Long Beach, the pier at Santa Monica, and downtown hotels and movie theaters—more closely monitored indiscreet behaviors by minority girls than by white girls, or at least more often filed charges against minority than against white girls for indiscrete behaviors.[12]

However, in general, the familial backgrounds of the male and female status offenders were similar. Both were likely to reside in a working-class household.[13] Approximately half of the children were living in single-parent/guardian households (45.2 percent of boys, 52.8 percent of girls). Hardly any of the children's parents were California natives, although most (except for the Hispanics) were native born, and most of the children were born in other states (70.8 percent of boys, 69.2 percent of girls).

Considerable family stress had characterized many of these children's upbringings, although not significantly more for one sex than for the other. Girls and boys were around equally likely to have been placed previously outside of their own homes to live (41.8 percent of boys, 45.6 percent of girls), to have experienced legally recorded or admitted family violence (14.1 percent of boys, 18.7 percent of girls), and to have an immediate family member with a criminal record (23.9 percent of boys, 15.4 percent of girls). Boys were more likely than girls to have substance-abusing parents (11.0 percent of boys versus 3.3 percent of girls),[14] although the reliability of parental admissions regarding alcohol or drug use seems dubious.

In sum, while the social backgrounds of the boy and girl status offenders were generally similar, there were significant differences in the types of offenses that brought them before the court, as well as differences by race and age.

Sanctions, Sex, and Disease:
Dismissal, Probation, Detention

How did the court deal with boy and girl status offenders? Did it treat them similarly or differently? Our descriptive analysis focuses on the apparent differences in treatment by the court—that is, in the observed outcomes experienced by boys and girls—and suggests possible reasons for any observed differences in treatment. Future analyses will examine the extent to which apparent differences seem more related to the youth's background characteristics or to the youth's sex per se.[15]

We have calculated five measures of the court's decision-making: (1) Was the petition dismissed? (2) Was the child placed on informal probation? (3) Was the child placed on formal probation? (4) Was the child detained in jail before and/or following the hearing? and (5) Was the child committed to a custodial facility?

Relatively few status offenders had their petitions, dismissed (7.5 percent of boys, 8.8 percent of girls). This suggests that the court regarded nearly all of them as at least minimally at risk and, further, that the court meant business and was not simply trying to scare a child into better behavior by threatening court intervention. The court also gave relatively few children the modest sanction of informal probation, although here an interesting gender difference emerged: 15.0 percent of the boys versus none of the girls were placed on informal probation.[16] Without additional data, we cannot seriously probe into the court's motivation for excluding girls entirely from informal probation. However, we would speculate that in the court's eyes more was at stake for a girl than a boy in youthful indiscretions. By definition, in other words, the court viewed girls as being more at risk than boys, hence they were more in need of official monitoring. In fact, the court placed girls on formal probation considerably more often than boys (47.2 percent versus 29.0 percent).[17]

The court's tendency to authorize more formal supervision over status-offending girls than boys was also evident in its use of detention, both before and following the courtroom hearing. To be sure, the most notable statistic with regard to prehearing detention was how frequently the court used it for *both* boys and girls. Nonetheless, girls were detained significantly more than boys (92.0 percent of girls versus 78.7 percent of boys).[18] To appear in court, then, carried with it a strong probability of doing jail time as well, especially for girls. Gender differences were equally notable in the use of detention following the hearing: 56.0 percent of the girls versus 35.5 percent of the boys were detained.[19] Both before and following their hearings, moreover, the girls were detained for lengthier time periods than the boys.

Why were girl status offenders detained in jail more frequently than boy status offenders? The most probable explanation derives less from the formal allegations lodged in the petitions than from a combination of two factors: first, the higher rates of sexual activity among the girls who were petitioned to court (to be discussed in part 3), and second, the health risks associated with sexual adventurism in the early twentieth century.

Venereal disease was still quite common in 1930, and no reasonably effective cure for it (most notably, penicillin) would emerge until a decade or so later.[20] Court officials vigorously asserted their public health obligations in the screening and treatment of venereal diseases. They probed into the sexual histories of their clients in great detail, not only better to understand their behavior patterns and home backgrounds, but, of more immediate concern, to determine whom to test for VD. At least this was their ostensible motivation; in practice, it appeared that hardly any of the boys were tested for VD, whereas virtually all of the girls were tested.

As it turned out, 33.0 percent of the status-offending girls were afflicted with syphilis or gonorrhea. To deal with this situation, the court generally insisted that treatment be formally begun while the girl was in custody (in a special hospital section of the jail, in the county hospital, or in private sanitaria) and that continuing treatment be monitored by the court afterward. A girl on probation who refused to receive the very painful Salvarsan treatments could be returned to the jail and be compelled to receive treatment.

In sum, the higher detention rate of female status offenders would appear, in good measure, to have been a product of the special public health responsibilities that the juvenile court exercised in the early twentieth century, which it applied with much greater vigilance over girls than over boys.[21]

Long-term Institutionalization

The bottom-line decision that juvenile courts make whenever a petition is filed is, of course, whether to return the child to her or his home or to place the child elsewhere to live. The most severe sanction that the court could impose in 1930, as today, was to commit the child to a custodial facility. Prior research has indicated that juvenile courts in the early twentieth century were twice as likely to institutionalize girl as boy delinquents. Did this pattern hold for status offenders in the Los Angeles Juvenile Court?

The answer would appear to be no: the court committed approximately the same fraction of girl and boy status offenders to custodial institutions in California (22.0 percent of girls, 18.3 percent of boys). Regardless of whether or not there were significant gender differences, however, the most interesting point about these data may be the high rate (approximately one of five) at which the court institutionalized status offenders, regardless of gender. The court clearly meant business in its dealings with status offenders. When it adjudged a child seriously at risk, the fact that she or he was accused only of a status offense, rather than a criminal offense, was not necessarily a deterrent to institutionalization.

2. STATUS VERSUS CRIMINAL OFFENDERS: PORTRAITS IN NUMBERS

The status offender best personified the children-at-risk concept in early twentieth-century juvenile justice policy. However, as we argued earlier, the principal spokespersons for the court went to some pains to blur the differences between children accused of status, versus criminal, offenses. They stressed the common adjustment problems, at home and in the community, that all delinquent children tended to experience. Every delinquent child, in their view, deserved to benefit from the court's (presumably) benign intervention.

During the past two decades, much historical commentary has centered on whether the founders' intentions, and the institution they invented to realize their intentions, were indeed benign, in theory or in practice. We address these broader debates about social control only obliquely here, via a new line of empirical inquiry.

We ask two key questions of our case data. First, were the background characteristics of status and criminal offenders essentially the same; that is, what distinguished these delinquents from one another as children at risk? Second, did status and criminal offenders receive similar sanctions; that is, did the court treat the two groups equally as children at risk, regardless of the formal accusations against them?

As previously, we present only descriptive statistics to answer these questions, with the additional limitation that due to small sample sizes (a result of the tiny fraction of girls petitioned for crimes) we cannot now compare girl status with girl criminal offenders. Our discussion will necessarily center, therefore, on comparisons between boy status and boy criminal offenders.

As demonstrated earlier, criminal offenders accounted for the great majority (over three-quarters) of the boys petitioned to juvenile court. The boy criminal offenders were accused overwhelmingly of property rather than personal, offenses, especially burglary, auto theft, and petty theft (77.4 percent of all criminal offenses). They rarely committed crimes alone: 33.6 percent committed their petition offenses with one accomplice, and 47.7 percent had two or more accomplices, mainly males around the same age.[22] Insofar as we could determine, 14.2 percent of the juveniles had formal or informal gang affiliations, and 10.8 percent possessed weapons at the scene of their crimes. (By definition, of course, status offenders were not reported for similar patterns of illegal conduct.) In addition, and not surprisingly, criminal offenders were far more likely than status offenders to have been referred to court by agents of law enforcement (71.3 percent versus 25.8 percent).[23]

Aside from their criminal behaviors, were the basic profiles of boy criminals like or unlike those of boy status offenders? Overall, several key points of dissimilarity tend to stand out, despite similarities in the boys' ethnic and economic backgrounds.[24] Status offenders were somewhat younger than criminal offenders (33.4 percent versus 49.4 percent age sixteen and over),[25] and were also less likely to live with two parents (54.8 percent versus 65.9 percent).[26] Two indicators of major family stress were substantially higher among status offenders than among criminal offenders: family violence (14.1 percent versus 4.8 percent),[27] and substance abuse (11.0 percent versus 3.5 percent).[28] On the basis of the above characteristics, it would not have been surprising if the court had tended to view status offenders as more at risk than criminal offenders due to their younger ages, less-intact family structures, and less-stable family situations.

Two additional features of the children's backgrounds would almost certainly have pushed the court to this conclusion. First, status offenders, though younger, were far more likely to have been placed previously outside of their own homes to live: 41.8 percent versus 22.4 percent.[29] This clearly attested to the greater prior instability of the status offenders' living environments. Second, and surely corroboratory evidence in the eyes of the court, status offenders were far more likely to have a prior history of running away: 42.2 percent versus 13.9 percent.[30]

Obviously, raw statistics of this type are a poor substitute for intensive analysis of individual family situations; various "push" factors toward crime in the homes of the criminal offenders may not be captured very well by our indicators, although they may have been transparent to a savvy judge. Still, comparison of the several indicators we have reported suggests that there were indeed significant differences between status and criminal offenders that the court was likely to integrate into its decision making.[31] At the very least, the court was unlikely to have viewed status offenders as less needy of court intervention simply because their "delinquencies" were not criminal. Indeed, quite the opposite. The court may well have been inclined to view status offenders as more at risk, in the long run, than criminal offenders, regardless of the different reasons each group had landed in court.

That the court was probably thinking along these lines is suggested by two patterns observable in its decision making. First, and very decisively, status offenders were detained following their hearings far more frequently than were criminal offenders: 35.5 percent versus 13.7 percent.[32] And second, the ultimate sanction, status offenders were placed in custodial institutions substantially more often than were criminal offenders: 18.3 percent versus 7.6 percent.[33]

It seems, then, that boy status offenders received harsher sanctions than boy criminal offenders. Not the criminal, but the noncriminal, got the stiffer penalty in the Los Angeles Juvenile Court, where decision making appeared to hinge—at least on the basis of this preliminary statistical overview—less on whether the child had formally broken the law, and more on an informal assessment of the child's vulnerability to harm at home.

Summary

In parts 1 and 2, we have statistically compared boy versus girl status offenders and boy status versus boy criminal offenders with regard to various aspects of their backgrounds, offenses, and treatment in the Los Angeles Juvenile Court in 1930. At several points, we have speculated on how these data appeared to reflect and to shape the court's decisions about which members of its clientele were more or less at risk.

Three major sets of findings strike us as most important:[34]

Boys versus Girls: Overall Differences
1. Boys and girls differed in the types of status offenses they were accused of committing.
2. Boys and girls differed in their likelihood of being petitioned for a criminal offense.

Boy versus Girl Status Offenders
3. Boy and girl status offenders shared similar socioeconomic and family backgrounds.
4. Girl status offenders were more likely to receive formal supervision and detention than their male counterparts but were no more likely to be sent to custodial institutions.

Boy Status Offenders versus Boy Criminal Offenders
5. The families of boy status offenders experienced considerably greater disarray and stress than the families of boy criminal offenders.
6. Boy status offenders were more likely to be detained in jail and placed in custodial institutions than boy criminal offenders.

3. GIRL STATUS OFFENDERS AND BOY CRIMINAL
   OFFENDERS: PORTRAITS IN MINIATURE

Inevitably, statistical portraits of the kind we have just presented flatten human experience. Juvenile court evoked intense emotions and dramatic personal encounters that statistical representation alone can barely begin to suggest. Fortunately, many documents that are contained in the case files of the Los Angeles Juvenile Court—especially pre- and posthearing reports and sporadic trial transcripts—have preserved much of the substance as well as the flavor of daily events in court. We now turn to these unique qualitative and anecdotal data.

Space limitations prevent us from incorporating here the enormous variety of information from individual cases that would be necessary to illustrate each of the major statistical findings summarized above. Instead, we have selected a small group of cases that will enable us to refine and go beyond our statistical findings by examining two points of unusual interest: first, in the case of girl status offenders, the greater centrality of sexual offenses than is revealed by formal analysis of the petitioning process; and second, in the case of boy criminal offenders, the tendency of the court to treat their lawbreaking activities fairly leniently.

Sex, Status Offenses, and Girls 'at Risk'

We observed earlier several differences in the offense patterns of girl and boy status offenders, notably the higher share of girls who were charged with incorrigibility and of boys who were charged with running away and truancy. We also observed that relatively few girls or boys were petitioned for sex offenses. While these data are accurate, they may be misleading.

First, they imply that law enforcement officials were rigorously concerned to apply the most appropriate legal label to each child's offense. This was simply not the case. The designation of a specific offense on a petition was intrinsically ambiguous; moreover, in practice it was a rather casually administered process. Different labels were often applied to similar behaviors, and the same labels were often applied to different behaviors.

Second, and more central to the following presentation, the formal labeling of a status offender—whether as an incorrigible, a runaway, or whatever—often obscured the fact that the matter of greatest concern to the court was the child's sexual behavior. This concern applied especially to the girl status offenders, 77.5 percent of whom were sexually active (as compared to 27.8 percent of the boys). Whether girls were formally petitioned as sex offenders or not, the court tended to assume that every girl in court was sexually active unless proven otherwise. To the juvenile court, a sexually active girl was virtually by definition at risk and in need of formal supervision. For girls, *incorrigibility* and *runaway* were generally euphemisms for out-of-wedlock sexual activity.

But it was not just the greater frequency of sexual activity that distinguished the cases of girl and boy status offenders, however. Rather, the girls' cases more often revealed a broader pattern of adolescent revolt: a conscious rejection by the girls of both parental discipline and social convention regarding the boundaries of acceptable female behavior. Unfortunately for the girls—as suggested both by the statistical data presented earlier and by several poignant case illustrations presented below—the physical and emotional stakes at issue in this adolescent revolt were high indeed, in light of the extraordinary frequency of venereal disease among girl status offenders in court.

Consider the troubles of seventeen-year-old MO, case #52596, an illegitimate child whose parents' whereabouts were unknown and who had been brought up by one of her several aunts in the Los Angeles area. After a relatively trouble-free adolescence, MO had recently begun to chafe under her aunt's refusal to allow her to go to dances unchaperoned, and the two had been quarreling regularly.

In the midst of these difficulties, the aunt suddenly took ill and had to be hospitalized. MO decided to move in with another aunt, who worked long hours outside of the home. Almost immediately, MO began having sex with a neighborhood boy. Quite tragically for MO, it turned out that this boy despised the aunt with whom she had moved in and intended to hurt the aunt through his sexual adventures with MO. The boy's motivations might be considered irrelevant, except that he knew (and did not tell MO) that he was a carrier of venereal disease.

Following a fight in which the boy beat up MO so severely that she had to be hospitalized, the two broke off their relationship. To make matters worse, while MO was in the hospital, the boy boasted throughout the neighborhood of their sexual adventures and of the fact that he had probably infected her with venereal disease. Hearing this scuttlebutt, the aunt who had raised MO petitioned her to juvenile court for incorrigibility. MO was immediately detained in juvenile hall where she did indeed test positive for venereal disease.

Following her court hearing, MO was detained in juvenile hall for two and one-half months to receive treatment and was then released to her aunt on probation, on the condition that she return regularly for additional treatments. In the court's eyes, MO's defiant attitude toward her aunt/guardian, her sexual adventurism, and her disease made her triply at risk and in need of court supervision. Chastened by her harsh experiences, MO cooperated fully with her probation officer and remained under supervision until shortly after her eighteenth birthday.

Many of the girls who were petitioned for status offenses had sought to demonstrate their freedom from parental restraint, and to carry out their sexual adventures, by consorting with sailors who congregated at teen hangouts in such coastal cities as Santa Monica, Long Beach, and San Pedro. The police, especially women officers of the city's crime prevention bureau, regularly patrolled these areas on the alert for outwardly indecent behavior by the girls and the sailors. But the numbers of police were far too few, however, to inhibit informal dating or the consummation of sexual activities in nearby hotels, cars, open fields or on the beach.

EB, case #50506, was a sixteen-year-old who, following regular battles with her stepmother about appropriate female behavior, began socializing with and having sex with sailors. Only after she had left on a train with a sailor for a tryst in San Diego, however, did her parents get disgusted enough to intervene. They asked the police to file a petition for incorrigibility and had EB arrested en route, returned to Los Angeles, and detained in juvenile hall. At her hearing, the court issued EB a strong reprimand and placed her on probation.

Though outwardly penitent during and following her court appearance (she was really more in love with another sailor than the one she was caught traveling with, she assured the court), EB continued her sexual adventures with new paramours—even after she realized that she had venereal disease. The court placed EB periodically in juvenile hall for chastening and medical treatment and threatened to commit her to the state reform school (she would take poison, she promised) if she did not control her sexual behavior.

Finally, after nearly a year of frenetic sexual adventurism, EB suddenly got married (to someone she had only recently met). The court, as was its custom, dismissed the case. No doubt the court continued to regard EB as seriously at risk and to question the wisdom of her quick decision to marry. But for sexually defiant mid-adolescent girls like EB, the court tended to view marriage as a far better alternative than any that the parents, or the court, had to offer.

EB's decision to marry came with little forethought and only after much sexual experimentation. For many girls who were petitioned to juvenile court as status offenders, however, sexual involvements and marital aspirations were more clearly linked from the start. The court was essentially asked to arbitrate between them and their parents regarding whether and when they should marry. The court accepted this responsibility, in part because it recognized, from long experience, that sexual activity of girls who were still living at home was likely to cause enough turmoil to undermine the emotional stability of the entire family unit.

Consider the situation of LP, case #53671, a seventeen-year-old whose mother had charged her with incorrigibility after she had run away from home. LP had been arguing with her mother for months because her mother refused to allow her to go to movies and to dances. LP's goal, in running away, was in part simply to escape her mother's incessant nagging. But LP's long-term intention was to be free so that she could marry her twenty-seven-year-old boyfriend, a well-paid Hollywood sound technician to whom her mother objected because of his alleged drinking (recall that Prohibition was in effect). LP's mother doubtless had other worries, too: her husband had left her recently, and LP, who was paid well as a studio dancer, provided her sole source of income.

Although LP was sexually active—she admitted that she had slept twice with a boarder in her home the previous year—she emphasized that she had never had sex with her prospective husband and desired to keep her sexual history secret from him. Unfortunately for LP, the physicians at juvenile hall discovered (to her surprise, she claimed) that she had venereal disease. Perplexed by her situation and unwilling to inform her boyfriend of the facts, she begged the court to help her consummate a devious plan. Following her release from juvenile hall, she would marry her boyfriend and then—immediately after the ceremony—she would feign illness, leave town for a protracted rest, check into a hospital to receive treatment, and return to live with her husband after she was cured. Of course, the court rejected this plan (the logic of which seemed impeccable to LP). While the court would agree to the marriage and would do what it could to reconcile the mother, it insisted that LP either get cured beforehand or be honest with her boyfriend about her venereal disease before marrying him.

Eventually this case became bogged down in bizarre uncertainties regarding LP's actual age, whether she had initially contracted venereal disease as a child, and whether the mother was

the natural, or an adoptive, parent. In the end, the court overrode the mother's objections and sanctioned the marriage—but
only after it had taken it upon itself to inform the prospective
husband of LP's health situation and to arrange for a cauteriza-
tion of LP's cervix (in order to contain her venereal disease).

Clearly, the juvenile court did not hesitate to become deeply
entangled in the intimate lives of children whom it considered at
risk. It was a rare sexually active girl, indeed, into whose personal life the court was not ready to intervene. In the court's
view, a girl's sexual activity per se placed her at risk; and it was
the presence or absence of sexual behavior, not the formal petition offense, that generally preoccupied the court in adjudicating
the cases of girl status offenders.

On Boys and Crime: The Criminal Offender as Innocent

In part 2, we observed the apparent anomaly that, among boys,
the criminal offenders were treated more leniently (i.e., were
less often detained and placed in custodial institutions) than
were the status offenders. We speculated there, on the basis of
several statistical indicators, that the more difficult family situations of the status offenders probably helped to explain this
result. The qualitative information in the case files suggests additional explanations for this pattern of greater leniency. We focus
our attention now not on what made the status offenders seem
more at risk, but instead on the types of crimes, and the attitudes toward children's crimes, that appear to have led the court
to dispense rather lenient treatment to children who were petitioned for criminal offenses.

Three related elements of the court's decision making seem
to have been involved. First was the relative unseriousness of
the actual criminal offenses with which most boys were charged.
Petty property offenses were the juvenile court's bread and but-
ter. Labels often made some of the more serious property crimes,
such as burglary or grand theft, appear more heinous that they
really were. Moreover, the fact that juvenile court, in order to
sustain a petition, did not have to prove guilt according to stringent due-process criteria, meant that boys were regularly petitioned to juvenile court for petty crimes that would almost never
have led to arrest or complaint in adult criminal court.

Second was the court's tendency to take a "boys will be
boys" attitude toward petty stealing behavior that occurred in

the face of overwhelming temptation. Stealing when tempted to do so, the court appeared to believe, was almost instinctual for young boys. At the least, it was readily understandable and even excusable behavior; it did not necessarily connote major problems in the boy's emotional life or in the quality of his parental and home environment. Children who committed minor crimes when confronted with a ripe opportunity, in other words, could not be assumed to be at risk; the court's attitude toward them was often to forgive and forget.

Third, the pattern of dispositions suggests that the court did indeed take seriously the special mission that had been defined for it by such pioneers as Denver's Ben Lindsey: that is, to educate, not to punish; to rehabilitate, not to determine guilt. The court's goal was to identify and assist children at risk, not to fulfill the classic criminal-justice goals of deterrence and retribution. The circumstances in which a child found himself, quite as much as the specific conduct of which he was accused, were what was on trial. The formal charges against a child were less important to the court than its own assessment of his prospects for normal future development.

In light of this philosophy, it was perhaps not inconsistent for the court to determine that a status offender was more seriously at risk, and more in need of major court intervention, than a criminal offender and to place the former rather than the latter in a custodial institution. Indeed, one might even suggest that a bias in this direction was built into the court's raison d'être.

We have chosen four cases to illustrate succinctly these three general points. As earlier, the anecdotal data are inevitably idiosyncratic and can only broadly suggest how the court dealt with children who were petitioned for criminal offenses. All four petitions were filed by the police; the first two were for petty theft, and the last two were for burglary.

LM, case #53091, was a thirteen-year-old boy who had been arrested, along with several other boys, for stealing vegetables from an open truck that was parked at a gas station. This type of theft was apparently quite common: a swarm of boys would move in rapidly while the driver was indisposed and the truck was being filled with gas by the attendant. The boys would jump the truck, steal whatever they could gather quickly, and run. Usually, if the cargo was not expensive, the thefts were too insignificant for the driver to complain about them to the police. However, the practice of theft at this filling station had become so regular that the police had prepared a stakeout. When the boys descended on the truck, the police nabbed as many as they could get their hands on. LM was one of these.

Or was he? As so often occurred when the police arrested large numbers of boys for thievery, questions arose as to whether all of the arrestees were culpable. LM claimed to be an innocent bystander who was inadvertently picked up in the police sweep. Doubtless the court was suspicious of LM's claim: from everyday experience, judges and probation officers well knew that children often lied about their behavior, particularly if they had already persuaded their parents of their innocence. In this case, though, the court was genuinely uncertain about the facts. When further investigation revealed that LM's parents, though desperately poor, were regular churchgoers and were attentive to their children's needs and that LM had a good school record, the court was inclined toward letting him off with a mild reprimand. And when LM's father further revealed that he had a new job in San Jose for which he wanted to leave the following week, the court decided to dismiss the charges entirely and to let the family be on its way.

Guilty or not, LM's was not the kind of stealing behavior that would usually lead the court to issue a stern warning to the child or his parent or to contemplate major intervention into the household. Even if LM did steal, boys would be boys. Hopefully, his experience in court would be sufficient to make him think twice before causing such trouble for himself and his parents again.

Fifteen-year-old PW, case #53796, was also accused of petty theft for stealing one dollar's worth of gas from a city parking garage. It seems that PW and a close friend, in trying to steal the gas, had initially succeeded in filling their gas can but had dropped it and run away when they became scared that someone had seen them. Later the same day, they returned to the garage in the friend's car. When they spotted the can where they had left it, PW—with the lack of guile so often evident in children's crimes—stepped out of the car to retrieve it. At this moment, the two boys were nabbed by the garage attendants and held for the police.

As in the case of LM, however, PW raised doubts about whether he was indeed guilty. According to PW, he had never participated in the initial attempt to steal the gas and did not know that the gas was stolen. Rather, he had been duped by his friend into going for a ride and retrieving the gas can so that they could achieve a quick getaway. According to PW, he had no idea that the gas can was not his friend's property; he just did as he was asked, out of friendship.

The friend disputed PW's account of the story and informed the judge that PW was a full partner in the botched theft. Following separate interrogations of the boys, the judge was clearly inclined to believe that PW was lying or at least was not telling the whole truth.

In the end, though, the "facts" of the case were really not what was at issue. Though the theft obviously demonstrated premeditation, planning, and determination to carry it through, the amount of gas stolen was minimal, and the boys apparently only wanted the gas to go for a pleasure ride. Boys will be boys, especially when their cars are involved—this was the assumption that appeared to guide the court's decision making. Thus, the judge dismissed the case against PW's friend—the one who fully admitted to planning and executing the theft—after mildly warning him not to do it again.

However, the court was not similarly lenient with PW. The judge placed him under formal supervision—not because he was certain that PW had not been duped, but, rather, because PW's failure to admit that he had done anything wrong conveyed an attitude of defiance. As the judge made clear in a long and rambling moral lecture, stealing behavior per se certainly did not indicate to him that a child was at risk. Had PW merely been a thief and admitted his wrongdoing, his case would have been dismissed with a simple reprimand, as was his friend's. But it was PW's hostile attitude that, in the judge's view, did indeed place him at risk because it portended future confrontations with institutions of authority. PW was therefore placed under the court's supervision for three months before his case was dismissed.

The law regards burglary as a more serious crime than simple theft, because it involves illegal entry as well as thievery, moreover, when the burglary is of a home, it carries the additional implicit risk of confrontation with the resident and, hence, of personal violence. Yet only infrequently did the burglaries committed by children take on menacing qualities. Children rarely seemed to plan their illegal entries with the intention of stealing expensive items for personal use or for resale, and almost always stole from homes they knew well or places where they worked. The opportunity for easy and unnoticed theft just seemed to present itself, and the boy could not resist the temptation: this was how the boys often explained their own actions. Interestingly enough, the court generally acted as if this explanation was reasonably persuasive.

To be sure, the court would never fully exculpate a burglar, as it might a petty thief; the intrinsic dangers presented by the act of illegal entry, however innocently pursued, were too great to turn the other cheek entirely. But while a boy who conducted a burglary was almost by definition at risk and in need of probation, he did not necessarily require, in the court's view, a more intrusive restriction on his freedom than if he had been a truant from school or a runaway from home.

JH, case #50941, was a fourteen-year-old boy accused of burglarizing a store with a friend. Before committing the burglary, the boys had been picking apples in an orchard, when they noticed from afar that the door to a nearby store was open and that no one was guarding the store's merchandise. They snuck into the store, stole a few wrapped packages, and quickly ran out to see what they had got. Unfortunately, the items were not anything they wanted, so the boys buried them in the apple orchard and went about their business. A while later, however, the burglary was reported, and the boys became prime suspects (exactly who had spotted them was unclear). Under questioning, they admitted the thefts and retrieved the items from the orchard for return to the store's owner.

JH was deeply contrite about his wrongdoing. The court, for its part, was understanding of the temptation that the open door had presented to him and his apple-picking friend. Harsh punishment for the boys was never a consideration, especially after JH's father—in a common tactic used by parents to assure the court of their concern and the adequacy of their supervision—promised to keep the two boys from seeing one another and to find JH a paper route to occupy his free time.

JH, in short, presented the court with an easy case, despite his having committed what, according to the law, sounded like a very serious crime. Neither JH's actions nor his home situation placed him seriously at risk, the court concluded; a short stay on probation would suffice to help him see the error of his thieving ways. JH cooperated fully with his probation officer and kept up his paper route. Within a matter of months, his case was dismissed.

If, as we have seen, the juvenile court was hesitant to punish children just because they had committed serious property offenses, what level of criminal activity did it take for the court to commit a boy who lived in a decent home to a custodial institution? The answer would appear to be—if we may exclude the few serious personal violence cases petitioned to juvenile court— quite a lot. The case of FM, #53856, illustrates the long leash that juvenile court judges were generally willing to give boys who were persistent criminal offenders before removing them to a custodial institution.

When arrested and petitioned for burglary in 1930, thirteen-year-old FM already had lengthy juvenile court experience behind him. The previous year he had been petitioned for petty theft and placed on probation; eventually his case has been dismissed. Shortly after completing his probation, however, FM ran away and hitched rides to San Diego. While there, he stole a car and was shortly afterward captured by the police while driving it. He was petitioned to juvenile court in San Diego and placed on probation there. While on probation, FM returned to Los Angeles and committed at least two burglaries. He was arrested for playing with one of two guns he had taken in the burglaries (the guns were the only remains from the many items stolen).

Thus, when FM appeared in juvenile court in 1930, he had already been placed on probation twice before, for petty thievery and car theft; he had recently perpetrated two substantial burglaries; and he had committed a weapons violation. FM readily admitted, moreover, that he had committed many other thefts for which he had never been charged. In addition, FM's mother wrote to the court requesting that he be committed to a custodial institution, as she and her husband were unable to control his behavior.

The court, however was not ready to commit FM. It decided once again to place him on probation, but this time—presumably because his parents no longer wanted him—in the home of a maternal aunt. The results were equally discouraging: FM ran away regularly, burglarized several homes, and then—the coup de grace—passed several bad checks in his aunt's name. The aunt returned FM to court and refused to have anything more to do with him.

At this point, the court finally decided it had no choice but to punish FM by committing him to a custodial facility.

Rather than sending him to the state reform school at Whittier, however, the court committed him to the Pacific Lodge, a minimum security facility in the nearby suburb of Woodland Hills. Immediately FM ran away from the institution, and was recaptured and returned; this pattern was repeated many times over a series of weeks. Finally the superintendent at Pacific Lodge kicked FM out—or at least tried to, for the court told him to take FM back and give him another chance to reform. While the court readily acknowledged that FM was a persistent criminal, it insisted that his lawbreaking was not yet so serious as to merit a commitment to state reform school.

Upon returning to Pacific Lodge, FM ran away again, and this time, before he was recaptured, he added another major burglary to his lengthy list of serious crimes. Having given FM multiple chances to reform, and having exhausted the patience and resources of his parents, relatives and a minimum security facility, the court at last decided it had run out of viable options. It therefore committed FM to Whittier (from which, incidentally, he escaped many times).

To us, the most interesting aspect of FM's case was how long a leash he enjoyed before being committed to a custodial institution. Even after his parents had given up on him, the court initiated another noninstitutional placement (with an aunt), despite not having seen any sign that FM was willing to give up crime. The court did not necessarily consider a child as seriously at risk merely because of a persistently criminal pattern of behavior.

In showing just how far a child had to go in criminal behavior before the court was willing to institutionalize him, the anecdotal data shed new light on the patterns of differential treatment that we observed earlier. As we argued before, it was not unusual for the court, or inconsistent with its philosophy, to perceive criminal offenders as being less at risk than status offenders and to place them less frequently in custodial institutions because of it. If that result appears suspect in hindsight, that is probably because we, unlike our Progressive Era forebears, have become skeptical about the knowledge base necessary to guide the subjective assessment of children at risk. Perhaps, too, we have become more deterministic in interpreting early criminal behavior as a sign of perverse developmental tendencies.

Conclusions

The present study offers a glimpse into the backgrounds and treatment of youth brought before the juvenile court in Los Angeles of the 1930s. Our analysis has illuminated a number of central issues regarding the operations of the court during its high point of popularity in this country. In particular, we have shown that status offenders comprised a minority of youth brought before the court in the early twentieth century. These youth experienced greater disarray and stress in their families than youth brought before the court for criminal offenses. In addition, status offenders, particularly the girls, were treated more severely by the court: Girl status offenders were more likely than their male counterparts to receive formal supervision and detention, boy status offenders were more likely to be detained in jail and placed in custodial institutions than boy criminal offenders.

Our statistical portraits are further illuminated by the case histories of the youth, which examine two points of particular interest. For girls, we found that the centrality of sexual offenses was often obscured by the formal petitioning process. For boys, we were struck by the apparent leniency shown by the court toward lawbreaking activities.

Our data focus on events more than half a century in the past. Since that time, a number of key events have helped reshape the mission and focus of the juvenile court. To what extent has the picture we paint here changed over time? We know, for example, that in 1987 status offenders shrunk to fewer than 2 percent of filed petitions in the Los Angeles Juvenile Court. We know, too, that while the percentage of overall petitions filed for girls was lower in 1987 than in 1930, girls still constitute half of all petitions filed for status offenses (data supplied to us by the California Bureau of Criminal Statistics). Moreover, we know from Greenwood et al. (1983) that the juvenile court still requires an extensive prior record before youth are incarcerated: Although prior record and severity of current crime are major determinants of harsh treatment by the Los Angeles Juvenile Court, they do not guarantee a sentence of incarceration. For example, of juveniles arrested for robbery with aggravating factors plus at least five prior arrests, only 39 percent received state time.[35]

As indicated earlier, this analysis draws from an ongoing,

large-scale study of juvenile delinquency and its treatment in Los Angeles between 1900 and 1960. As we continue to analyze these data, the snapshot we have presented here will develop into a more comprehensive picture of children at risk in the Los Angeles Juvenile Court.

NOTES

1. On the founding of juvenile courts, see Steven Schlossman, *Love and the American Delinquent* (Chicago: University of Chicago Press, 1977); Ellen Ryerson, *The Best-Laid Plans* (New York: Hill and Wang, 1978); and David Rothman, *Conscience and Convenience* (Boston: Little Brown, 1980).

2. See Ira Schwartz, *(In)Justice for Juveniles* (Lexington, Mass.: D.C. Heath, 1989).

3. See Daniel Curran, "The Myth of the 'New' Female Delinquent," *Crime and Delinquency* 30 (July 1984), 386-99.

4. This represents an approximate 10 percent sample of all delinquency petitions filed in Los Angeles Juvenile Court in 1930.

5. This was approximately 26 percent of the total petitions filed (i.e., the total includes dependent, neglected, and abused children, as well as sundry others). This estimate was based on a sample of seven hundred cases handled by the juvenile court in 1930.

6. Chi-square [5] = 25.5, p < .00.

7. This category also included: no parental control; no proper guardianship; danger of leading an immoral life; and refuses to obey.

8. As we shall demonstrate later, the share of girls who were sexually active, and whose sexual activity influenced the processing of their cases, was much larger. These offense statistics derive entirely from the most serious formal allegation listed in the petition.

9. Chi-square [3] = 7.8, p < .05.

10. Chi-square [2] = 6.0, p < .05.

11. Chi-square [1] = 6.1, p < .01.

12. Of course, it may also be that minority girls in Los Angeles were more likely to be indiscreet in manner, and perhaps more sexually active as well, at younger ages than white girls, and hence ran a greater risk of being caught.

13. Of boys, 42.9 percent, and of girls, 53.1 percent. Note that approximately one-third of the households for both boys and girls contained no male guardian. We define a working-class as a household with a resident male guardian whose occupation was as a skilled or unskilled laborer; a member of the armed forces; a farmer or agricultural worker; a public-works program participant; or someone with no regular occupation.

14. Chi-square $[1] = 4.0$, $p < .05$.

15. Our present analysis takes a simple approach to the data. A more sophisticated technique would be to ask whether, given similar background and offense characteristics, the court treated boys and girls similarly. This would entail multiple regression modeling in which the outcomes of interest were predicted as a function of offense, background characteristics, and sex of youth. While this latter technique is most appropriate for addressing differential treatment of similar offenders, it is beyond the scope of the present paper and will be explored in future analyses. See Steven Schlossman and Susan Turner, *Race and Delinquency in Los Angeles Juvenile Court, 1950* (Sacramento: Bureau of Criminal Statistics, California State Department of Justice, 1990).

16. Chi-square $[1] = 14.8$, $p < .00$.

17. Chi-square $[1] = 6.5$, $p < .01$.

18. Chi-square $[2] = 7.9$, $p < .02$.

19. Chi-square $[1] = 7.8$, $p < .00$.

20. See Allen Brandt, *No Magic Bullet* (New York: Oxford University Press, 1985.

21. Another factor contributing to higher posthearing detention rates for girls was, in all likelihood, the practice of holding sexually active girls in custody for testimony in rape proceedings in criminal court against adult paramours. We have not yet determined how common this practice was.

22. These data are consistent with what we know about male juvenile crime patterns today.

23. Chi-square $[1] = 62.5$, $p < .00$.

24. Both groups of "delinquents" came from predominantly working-class households: 42.9 percent among status offenders and 52.9 percent among criminal offenders (see n. 7 for further explication). While fewer racial minorities appeared among status offenders than among criminal offenders (19.3 percent versus 29.3 percent), the differences did not reach statistical significance.

25. Chi-square [3] = 11.4, p < .01.

26. Chi-square [1] = 3.9, p < .05.

27. Chi-square [1] = 9.5, p < .00.

28. Chi-square [1] = 7.9, p < .00. While not reaching conventional significance, a history of criminality among other family members was also higher among status than criminal offenders: 23.9 percent versus 16.4 percent, chi-square [1] = 2.7, p < .10).

29. Chi-square [1] = 13.4, p < .00.

30. Chi-square [1] = 34.5, p < .00.

31. In fact, separate analyses revealed that the court was significantly more likely to place in detention or place in a custodial institution children who: did not reside with two parents or guardians; had violence in the family; had prior placements; had previously run away; and acted alone; were referred by parents; had criminality among other family members; and had alcoholic parents.

32. Chi-square [1] = 22.4, p < .00.

33. Chi-square [1] = 9.0, p < .00. The pattern of two additional sanctions pointed in the same direction but did not reach conventional significance. Despite the noncriminal nature of the offenses lodged against them, status offenders had their cases dismissed slightly less often than criminal offenders (7.5 percent versus 12.4 percent). Status offenders were also less likely than criminal offenders to be placed on informal probation (15.0 percent versus 22.9 percent). That is, criminal offenders more often received this minimalist form of supervision than noncriminal offenders.

34. All of which tested significantly at p < .05.

35. Peter Greenwood, Albert Lipson, Alan Abrahamse, and Franklin Zimring, *Youth Crime and Juvenile Justice in California: A Report to the Legislature* (Santa Monica, Calif.: RAND Corporation, June 1983, R-3016-CSA).

3

Structuring Risks:
The Making of Urban
School Order

INTRODUCTION

Consequent to effective turn-of-the-century compulsory attendance laws, schools developed procedures and rules to deal with difficult pupils, from special rooms to lowered performance standards and increasingly indiscriminate exclusion from regular curricula. Benevolent rhetoric, "scientific" pupil diagnosis, bureaucratic "efficiency," progressive pedagogues, and tacit understandings helped school authorities adapt formal programs into mechanisms for preserving a school order that increasingly placed pupils at risk. This chapter documents the evolution of that order.

EXCLUSION AND SEGREGATION BEFORE 1920

School authorities were not "anxious to receive in their well-ordered classes those who, by taste or necessity, placed fore-

most the bread-winning pursuits."[1] Once in the schools, as long
as the unruly or backward pupil was free to leave, this was
"good, from the teacher's point of view, because the class would
be easier to manage without him."[2] In a 1909 school report, a
Philadelphia administrator, reflecting on earlier times, stated
that "the pupil who failed to keep step with his fellows, or who,
because of physical or moral defect seriously interfered with the
regular work of a class, tended to drop out, or to be forced out, of
school and the problem of the exceptional child disappeared
with him."[3] Teachers and administrators learned that exclusion
of unwanted pupils was an effective organizational practice.

Though turn-of-the-century compulsory attendance laws
challenged exclusionary practices, many school systems were
unwilling to relinquish them. Even after these laws were passed,
some systems had "their own way regardless of law."[4] One Baltimore official, in a 1903 report, points out "with a great deal of
hesitancy" that "candor compels me to say that in instances the
work of the Attendance Officers has been made very grievous . . .
on account of lack of effort on the part of some teachers."[5] School
boards were even threatened with the loss of state funds for not
enforcing attendance laws.[6]

Schools required an alternative that would enable them to
comply with the law while supporting the sentiment for exclusion. Special classes provided that alternative. They moderated
resistance to attendance laws by providing within-school alternatives to past exclusionary practices. For example, Philadelphia, with a school population of 143,000 in 1897, and Baltimore, with a school population of 63,000 in 1902, had no special
classrooms. Yet both systems created them after their compulsory attendance laws took effect: Philadelphia implemented special schools in 1898 after Pennsylvania's 1897 legislation, while
Baltimore implemented ungraded classes in 1903 after Maryland's 1902 law.[7]

Such classes are not explained by increased enrollments or
attendance rates, after attendance legislation.[8] Rather, they orga-
nizationally embodied past exclusionary practices, as Baltimore's
superintendent pointed out in 1902: "When the school attendance law goes into operation in January, some special provision will need to be made for . . . boys who are unmanageable in
the regular schools."[9] That "special provision" was special classes,
which allowed urban schools to preserve order in the regular
classroom and comply with the law. Decades of learning pro-

duced exclusionary practices, not an organizational model for universal education, practices that were not altered by more stringent legislation compelling attendance.

Amorphous categories were used to place pupils in these early special classrooms; for example, in Philadelphia, Baltimore, and Detroit, pupils were classified as "irregular attendants, and neglected children,"[10] "unmanageable in the regular schools,"[11] "incorrigible, backward and otherwise defective pupils,"[12] "a type who could not be effectively taught in the regular classes,"[13] and immigrant's children.[14] These diverse pupils had a common denominator: their threat to classroom order. Not surprisingly, the students placed in special classes were overwhelmingly male. The enrollment in Philadelphia's special classes illustrates this (table 1).

Table 1
Philadelphia Special Class Enrollments, 1900 to 1906

	Male	Female
1900	152	0
1901	146	8
1902	339	9
1903	510	16
1904	725	17
1905	1,055	17
1906	991	17

Source: *Philadelphia School Report*, 1899-1900 to 1905-6.

Special classes were limited until distinctions between behavioral and learning problems were made. Then, greater legitimacy and capacity in segregating pupils were acquired, especially in placing females in special classes. There was an increase of females in Philadelphia's classes, once "disciplinary" and "backward" distinctions were made (table 2).

Administrators were well aware of the risks associated with these classes; for example, Baltimore's 1902 report warned that "we ought certainly to do everything in our power to prevent the evolution of the unmanageable pupil and the truant."[15] However, actions belied concerns: pupils in special classes increased in Baltimore from 511 to 1,422 (1916-26), in Detroit from 172 to 1,484 (1905-15), and in Philadelphia from 852 to 2,468 (1909-19), proportions far greater than those for overall school enrollments.

Table 2
Philadelphia "Disciplinary" and "Backward" Enrollments,
1910 to 1919

	Orthogenic Disciplinary		Orthogenic Backward	
	Male	Female	Male	Female
1910	454	0	410	120
1911	514	2	764	200
1912	600	12	711	259
1913-16	[Sexes not distinguished]			
1917	594	17	1,215	503
1918	556	15	1,277	587
1919	514	20	1,314	620

Source: *Philadelphia School Report*, 1909-10 to 1918-19.

Still, early undifferentiated special classrooms contained a small proportion of the schools' population. From 3 to 8 per 1,000 Baltimore elementary pupils were enrolled in these classes from 1906 through 1916, while only 1 per 1,000 were enrolled in Philadelphia in 1900. Even after they were transformed into "disciplinary" and "backward" or "subnormal" classes, enrollments remained small: for every 1,000 pupils, Detroit had 21 enrolled (1912); Philadelphia, 12 (1919); and Baltimore, 19 (1925).[16] Though special classes did not involve a large number of pupils, they both institutionalized and increased the phenomenon of "the unmanageable pupil," effecting what school rhetoric claimed to prevent. Also, they identify the preservation of exclusionary practices, abetted by bureaucracy and benevolent rhetoric.

School order was as much dependent on attrition as on segregation of selected pupils. In the decade preceding this century, only one-third of the pupils entering the Baltimore schools advanced to the fifth grade;[17] in Massachusetts, over one-third in Somerville and almost one-half in Cambridge failed to reach this same grade.[18] This was typical. In this century's first decade, a general model indicated that only 190 out of every 1,000 pupils entering the first grade would reach the eighth grade. These figures indicate failure to progress through the grades as well as attrition: in Baltimore in 1913, over 25 percent of the white, and 40 percent of the "colored," first-graders were not promoted; in Philadelphia in 1920, over 27 percent of the first-grade (1A) class did not pass; in Kent County, Delaware, in 1921, over 32 percent of the white students failed.[20] Attrition served both school order and academic standards, allowing schools to maintain performance norms while awaiting the departure of pupils who did not do well. Attrition also moderated the need to segregate pupils. But this situation was changing.

Baltimore's school authorities noted in a 1909 report that pupils were remaining in school longer.[21] Though supporting this trend, they suggested curricular changes: "Children should be held in school as long as possible after the law allows them to drop out; but when they do stop going to school, especially if this occurs at an early age, they should possess either some little skill in a productive industry or such manual dexterity as will enable them quickly to acquire the special skill needed."[22] Such suggestions became policy the very year Maryland law limited child labor; as stated in the 1912 report,

> It becomes one of our greatest problems, therefore, to revise and simplify our course of study. . . . May it be sufficient to state that the newer subjects—manual training, sewing, drawing, nature study and domestic art—have come to stay, that they will be developed and that we shall attempt to make the school a medium in which the conditions of the social spirit are not wanting.[23]

Rhetoric notwithstanding, the law effectively returned 913 working children to the system in 1912-13, almost one-half of its enrollment increase. Baltimore responded with a "nature study" curriculum. Though tenuous as preparation for an urban economy, simplified courses aided school order facing an increase in working-class youth. A class for "subnormals," as well as a manual curriculum became operative the same year that working permits were revoked, returning working children to the schools.[24] As special classes provided an alternative to exclusionary practices, consequent to effective attendance laws, manual curricula provided an alternative to attrition with the passing of child labor legislation.

THE CASE OF DETROIT

Classes, curricula, and annual-report rhetoric identify formal organization. They do not exhaust the understandings and rules school actors develop and actions they take to moderate problems with difficult pupils, which can transform formal programs into instruments for school order. Here, the historical development of special classes and students, manual curricula, and benevolent rhetoric may reveal not only formal structures and goals but also tacit understandings, rules, roles, and actions—suggested by Detroit data.[25]

Detroit opened a "truant" school in 1883, and its police implemented a truant squad.[26] This school was a depository for truants apprehended by the police until 1898, when it underwent "some changes in name and organization," becoming Ungraded School No. 1.[27] According to Detroit's 1906 report, the ungraded rooms of 1898 served "pupils mostly below the fifth grade," former parochial school students, pupils returning from the work world, incorrigibles, truants, and others "sent because in these rooms the studies [were] better adapted to their needs than in the ordinary school room."[28] This ungraded school, like the classes in Philadelphia and Baltimore, used similarly inclusive categories for difficult pupils. The qualifier "pupils mostly below the fifth grade" suggests that these difficult pupils dropped out of school by that grade.

As in other cities, Detroit's ungraded classes were followed by special rooms for backward pupils and benevolent rhetoric.[29] Its 1907 report argued that these rooms were to "be reserved for the high grade backward students" who "should under the stimulus of individual attention soon become prepared to re-enter the regular grades."[30] The 1911 report affirmed this: "It is not intended that pupils entering the ungraded schools shall stay there indefinitely."[31] Here, too, actions belied rhetoric: the 1912 report admitting that these rooms had become "a clearing house to eliminate low grade children from the schools."[32] Program distinctions between the obstreperous and the dull, imprecise classification of pupils, and informal rules of segregation allowed "clearing houses" for difficult pupils, in many systems.[33]

Child labor laws and longer stays in school made it difficult to rely on attrition and poorly rationalized segregation. Changes were needed to better rationalize the management and control of pupils. This process is illustrated in Detroit. Its superintendent appointed a Child Study Committee in 1907.[34] By 1908, forms were devised to report pupils with "marked defects" to the committee and to request that parents "consult their family physician."[35] By 1910 a "Binet Examiner" was employed on a part-time basis, and by 1912 a psychological clinic and testing and placement procedures for special classes were in place.[36] These efforts provided a "scientific" rationale for differentiating among students and their treatment. Though specialized staff and "scientific" standards legitimized special programs, they often conflicted with proven practices for dealing with difficult pupils and preserving order in the regular classroom.

Conflicts between staff procedures and tried practices for school order were moderated by affirming order while not denigrating formal procedures. Detroit's 1912 report affirmed the primary importance of order by noting the place of diagnosis and placement of pupils in the school context; it stated that, while science "is the guiding principle, still it is by no means closely adhered to, as the condition of the child frequently shows that he should be placed in a special room, even though his classification indicates otherwise."[37] The phrase "the condition of the child" suggests a euphemism for pupils the teachers were unable or unwilling to deal with in the regular classroom—a "condition" framed by tacit understandings and rules for school order, not "scientific" procedures.

"Scientific pedagogy" was encapsulated in a bureaucratic order. Conflicts between official procedures and tacit understandings and practice were reduced when school actors learned the primacy of the latter and when programs developed that accommodated practice and "scientific" differentiation of pupils. This allowed staff to expand, legitimize, and interrelate the segregation of pupils and curricula changes. Vocational education in Detroit illustrates this process.

The roots of manual training were in nineteenth-century curricula. Manual courses were also evident in the early part of this century. Prevocational curricula or industrial education that developed in the second and third decades of this century were different: less a part of common school or handicraft traditions, more an extension of special classes.[38] Detroit's 1914 report stated that prevocational classes were to "take children from our special classes," classes in which a "maximum of manual arts and a minimum of academic subjects are taught."[39] They were for "defectives" without working permits who remained in school past their fourteenth year. Prevocational curricula accommodated concerns for order with a rhetoric suggesting that they "best fit" the child.[40]

Though the prevocational program harmonized legitimizing rhetoric, staff classification of "defectives," and the use of special curricula for preserving school order, problems remained for teachers who wanted difficult pupils, whom staff could not classify as "defective," out of their classrooms.[41] Conflicts between the need to place difficult children outside of the regular classroom and diagnostic criteria were reduced by programs that had few or no criteria for such placement. For example, in 1914, Detroit introduced a "special preparatory" curriculum "for girls over fourteen who, for reason other than mental deficiency, had fallen behind grade."[42] The following year a dressmaking curriculum was added as an alternative to the special preparatory courses.[43] Segregating practices and staff integrity were preserved by programs for girls who could not, or need not, be classified as defective. These programs for girls complemented the ungraded classes, which were almost exclusively male. In this way, staff was better able to rationalize and expand segregation through special curricula; Detroit had, in 1911, nine ungraded classes and nine special rooms; by 1916 there were ungraded classes in seventeen schools, twenty-nine special classes, and five prevocational classes, in addition to special preparatory and dressmaking classes for girls.[44] These developments were enthusiastically advocated.[45]

Factors affecting Detroit's expansion of special classes were common in many systems: tests to measure individual differences; specialized staff to use the tests to classify pupils; administrators concerned with school order and rationalizing pupil management. Child labor laws were also a factor. In 1911 a law made the Detroit schools responsible for monitoring child labor. As a result, hundreds of youth who would have been in the work force were returned to the schools.[46] After the law was enacted, prevocational and special preparatory classes began for fourteen- to sixteen-year-olds—the school-age population most affected by the law. Special classes and curricula were influenced by concerns for school order and by child labor laws, which threatened that order.

The growth of special classes was aided by "laggards," pupils behind in normal progress through the grades. This was known as "retardation" and, when aggregated, its inverse became a measure of "efficiency," whose costs to taxpayers were published. Reducing retardation became an important political and bureaucratic, if not pedagogical, indicator of efficiency, evidenced in the "grade-age" sections of annual reports.[47] Detroit's

1915 report suggests how special classes abetted efficiency: "The increased number . . . in special classes has been felt throughout the entire school system, noticeable in the Grade-Age Report for this year, the percentage of retardation of three and more years having dropped from eight per cent in December, 1913, to six and six-tenths per cent in December, 1914. We think this is partly due to the greater numbers now in Special and Prevocational Classes."[48] Special classes were "ungraded" and not included in the calculation of retardation. In this way, the growth of special classes related to "efficiency."

Issuing work permits to children under the compulsory attendance age also reduced retardation and aided school order. After Detroit's 1911 child labor legislation, more children were released from its schools through work permits than through special or ungraded rooms; in 1915 the special population was 1,424, while the number of work permits was 2,470.[49] This was common, as indicated by Philadelphia data in table 3.

Table 3
Philadelphia "Disciplinary" and "Backward" Enrollments
and Work Permits Issued, 1916 to 1919

	Disciplinary	Backward	Work Permits
1916		2,124	11,104
1917	611	1,718	13,307
1918	571	1,864	21,220
1919	534	1,934	19,345

Source: *Philadelphia School Report*, 1915-16 to 1918-19.

The work permit reduced the number of pupils the schools were unable or unwilling to educate. In some jurisdictions, school order was so dependent on issuing work permits that authorities violated the law in issuing them. Permits were issued to pupils who had not met "schooling requirements," who were "entirely illiterate"; "careless certification" included "only an affidavit of a parent as evidence of date of birth."[50] Still, the ill effects of school actions were moderated by the demand for labor. This is illustrated in a 1915 study of one hundred children over sixteen years of age who had attended Detroit's special classes and were characterized as "feeble-minded" or "high-grade moron": 78 percent of the boys who could be located in the community were employed, and 68 percent of the girls were either married or working.[51] Many implications of the schools' evolving organization were masked by the demand for unskilled labor.

THE IMPACT OF PROGRESSIVE REFORM

Segregating difficult pupils aided teachers in dealing with day-to-day problems of regular classroom order while serving administrators by increasing special curricula and staff—even aiding their efficiency by not including special students in the calculation of the system's promotion rate. Yet there were limits to labeling students "special" and elaborating curricula to increase the promotion rate and, thereby, efficiency. Changing promotion standards was another administrative solution. This policy was more difficult to implement than increasing curricula and special pupils: it conflicted with an educational tradition that placed promotion in the hands of teachers.

Early school reports, such as Detroit's 1898 report, affirmed promotion criteria: "It should not be forgotten that the results of examinations of whatever nature must still take an important place as a factor in all promotions."[52] Baltimore's 1901 report was similar: "The weakest group would require more than a year for the completion of the same work. It is just as necessary in this case to withhold promotion till the work is well done."[53] These principles conflicted with concerns for efficiency and were replaced by other rationales. By 1908 the Detroit system suggested that pupils "are not getting that form of instruction to which they are entitled, namely instruction which will advance them progressively without the ruinous effect upon them and the schools of having this large number instructed in classes with pupils from two to six years younger";[54] its 1909 report even chided teachers who supported the importance of examinations for promotion.[55] Performance standards were bureaucratically transformed.

Changing promotion standards received ideological support. University pedagogues, through child-centered or "progressive" ideology, provided this.[56] They had a major impact on urban systems through the school survey, which "became a favorite technique to spread the program of administrative progressives."[57] Professor Strayer's 1921 report of his survey illustrates the support provided for different promotion criteria: "Baltimore teachers must think of the school more definitely as a place for instructing pupils and improving their abilities and to consider the school no longer as a place for holding pupils until their abilities reach certain arbitrary standards. . . . Teachers tend quite naturally to feel that those pupils who do the work offered in school are 'superior' to those who do not succeed in school, and it will take a considerable amount of patient supervision to bring them to 'lower their standards' and to think of other interests as being just as 'noble' and 'worthy' as the academic life."[58] This rhetoric fit well with administrative concerns of efficiency. However, financial, as well as psychological, considerations affected promotion, as pointed out in Baltimore's 1921-22 report: "In 1920-21 the number of unpromoted pupils in elementary schools alone was 11,021. Estimating the cost per pupil per year at $52.00 this amounts to a loss of over $500,000."[59]

Though many factors worked to transform traditional understandings and practices, classroom teachers, too, realized the benefits of "passing on": not having to confront certain difficult pupils the following year. In this way, changing promotion rules came to satisfy teachers' interest in classroom order as well as administrators' interest in efficiency. The increase in promotion rates for Baltimore's elementary pupils after the 1921 Strayer Report was submitted suggests a consequence (table 4).

Table 4
Average Percentage of Promotions in the
Elementary Schools of Baltimore, 1913, 1924, and 1927

	Whites		Coloreds	
	Boys	Girls	Boys	Girls
1912-13	77.2		69.7	
1923-24	87.7		78.5	
1926-27	90.1	92.9	88.1	91.2

Source: *Baltimore Board of School Commissioners Annual Report*, 1912-13, 1923-24, 1926-27.

Progressive pedagogues, administrators concerned with bureaucratic efficiency, and teachers helped to marginalize performance as a criterion for promotion. As segregation was affirmed over diagnostic results, "passing on" was affirmed over performance. Yet convoluting relations among promotion, performance, and progress produced organizational outcomes and interdependencies that were difficult to anticipate or control:

Simplified courses of study, concomitant to child labor legislation, encouraged changing promotion standards; "special promotion rooms" were created to augment passing-on policies;
special promotion rooms, in turn, required special preparatory
classes in secondary schools to advance pupils with minimum
progress.[60] Devalued performance standards aided pupil pro-
gression through the grades and, as stated in Baltimore's report
of 1927, became "fixed": "Trial promotion which has been
employed for a number of years in the case of pupils whose
scholastic achievements were borderline has become a fixed policy in the elementary grades."[61]

Child-centered rationales transformed the meaning of promotion and encouraged exclusion of pupils from the regular
classroom. In the latter case, a teaching tradition was not challenged; rather, tried practices for school order were affirmed,
even given license. This is shown by Baltimore's selective
responses to the Strayer Report's recommendations. Classroom
order was challenged more by pupils difficult to control than
by the physically deformed. Consequently, although Strayer recommended 150 additional ungraded rooms for overage or
undergrade pupils ("subnormals") and at least fifty special
rooms for the "cardiac, crippled, blind, and the like," there was a
bias for "subnormal" classes and enrollments, compared to
"open air," "crippled," and "deaf," after the recommendations
were implemented in 1921-23 (table 5).[62]

Table 5
Baltimore Special Class Enrollments, 1921 to 1923

	1920-21		1921-22		1922-23	
	Classes	*Pupils*	*Classes*	*Pupils*	*Classes*	*Pupils*
Open Air	4	172	4	152	5	177
Crippled	4	129	4	117	5	149
Deaf	1	19	1	13	1	15
Subnormal	3	46	4	80	22	561
Disciplinary	14	342	16	383	12	256

Source: *Baltimore Board of School Commissioners Annual Report*, 1922-23.

Control problems posed by the obstreperous or the dull
were moderated by their isolation from the regular classroom.
Such affixed labels are administratively interchangeable; for
example, expanding subnormal classes provided opportunities

for removing disciplinary problems from regular classrooms; concomitantly, the need for disciplinary classes was reduced. There was a decline in "disciplinary" classes and enrollments, consequent to the expansion of "subnormal" classes (table 5). Still, the special pupil population grew as shown by the rapid increase in Baltimore's "subnormal" population after the Strayer Report was implemented (table 6).

Table 6
Baltimore "Subnormal" Enrollments, 1921 to 1925

	Subnormal
1920-21	56
1921-22	80
1922-23	561
1923-24	860
1924-25	1,179

Source: Baltimore Board of School Commissioners Annual Report, 1920-21 to 1924-25.

The Strayer Report licensed an immediate increase in special populations and provided plans for their long-term expansion through organizational restructuring. Staff and line functions and classifications of pupils were developed that aided this growth: so-called child guidance clinics, special class clinics, special education, psycho-educational clinics, "Z" children, dull normal first-graders, prevocational education, adjustment classes, and so on. Ostensibly, this made detection, diagnosis, and placement of pupils more precise and rational. Yet the interchangeability of pupil and program classifications belied rationalization. "Prevocational education" suggests a curriculum with an occupational orientation, not a disciplinary or ungraded class. However, it was administered in Baltimore's elementary grades for "over-age pupils who will probably leave school at the first opportunity"[63] and to meet "the needs of the child of less than normal mental ability."[64] One program could augment or eliminate another; one classification could replace another. The "condition of the child" was flexible enough to accommodate one program or another. Tacit understandings, exclusionary practices, and lowering expectations belied bureaucratic rationality.

An indication of interrelationships among programs' rationalization and interchangeability that underwrote the overall expansion of the special population is provided by the demise of the "disciplinary" population, transformation of the "subnormal" into the "mentally handicapped," inception of the "prevocational" and "vocational" programs, amidst the overall growth of the special pupil population, subsequent to the Strayer Report (table 7).

Table 7
Baltimore Special Program Enrollments, 1926 to 1936

	Disciplinary	Subnormal	Vocational	Prevocational	Mentally Handicapped	Total
1926	269	1,152				1,421
1927	225	1,264	746			2,235
1928	228	1,316	886	255		2,685
1929	186	1,375	847	314		2,722
1930	156	1,605	975	482		3,218
1931	208		1,152	884	2,024	4,268
1932	168		1,304	891	2,475	4,838
1933			1,566	964	3,801	6,331
1934			1,629	2,370	4,485	8,484
1935			1,606	2,702	5,339	9,647
1936			1,828	2,745	6,383	10,956

Source: Baltimore Board of School Commissioners Annual Report, 1925-26 to 1935-36.

Table 7 does not include "Z" (below average) pupils, a classification of children commencing in Baltimore in 1926-27. The "Z" group approximated 20 percent of the remaining pupil population—exceeding all the groups in Table 7 combined.[65] Though these programs were justified through children's "needs," they served administrators' needs as well.[66] They enabled bureaucratic processing and placement of pupils the teachers could not control. However, the Great Depression severely challenged this school order.

EFFECTS OF THE GREAT DEPRESSION

School order was aided as older pupils dropped out to work or younger ones obtained permits to work. This changed during the depression, when pupils remained longer in school and the number of work permits declined—which amplified special classes and their populations.

Baltimore increased its special pupil population during the depression, largely through its prevocational program; its 1933 report provided a program rationale: "For children of the elementary grade who have been unsuccessful with the academic and rather bookish approach of the traditional schools a program has been developed that features shop activities with academic subjects as supplementary and interpretive."[67] Designed for thirteen- to fourteen-year-olds, a new policy extended it to fifteen- and sixteen-year-olds.[68] Also, in school year 1933-34, principals were authorized to transfer slow pupils, ages thirteen to sixteen, to a special class or a prevocational center. The enrollment consequences were clear (table 7): the prevocational enrollment increase, from 1933 to 1934, was more than twice that of the entire school system: 1,406 to 623. Prevocational teachers increased threefold the year the program was implemented, over 90 percent of the teacher increase for that year.[70]

The depression reduced the number of working young people. In 1929 in Detroit, school-issued work permits averaged 86 per month for fifteen-year-olds and 334 for sixteen-year-olds; two years later the figures were 19 and 105, and by 1933, 4 and 30.[71] There was a similar trend in Philadelphia (table 8).

Table 8
Philadelphia Work Permits Issued, 1927, 1931 to 1934

	1927	...	1931	1932	1933	1934
Work Certificates	23,317		10,783	6,051	3,240	110

Source: Philadelphia School Report, 1926-27, 1930-31 to 1933-34.

The depression seems to have transformed schools into custodial institutions, when school authorities admitted that "any effective program for meeting this situation must be predicated upon the thought that many of these compulsory students can not benefit from the standard curricula"[72] and "schools have emphasized social trends and personal use because these pupils are incapable of reaching vocational standards."[73] Krug points out, "Here were the beginnings of what would later be called life adjustment education and of the categorizing of students into the academic, the vocational, and those neither academic nor vocational."[74] Such characterizations of pupils and their curricular needs echo the rhetoric of earlier decades. The depression forced the schools to confront many pupils who had once departed, but the tacit understandings and tactics for coping with them had developed long before. The depression affirmed these tactics and made their excesses more apparent: In 1922, in Baltimore, 1 out of every 205 pupils was considered a "special," excluding the physically handicapped; by 1936 it was 1 out of 11. In that same system the school population increased by 11 percent between 1929 and 1933, while the mentally handicapped increased by 276 percent.[75]

During the depression, many ways to lower performance expectations were developed for older pupils who returned to, or remained in, school: limiting required courses, introducing "life adjustment" classes, supporting "antifailure" policies and "antihomework" campaigns, reducing criteria for high school graduation.[76] Still, these were consonant with tacit understandings and rules that developed earlier to devalue promotion criteria, which, again, were especially useful when resources were scarce. Many summer school programs were limited or eliminated during the depression. Such losses were compensated, in part, with a version of the "passing on" rule, suggested by Baltimore's 1937 report: "The continued operation of the retardation rule automatically eliminates a number of pupils who formerly were sent to summer school to make up two deficiencies." Though the depression affirmed tacit understandings and rules for school order, it also challenged the school's ability to control older pupils.[77]

Special classes developed consequent to effective attendance law, while manual curricula expanded consequent to child labor laws. These classes and curricula contained pupils who were not doing well and were, presumably, waiting to leave for work. While prevocational programs contained thirteen- and fourteen-year-olds waiting to leave, the work permit allowed many fifteen- and sixteen-year-olds to exit.[78] However, the depression changed this. "Terminal curricula" then contained increasing cohorts of waiting-to-leave fifteen- and sixteen-year-olds. Older and more difficult "terminal" pupils remained in the schools longer, which exacerbated problems of school order.

The depression threatened school order in other ways. With diminished labor demand came support for the schools' "custodial role," even arguments for students' remaining up to age twenty-five. This challenged the predepression high schools' status quo. Also, vocational programs, given their economic irrelevance, were challenged, which further threatened school order. Though such ideas suggest structural problems, pupils were often perceived as the source of problems.[79] Here, older and "terminal" pupils, with ominous out-of-school futures changed staff's views of their responsibility to older pupils, no longer advocating special programs for them.

Changing rhetoric and disciplinary procedures devalued the professional's place, as illustrated in Baltimore's attendance and child diagnostic offices.[80] "Conceptions" changed, as noted in Baltimore's 1938 report:

> In the earlier conceptions of attendance service the compulsory or police function was paramount. . . . Attendance officials, eventually realizing the futility of coercing attendance by means of legal authority, have gradually developed a technique involving social investigation, school adjustments, cooperative social remedial work, relief services, and health service, a procedure which emphasizes the welfare of the child and depends upon compulsion only as a last resort.[81]

The 1937 report suggests this benign view's implication: "The basic responsibility for securing prompt and regular attendance on the part of pupils rests upon their teachers and principal."[82] The diagnostic approach shifted enforcement responsibility to the school actors least concerned about the absence of difficult pupils. In 1937 this same office recommended that staff efforts "be directed toward problem cases at lower age levels than formerly in order that preventive measures might be undertaken more effectively."[83] Within a year, the office reduced its population of clients who were over age twelve from almost 82 percent to under 50 percent, as it reduced its percentages of black and special pupils.[84] Baltimore's attendance office was not the only one to show timidity vis-à-vis older compulsory-age youth.

In 1934 the "psycho-educational" clinic was "to diagnose and adjust any problem child in the public system"[85] by handling "cases of serious misconduct, actual or potential psychiatric problems, delinquency, social and economic maladjustment, and emotional instability."[86] Yet by 1940 the clinic argued its "program of prevention should be restricted almost wholly to cases under 14 years of age at the time of referral."[87] A year later, the clinic reported that "it was encouraging, therefore, to discover that the average of new cases was reduced this year by more than two years. Only 23 cases, or 3.7 per cent of the total number, were 16 years of age or over at the time of referral to the clinic."[88] Those who once promised to rationalize the management and control of all pupils now disclaimed interest in the older, more difficult, ones. Professional rhetoric, staff offices, and formal procedures decreasingly provided support for school problems. Schools seemed to have exhausted their in-school options in trying to control difficult pupils. However, World War II provided the schools some respite.

During World War II some urban school enrollments actually decline, and more youth were working, either part- or full-time. The St. Louis system issued only 21 work permits in 1939, but in 1942 it issued 656.[89] The office in Baltimore reported a continuous increase in students withdrawing for work: 105 in 1938, 178 in 1939, 226 in 1940, 249 in 1941, 257 in 1942, 272 in 1943.[90] Yet there was evidence that exclusion from the school had become, as it was in the nineteenth century, a means for school order. Suspension of students and toleration of nonattendance identify such means.

Though Baltimore reported in school year 1930-31 that "the rate of truancy . . . in the prevocational schools and certain classes is ten times higher than it is in the normal elementary grades,"[91] attendance-office policy reduced special-class clients, as a proportion of all cases and absolutely.[92] In Detroit, the number of attendance officers and the officer-to-pupil ratio declined from predepression levels through the 1940s.[93] St. Louis investigations for nonattendance show a steady decline, from 79,417 in 1940-41 to 42,968 in 1947-48. Keeping pupils in school was not a priority. Indeed, St. Louis officers found "suspension" to be an increasing reason for nonattendance, increasing from 209 to 339 in the mid to late 1940s.[44] "Suspension" is a curious reason for nonattendance, because statute limits its duration. Either communication within the school system was failing, or, more likely, teachers learned, or relearned, that sustained absence aided school order—a long-standing tactic whose excesses would become notorious in subsequent decades.[95]

CONTINUED PATTERNS OF EXCLUSION

Increasing enrollments, difficulties of family and race, lack of employment opportunities for urban youth, and decline in teaching authority exacerbated problems of urban school order after World War II.[96] Tactics used to cope with these problems were more elaborate versions of those developed in earlier decades: "diagnostic" or special program exclusion, lowering expectations, suspension, and toleration of nonattendance. However, consequences were more public and severe.

Decades-long practices of segregating difficult pupils in special classes were amplified and refined, primarily through a staff office commonly entitled "Pupil Personnel Services," whose predecessor was the "psycho-educational" clinics of the 1920s and 1930s. Unlike in earlier decades, such practices were often successfully challenged in the courts, which, in turn, challenged the system's ability to satisfy teachers who sought the removal of difficult children from their regular classrooms. However, the courts did not address the tacit understandings and rules that supported exclusionary practices; they addressed equity and formal procedures, not a school culture. Consequently, the removal of difficult pupils from the regular classrooms did not stop with court strictures. As in the past, schools responded by relabeling pupils for placement in programs not strictured by law, as with such relabeling in the District of Columbia school system (table 9), consequent to the impact of Judge Wright's decision in the *Hobson v. Hansen* case (1967-68).

Table 9
Reasons for Referral to Pupil Personnel

	1963-64	1964-65	1965-66	1966-67	1967-68
Academic	3,158	2,679	1,953	1,703	607
Behavioral	1,386	1,816	1,263	1,106	2,763

Source: Public Schools of the District of Columbia, Department of Pupil Personnel Services, annual reports.

This relabeling resulted from the court's eliminating the "basic track" program for excluding "academic," but not "behavioral," problems from the regular classrooms. Consequently, teachers changed the label of difficult pupils from "academic" to "behavioral," which shows how entwined the formal request-diagnosis-prescription process was with the tacit understandings and rules for school order. Diagnostic recommendations, like reasons for referral, accommodated the court's decision (table 10).

Table 10
Recommendations for Placement from Child and Youth Study

	1963-64	*1964-65*	*1965-66*	*1966-67*	*1967-68*
Regular	399	n.a.	628	692	1,374
Special	2,146	n.a.	1,727	1,079	951

Source: Public Schools of the District of Columbia, Department of Pupil Personnel Services, annual reports.

Administrators also accommodated to school order. They implemented a new program the year the court's decision was binding. Entitled "MIND," an acronym for "Meeting Individual Needs Daily," the program accommodated the exclusion interests of teachers who relabeled their pupils "behavioral" or "emotional." By school year 1968-69, the MIND program enrolled 2,913 students, more than the number of pupil referrals made prior to *Hobson v. Hansen*.[97]

Formal procedures and exclusionary practices were deeply entwined in school order, an order elusive to outside control. Though the system appears insidious, teachers and staff were not entirely arbitrary in describing their pupils as behavioral or academic problems. Obstreperous behavior and poor performance are often cause and consequence of teachers' inability or unwillingness to control pupils; under duress they were not dishonest in relabeling the "condition of the child." Yet exclusionary practices, which affected disproportionate numbers of minority pupils, resulted in closer scrutiny and monitoring by the courts. However, other exclusionary practices, such as suspending students, compensated for those lost through legal strictures.

Reliance on suspension was dramatically evidenced in the District of Columbia. When, in May 1969, its school board ordered that suspensions cease until policy was clarified, the teachers staged a walkout. They walked out because school-level suspensions were threatened.[98] Principals had statutory and administrative authority to exercise these suspensions, for which data are usually not available. However, the Baltimore school system conducted a survey on such suspensions. Baltimore's annual report listed 841 suspensions for school year 1967-68, but the number of school-level suspensions acknowledged in the survey for only part of the following year was over 11,000.[99] Other suspensions were exercised, often at the teacher level, that were not sanctioned by law or policy and for which no good data have been found. Still, an administrator in the Detroit system estimated that compared to a reported 1,827 suspensions, all suspensions for that same year might reach 100,000.[100]

Suspensions became visible and controversial by the 1960s. Highly publicized studies documented their excesses.[101] A Supreme Court decision mandated due process.[102] Suspended pupils created a number of problems in the community, which involved the police.[103] Lastly, suspension was a devalued sanction for students to whom it was applied. One report acknowledged that suspension "seems to place a premium on objectionable behavior in the classroom."[104] Junior high principals stated: "It's a vacation for them" and "Suspension is like throwing B'rer Rabbit in the briar patch."[105] Yet, another practice moderated some of the problems created by suspensions: toleration, or acceptance, of nonattendance.

Responsibility for investigating nonattendance is spelled out in statute.[106] The ratio of investigation requests relative to school absences provides a measure of the enforcement of attendance laws. Data show this ratio decreasing steadily during the 1950s and 1960s in American cities, such as Detroit, Washington, D.C., and Philadelphia.[107] Still, such measures are conservative; they show homeroom, not full-day, attendance. For example, during a two-week period in school year 1968-69, a Washington, D.C., junior high showed a homeroom attendance rate of 76 percent, while its principal reported that "easily 50 percent" of the students left the school sometime after the homeroom period, suggesting a full-time attendance rate of less than 40 percent.[108] Also, teachers did not always record absences of particularly troublesome students on the sheets forwarded to central administration. One junior high school teacher said not reporting the absence of undesirable students was accepted procedure—"everybody does it."[109]

Toleration of nonattendance vis-à-vis difficult pupils is shown in table 11. These data are particularly striking because many, if not most, of the students enrolled in those special schools would have been on juvenile court probation, a condition of which is regular attendance at school.

Other dimensions of tolerating nonattendance suggest how ingrained a part of school order it had become: In Detroit there was a decrease in the number of attendance officers and their investigations, comparing the 1920s with the 1950s;[110] in Balti-

Table 11
Attendance Rates for Special Schools with
Behavioral Problems, Detroit

School	1967	1968	1969
I	77.7	79.1	69.6
II	84.0	68.6	57.3
III	70.9	59.6	63.2
IV	76.2	76.4	68.5
V	60.8	66.1	64.6
VI	71.6	57.6	49.4

Source: Office of Attendance, Detroit Public Schools.

more, investigating truancy changed from visiting the family
and community to the use of mails and the telephone;[111] memo-
randa instructed District of Columbia attendance officers not to
transport truants in their cars or to approach groups of known
truants in the streets.[112] A clinical ideology gave support for
enforcement inactivity:

> Traditionally, the function of the attendance service was
> conceived as solely compulsory in character. The duty of
> an attendance officer was considered to be that of receiving
> from principals lists of the children who failed to appear at
> school from day to day and making sure that such children
> did appear. Another duty was to seek out truants upon the
> streets or in loitering places and to take them directly to
> school. Modern attendance operates on a higher profes-
> sional plane.[113]

Lack of enforcement rigor by attendance officers does not
suggest independent malfeasance. Lack of rigor in reporting
absences and ineffectiveness in investigating them were recip-
rocal consequences of school order, which suggests the effectiveness of tacit understandings. The rhetoric and inaction associated with the attendance office are consonant with the
evolution of practices for dealing with difficult pupils. Yet tactics
of exclusion that served urban schools for much of the century
exacerbated problems in the 1960s.

As the ineffectiveness of exclusionary practices became
transparent during the depression, suspensions and toleration of
nonattendance became so in the 1960s: no longer were difficult

pupils removed from the schools. Numbers of nonattending young people, so-called outsiders, frequented the schools and became a well-known and well-publicized problem for the schools in the 1960s.[114] Outsiders' behavior ranged from simply frightening students to stealing, extortion, fighting, carrying weapons, and selling drugs. Outsiders posed a formidable problem for school authorities; a principal stated it simply: "I cannot handle an outsider."[115]

An implicit outcome in the evolution of urban school order was deviant behavior. While the economy productively engaged young people, it offered the schools some relief and masked this outcome. However, by the 1960s, urban school order clearly produced not only poor performance and discipline problems but delinquency as well; for example, in Los Angeles, when the police cracked down on truancy, daytime burglaries and auto thefts were reduced by 30 percent and daytime thefts from autos by 75 percent.[116] Increasingly, the police had to rationalize their responses to school problems in terms of criminal justice; for example, they instituted unlawful-entry complaint procedures for school authorities when the latter summoned the police. Data from this procedure when first instituted in Washington, D.C., suggest the deviant outcome of school order: difficult pupils did not achieve senior high status.

Table 12
Unlawful Entry Complaints Filed by District of Columbia
Public Schools, 1968-69

	Elementary	Junior High	Senior High
Complaints	62	752	35
Number of Schools	21	29	9

Source: Youth Division, Metropolitan Police Department, Washington, D.C.

The U.S. Senate produced a report in which school problems were cited: assaults on teachers, comparing 1964 to 1968, increased from 25 to 1,801; assaults by students on students, from 1,601 to 4,267; crimes by nonstudents, from 142 to 3,894; students expelled for incorrigibility, from 4,884 to 8,190. More importantly, this report pointed out that "the chief trouble-maker in many schools is the drop-out who returns to his old school to destroy it because he harbors a deep fury against the school which, through lack of discipline or lack of interest, has rejected him."[117]

CONCLUSION

Turn-of-the-century compulsory attendance legislation produced an organizational dilemma by making urban schools responsible for a universal education to which their personnel could not or would not entirely comply—a dilemma partially resolved by lowering performance expectations and excluding selected pupils from the regular classrooms. By continually adapting classes, rhetoric, and curricula to these mechanisms for school order, teachers and administrators preserved organizational, if not pedagogical, integrity.

Incipient consequences of such practices were innocuous compared to the task of assimilating pluralist youth into industrial society. Yet reliance on within-school exclusion, lowered standards, and changing labor demands began to produce a population whose personal development and productive role were problematic. Debilitating, long-term consequences became clear when large numbers of older youth remained in the schools' custodial-like programs during the depression. World War II provided some respite through decreased enrollment rates and increased work opportunities, but postwar demographic changes and swelling enrollments refueled challenges to school order. By that time, lowered expectations and exclusion from regular classes had become entrenched parts of urban school order. Courts, curricular reform, and federal monies tried to limit school order's adverse consequences—but did not confront the tacit understandings and rules upon which it was based. Still, within-school exclusion was made more difficult, which amplified exclusion from the schools proper.

In retrospect, order within schools was secured at the cost of future problems. Lowered performance expectations, segregation in special classes, and exclusion generated poor performance and poor discipline, negative school ascriptions, and limited future possibilities for many young people. The elaboration of these practices and the flight of capital from central cities contributed to the criminalization of youth as well. If the history of the school order documented in this research is accurate, then new or old forms of exclusion can be expected to accompany efforts to raise performance norms, and children will continue to be at risk in a domain in which their attendance is mandated by law.

NOTES

1. Forest Chester Ensign, *Compulsory School Attendance and Child Labor* (Iowa City: Athens Press, 1921), 234.

2. David Swift, *Ideology and Change in the Public Schools: Latent Functions of Progressive Education* (Columbus, Ohio: Merrill, 1971), 38.

3. *Philadelphia School Report* (Philadelphia, 1909), 58.

4. Mary A. Clapp and Mabel A. Strong, *The School and the Working Child* (Boston: Child Labor Committee, 1928), 162; Ensign, *Compulsory School Attendance*, 234.

5. *Baltimore Board of School Commissioners Annual Report* (Baltimore, 1903), 43.

6. *Philadelphia School Board Minutes*, (Philadelphia, 1902), 38-40; Ensign, *Compulsory School Attendance*, 146-147.

7. *Baltimore Annual Report*, 1902, 39, 1903; *Philadelphia School Report*, 1909; *Philadelphia Minutes*, 1898. Also, see discussion in: *Detroit Public Schools Annual Report* (Detroit, 1897), 76-81.

8. Enrollments increased by 1 percent from 1897 to 1898 in Philadelphia and by 4 percent from 1902 to 1903 in Baltimore. Baltimore's average attendance decreased by one percentage from 1902 to 1903.

9. *Baltimore Annual Report*, 1902, 39.

10. *Philadelphia Minutes*, 1898, 124.

11. *Baltimore Annual Report*, 1902, 39.

12. *Philadelphia School Report*, 1909, 58.

13. *Philadelphia School Report*, 1916, 13.

14. *Philadelphia School Report*, 1911, 52; *Detroit Annual Report*, 1914, 145.

15. *Baltimore Annual Report*, 1902, 40.

16. *Baltimore Annual Report*, 1916-1926; *Detroit Annual Report*, 1905-

1915; *Philadelphia School Report*, 1909-1919.

17. *Baltimore Annual Report*, 1912.

18. Lazerson, Marvin, *Origins of the Urban School: Public Education in Massachusetts, 1870-1915* (Cambridge: Harvard University Press, 1971), 140.

19. Leonard Porter Ayres, *Laggards in Our Schools: A Study of Retardation and Elimination in City School Systems* (New York: Charities Publication Committee, 1909), 31.

20. *Baltimore Annual Report*, 1913, 201, 248; *Philadelphia School Report*, 1920, 107; Richard Watson Cooper, *Better Attendance in Delaware Schools* (Wilmington, Del.: n.d.), 47.

21. *Baltimore Annual Report*, 1909, 39.

22. *Baltimore Annual Report*, 1908, 42.

23. *Baltimore Annual Report*, 1912, 57.

24. *Baltimore Annual Report*, 1913, 71.

25. Participant observation aids identifying social rules, roles, and knowledge shared among school actors but not with the public; for example: Gerald E. Levy, *Ghetto School* (New York: Pegasus, 1970). Historical work can aid knowledge by linking this social order's evolution to its bureaucratic context.

26. *Detroit Annual Report*, 1911, 44; *Detroit Police Department Annual Report*, 1917, 75.

27. *Detroit Annual Report*, 1898, 79.

28. *Detroit Annual Report*, 1906, 81-82.

29. *Detroit Annual Report*, 1914, 104.

30. *Detroit Annual Report*, 1907, 75.

31. *Detroit Annual Report*, 1911, 47.

32. *Detroit Annual Report*, 1912, 78.

33. Baltimore reported likewise: a three year average of under 4 percent "restored"—special room pupils returned to the regular grades; *Baltimore Annual Report*, 1932, 42.

34. *Detroit Annual Report*, 1911, 109.

35. *Detroit Annual Report*, 1908, 75; 1912, 75.

36. *Detroit Annual Report*, 1914, 10; 1912, 81.

37. *Detroit Annual Report*, 1912, 76.

38. Lazerson, *Origins of the Urban School*, 76; *Detroit Annual Report*, 1904, 190-191.

39. *Detroit Annual Report*, 1914, 105-106.

40. *Detroit Annual Report*, 1913, 67.

41. *Detroit Annual Report*, 1914, 104.

42. *Detroit Annual Report*, 1915, 178; 1914, 210.

43. *Detroit Annual Report*, 1915, 252; 1916, 96.

44. *Detroit Annual Report*, 1911, 6; 1916, 90, 130.

45. See: *Detroit Annual Report*, 1912, 74-81; 1913, 126-140; 1914, 104-119, 144-147; 1915, 137-147.

46. *Detroit Annual Report*, 1912, 150-151.

47. Ayres, *Laggards in Our Schools*; Leonard Porter Ayres, *The Binet-Simon Measuring Scale for Intelligence: Some Criticisms and Suggestions* (New York: Russell Sage Foundation, 1911), reprinted from *The Psychological Clinic: A Journal of the Study of Mental Retardation and Deviation*, November 15, 1911.

48. *Detroit Annual Report*, 1915, 137.

49. *Detroit Annual Report*, 1912-1916, 1918.

50. Ensign, *Compulsory School Attendance*, 143-144.

51. *Detroit Annual Report*, 1915, 144-147.

52. *Detroit Annual Report*, 1898, 62.

53. *Baltimore Annual Report*, 1901, 24.

54. *Detroit Annual Report*, 1908, 86-87.

55. *Detroit Annual Report*, 1909, 78-79.

56. Swift, *Ideology and Change*.

57. David B. Tyack, *The One Best System: A History of American Urban Education* (Cambridge, Massachusetts: Harvard University Press, 1974), 191.

58. *Baltimore Annual Report*, 1921-22, 46-47.

59. *Baltimore Annual Report*, 1921-22, 271.

60. *Baltimore Annual Report*, 1912, 57; *Detroit Annual Report*, 1916, 90; 1918, 25-26.

61. *Baltimore Annual Report*, 1927, 11.

62. *Baltimore Annual Report*, 1922, 42.

63. *Baltimore Annual Report*, 1928, 24.

64. *Baltimore Annual Report*, 1932, 44.

65. *Baltimore Annual Report*, 1927, 34.

66. Tyack, *The One Best System*, 208-209.

67. *Baltimore Annual Report*, 1933, 81.

68. *Baltimore Annual Report*, 1933, 20.

69. *Baltimore Annual Report*, 1933, 83.

70. *Baltimore Annual Report*, 1934, 22-25.

71. Jeffrey Mirel and David Angus, "Youth, Work and Schooling in the Great Depression," *The Journal of Early Adolescence* 5 (No. 4, 1985) 489-504.

72. Albert J. Kaplan, cited in Edward A. Krug, *The Shaping of the American High School, Volume Two: 1920-41* (Madison, Wisconsin: University of Wisconsin Press, 1972), 218.

73. Mary Stuart, cited in Krug, *The Shaping of the American High School*, 219.

74. Krug, *The Shaping of the American High School*, 219.

75. *Baltimore Annual Report*, 1922-1936.

76. Krug, *Shaping of the American High School*, 218-219, 279-281.

77. *Baltimore Annual Report*, 1937, 24.

78. *Baltimore Annual Report*, 1926, 78.

79. Krug, *Shaping of the American High School*, 311, 307.

80. *Baltimore Annual Report*, 1928, 135.

81. *Baltimore Annual Report*, 1938, 30-31.

82. *Baltimore Annual Report*, 1937, 47.

83. *Baltimore Annual Report*, 1938, 33.

84. *Baltimore Annual Report*, 1938, 32.

85. *Baltimore Annual Report*, 1934, 107.

86. *Baltimore Annual Report*, 1940, 25.

87. *Baltimore Annual Report*, 1940, 27.

88. *Baltimore Annual Report*, 1941, 94.

89. *St. Louis School Report* (St. Louis, 1943), 137.

90. *Baltimore Annual Report*, 1938-1943.

91. *Baltimore Annual Report*, 1931, 50; 1938, 32.

92. *Baltimore Annual Report*, 1938, 32.

93. "Attendance Officers Work Report, 1930-1958," Detroit Public School Attendance Office.

94. *St. Louis School Report*, 1941-1948.

95. Children's Defense Fund, *Children Out of School in America: A Report* (Washington, D.C.: The Fund, 1974) and Children's Defense Fund, *School Suspensions: Are They Helping Children?* (Cambridge, Massachusetts: The Fund, 1975).

96. Gerald R. Leslie, *The Family in Social Context* (New York: Oxford University Press, 1967), 586, 602; Paul H. and Lois N. Glasser, eds., *Families in Crisis* (New York: Harper & Row, 1970), 35; National Education Association Research Division, "Teacher-Opinion Poll," *National Education Association Journal*, Volume 53, Number 6, September, 1964, 25; National Education Association Research Division, "Major Problems of Teachers," *National Education Association Research Bulletin*, 49, December, 1971, 105; Bennet Harrison, "Education and Underemployment in the Urban Ghetto," in *Problems in Political Economy: An Urban Perspective*, ed. by David M. Gordon (Lexington, Massachusetts: D.C. Heath, 1971), 185; United States Department of Labor, Bureau of Labor Statistics, Middle Atlantic Regional Office, *The Working Age Population: Initial Findings* (New York: U.S. Department of Labor, 1969), 2.

97. Public Schools of the District of Columbia, *Pupil Personnel Services*, 1968-69.

98. Herbert H. Denton, "Forty Eliot Teachers Walk Out," *Washington Post*, 9 May 1969 and "Teacher Walk Out Grows," *Washington Post*, 10 May 1969; Public Schools of the District of Columbia, *Pupil Personnel Services, 1967-68*, 24; Joseph L. Tropea, "The Development and Implemen-

tation of a Behavioral/Systems Approach for the Prevention and Control of Delinquency and Crime," Second National Institute of Law Enforcement and Criminal Justice Report, December, 1969, 20.

99. "Informally Suspended Students," Baltimore City Public Schools Circular N. 244, Series 1968-69, (27 Mar. 1969).

100. Joseph L. Tropea, "Family, Productive Organization, Formal Authority, and the Generation of Deviant Youth: Toward a Social Structural Theory of Social Control and Socialization" (Ph.D. diss., George Washington University, 1973), 235.

101. Children's Defense Fund, *School Suspensions.*

102. *Goss v. Lopez*, 419 U.S. 565, 95 D. Ct. 729 (1975).

103. Baltimore Schools Circular, No. 245, Series, 1968-69 (1 Apr. 1969) and No. 89, Series 1969-70 (15 Oct. 1969).

104. *Pupil Personnel Services, 1963.*

105. Tropea, Second National Institute of Law Enforcement and Criminal Justice Report, Dec. 1969, 12.

106. *D.C. Code Ann.*, paragraphs 31-37 (1967).

107. Tropea, "Family, Productive Organization, Formal Authority, and the Generation of Deviant Youth," 240-241.

108. Tropea, "Family, Productive Organization, Formal Authority, and the Generation of Deviant Youth," 243.

109. Tropea, "Family, Productive Organization, Formal Authority, and the Generation of Deviant Youth," 244.

110. Tropea, "Family, Productive Organization, Formal Authority, and the Generation of Deviant Youth," 247.

111. Tropea, "Family, Productive Organization, Formal Authority, and the Generation of Deviant Youth," 248.

112. *Pupil Personnel Services, 1965-66, 1967-68.*

113. Tropea, "Family, Productive Organization, Formal Authority, and the Generation of Deviant Youth," 249.

114. U.S. Congress, Senate, Hearings before the Public Health and Education, Welfare, and Safety Subcommittee of the Committee on the District of Columbia, Crime in the National Capital, Part 5 (Washington, D.C., 1969), 1573-81, 1645.

115. Tropea, "Family, Productive Organization, Formal Author-

ity, and the Generation of Deviant Youth," 254.

116. Robert Kistter, "Campaign on Truancy Cuts Crime," *Washington Post*, February 13, 1971.

117. United Press International, "Study Cites Surge in School Violence," *Washington Post*, 13 Jan. 1970, A2.

Part II

Reconceptualizing
Children at Risk

4

Making Controversy:
Who's "At Risk?"

The language of risk is upon us, piercing daily consciousness, educational practices, and bureaucratic policy-making. It
satisfies both the desire to isolate children (by the Right) and to
display them (by the Left). We have all been quick to identify
those who presumably suffer at the mercy of "risk factors." This
essay waves a reminder: The cultural construction of a group
defined through a discourse of risk represents a quite partial
image, typically strengthening those institutions and groups that
have carved out, severed, denied connection to, and then
promised to "save" those who will undoubtedly remain "at risk."

With the image of "youth at risk" comes the litany of threats
now saturating the popular, policy, and academic literatures.
Unless public education in the United States improves substantially, the Japanese will conquer the international marketplace.
Hardworking Anglo-Americans will be swallowed by nonwhite,
noneducated nonworkers. As the general population ages, too

few will be able or willing to support us through Social Security payments. City streets will grow increasingly unsafe. And out-of-wedlock births will swell.

The one-liners ring so familiar because they chant so ritualistically. Filling public talk, shaping public policy, they traumatize and inhibit public imagination. This is the shaping of discourse. This is the making of controversy. And this is the perversion of possibility. Perhaps no field surpasses public education as the space into which public anxieties, terrors, and pathologies are so routinely showered, only to be transformed into public policies of what must be done to save *us* from *them*.

This essay peels through the constructed and impacted layers of debate that give ideological shape to today's dropout problem. This analysis of the borders of the debate surrounding (and, therefore, creating) dropouts distinguishes between concerns that have been fronted as the central intellectual controversies of the dropout problem and concerns that have been shadowed, trivialized, or silenced. We begin by eavesdropping on a debate about dropouts printed in the pages of the summer 1989 issue of *The Public Interest* between former assistant secretary of education Chester Finn and Rutgers professor Toby Jackson. Within that narrow space opened by the conservative discourse on education, Finn and Jackson find themselves in opposition, which they seem to think quite ironic. Jackson writes:

> We are brothers-in-arms in the educational-excellence movement. Apparently he [Finn] thinks it is easier than I do for adults to coerce young people to do what we consider good for them. I agree that coercion works for at least three quarters of the fourteen to eighteen year olds. They want to live up to our expectations. Hence we can force them to remain enrolled or persuade them to do so without coercion, as Japanese high schools demonstrate. The remaining quarter constitutes the problem. (Jackson 1989, 136)

Jackson wants to lower the compulsory age limit for high school students, enabling their early exit and ridding schools of adolescents who simply don't want to be there. Finn worries about giving adolescents too much say about departing from school, and he writes, instead, in support of a strategy first implemented in West Virginia and now popular elsewhere:

[The] recently enacted "no pass, no drive" law . . . denies driver's license to dropouts under the age of eighteen. [Exceptions are made for hardship cases.] This law is reportedly drawing dozens of youngsters back to school, though not necessarily for the sheer love of learning. . . . The underlying idea, of course, is to make life at least mildly unpleasant for prospective dropouts by exacting an immediate cost of the sort that most adolescents will hate to pay. (132)

The contours of this debate position "adolescent choice" (let youngsters leave high school as early as they wish) against "adolescent coercion" (punish those who leave, as an incentive for those who stay). The sense of possibility within this ideological space is remarkably slim and not at all about education. These two choices ignore any image of collective educational engagement, inquiry, passion, democracy, or critical excitement in the minds of secondary school students.

Toby Jackson does not want to "keep bodies in" that don't wish to be there. And Chester Finn does not want to let those bodies out. As these men dicker over these bodies as public property, the minds, collective educations, and critiques of those most likely to drop out are rendered simply irrelevant to the arguments postured. For Jackson, these young women and men constitute the worrisome 25 percent. And for Finn, they are, as he has written elsewhere, a "manifestation of linked social pathologies and inherited characteristics" (Finn 1989, 16). Either way, they are not "us." And they are not even very closely related to us. To the extent that a connection between us and them is acknowledged, it is not in the creation of urban decay—for there *they* have lead themselves astray—but in *our* rehabilitation of the Other, who survives "at risk."

Public and Subjugated Controversies
Surrounding the Dropout Problem

We live in a country in which 25 percent of adolescents fail to graduate from high school. Urban adolescents drop out at rates estimated to be up to 60 to 70 percent of blacks and Latinos in the comprehensive high schools of New York City, Boston, and Chicago. And in urban areas, only 35 percent of all dropouts and 25 percent of females return within two years for a GED or a diploma (Kolstad and Ownings 1987). The remainder of this essay takes as its task the analysis of "the dropout problem" as represented in public discourse. It offers an analysis of the issues that surface as public controversies and those that remain sub-jugated. Issues that have been constructed to *make controversy* offer a sharply individualized lens on the dropout problem. Those that have been *subjugated* conceal far more about deep social interdependencies and the shallowness of proposed "solu-tions." This essay offers a cultural journey through the ideologi-cal constructions and constrictions of Youth at Risk.[1]

CONTROVERSIES OF INDIVIDUALS: ISSUES THAT FLOAT "UP" INTO PUBLIC DISCOURSE

Measurement

> September 1984. Mr. Stein, Comprehensive High School principal, at the first Parent-Teacher Association meeting of the year: Welcome to —— High School. We are proud to announce that 80 percent of our graduates go on to college.

> I jotted that down in September, not knowing why it would be useful—but anticipating that it would be. After an archival cohort analysis of 1,430 incoming ninth-graders, conducted to assess their high school survival rate, I dis-covered that only 20 percent of the incoming ninth-graders ever graduate. And so it is true that 80 percent of 20 percent *do* indeed go on to college.

Perhaps the greatest public controversy around high school dropouts surrounds concerns of *measurement* (Mann 1986). If we are to assess the depth of the problem, understand the need for differential intervention, and hold schools, communities, and cities accountable, then it makes good sense to standardize a way of thinking about the scope of the dropout problem. And so we do certainly need to consider whether we calculate dropout rates within a static or a cohort frame; whether we "count" home instruction, GEDs, or imprisoned youngsters as "on register" or "dropouts"; whether we include special education placements and GEDs in aggregate graduation rates. These issues fill the measurement debate. While they are by no means frivolous, measurement itself has grown into a national fetish. Debates

about the magnitude of the problem have become, for some policymakers, districts, and advocates, *the* focus of policy debate,
with estimates ranging from 40 to 60 percent. For now we must
ask: for whom is the question, really, how *big* the problem is?

Early versus Late Intervention

> Guidance counselor at an urban high school: By high
> school, it's already too late. Look at their incoming records,
> and you can predict who's going to drop out. You need to
> start young, before school. We need to get to them before
> they are turned off to school—that happens at home.

> This is offered to me as an argument for early inter-
> vention and an explanation of why transformations of high
> schools are impossible and naive.

The second major public controversy involves *when to intervene* to reverse students' biographies of academic failure. Early
intervention and later intervention are posited as if in competi-
tion. The evidence on early intervention is unambiguous. Consistently, data on early intervention confirm the prophylactic
effects of early intervention on academic achievement, retention, delinquency, and college attendance rates. Indeed the Committee on Economic Development (1987) has recommended the
public and universal provision of preschool experiences for all.

At meetings among urban administrators concerned with
the dropout problem, however, the debate inevitably turns to
where limited public monies should be targeted. The artificial
choice pits little people, about whom romance and a sense of
hope swoon dramatically, and adolescents, about whom most
are highly ambivalent. If we opt for little, we write off the current generation of urban adolescents (who are parents of the
next generation). We legitimate the illusion that "at-risk" adolescents cannot be turned around academically. We produce a
generation of low-income youngsters who will be relatively skill-
less, jobless, and optionless and will do what adolescents without
skills do (disproportionately): parent (Children's Defense Fund
1987), get involved in criminal wage-producing activities, and/or
enroll in one of the proprietary schools, which have dropout
rates of 70 percent or more (Fine 1987). Although many teen
parents are fully skilled, talented, and educated, evidence col-

lected by Andrew Sum for the Children's Defense Fund suggests that female adolescents who experience academic difficulties are substantially more likely to become teen mothers than their average- or above-average-scoring peers (Children's Defense Fund 1987). The controversy over early versus later intervention derives from a contest over fiscal crumbs, an acceptance of squeezed and reduced budgets, and is, in the final analysis, an ideological diversion.

The Promotion/Retention Controversy

Conversation among educators:
Urban district superintendent: We need standards, and a promotion policy assures that standards are in place.
Advocate: But all the evidence suggests that promotion policies only encourage kids to stop trying and perhaps facilitates their dropping out!
Superintendent: What about the positive effect on the kids who are not flunking out? You don't measure that!

Conversation among adolescents:
Tanya: I stopped tryin' after they held me over. Felt real bad, stupid, you know. How would you feel?
Patrice: I understand why they doin' it, want to know it's a degree worth somethin', but it hurt sometin' bad. 'Nough to make me drop out and just stop carin'.

The third major public controversy involves the now-popular implementation of *promotion/retention policies* (Fine 1991). At specified academic levels, students in many districts are tested with standardized instruments, and to the extent that they do not pass the examination within an acceptable range, they are retained in grade. Inspired to cease the social promotion of students who weren't learning at "appropriate pace" and to enable educators to identify and remediate students in need of help, the program was designed to contain and resolve problems before they accumulated into a lifetime of academic failures.

Yet over the past decade, from across the country, evidence has been collected that confirms that retention per se (usually with little or no remediation, high stigma, and terribly low expectations) does not enhance learning substantially or in a sustained way and assuredly increases the likelihood of dropping out (Labaree 1983).

As policies for tougher promotion and graduation standards are put in place across the country, we are again obligated to ask, Whose risk is being lessened by this now quite popular intervention? Given that retention doubles the likelihood for students reading at or above grade level (see McDill, Natriello, and Pallas 1985), whose children are being sacrificed?

Discipline

> Assistant dean in charge of discipline: I see my job as the pilot of a hijacked plane. My job is to throw the hijacker off, even if that means bodily.

The fourth public controversy concerns *discipline, suspension,* and *expulsion.* We know from the National Coalition of Advocates for Students that, nationally, black and Hispanic students are significantly more likely to be suspended, placed in special education, and expelled than are white students, and that social class mediates this relationship. And we know from ethnographic evidence (Fine 1991) that being suspended substantially enhances the likelihood of further cutting of classes, ultimate failure, and expedited dropout rates. It is the rare educator who has the time or energy to welcome back a student who has been suspended or even out for an extended period of time for a "good" reason.

In the 1980s we heard little about alternatives to suspension and expulsion policies, some about the creation of special placements for violent (and, in some communities, "previolent") adolescents, and much about urban schools as jungles, infested with violence and lack of discipline. Violence inside schools, communities, and homes is clearly a major social problem that cuts across social classes and racial/ethnic groups, rendering low-income students and their kin particularly vulnerable to violence and to the absence of legal protection from that violence.

But while violence *is* a significant social issue, the move to identity "previolent" adolescents or "passively violent" youths, and the move to create special schools for them, represents a strategy of blaming individual students (which may need to be done for a few—but not for upward of 40 percent), not a strategy for educating urban youths. The presumption that life inside such an "alternative" school will motivate a student to gain access to a traditional comprehensive high school remains compelling—but undocumented. Instead, quantitative and qualitative evidence confirms that, once segregated inside the public education arena, one rarely escapes. For whom, among low-income youths, are suspension and expulsion policies, increased special education labeling, and alternative disciplinary school placements being designed? Whose children are sacrificed in the process? Has another false and diversionary dichotomy been created by positioning Self ("good kids") against the Other ("bad kids") and by obscuring *contexts* that enable violence versus *contexts* that inhibit violence?

Minimum Age of Exit

Administrator for a major urban school district speaking to a group of advocates: Isn't it just your middle-class values that make you think we should keep kids until they are seventeen? Why not let them leave at fourteen? Become a carpenter or contractor apprentice. They are entitled to come back up to age twenty-one. But let them go if they don't want to stay.

Advocate: What would you do if your child said that he wanted to drop out of high school at fourteen?

A fifth controversy concerns *minimum age of exit* from compulsory education, echoing the Jackson-Finn debate. It has been argued that, ironically phrased in the language of student rights, adolescents should be "allowed" to leave high school prior to age sixteen or seventeen (depending on state mandates) rather than "forced" to stay. Hanging around the public halls of education, one quickly becomes suspicious whenever students' rights are defended by persons other than students and their parents. Perhaps in a world in which meaningful employment, travel, Job Corps, Peace Corps, or other public service opportunities were available to adolescents in ways that enabled education, housing, health care, experience, adequate income, and a strengthened sense of one's own competence, perhaps then I would be more in agreement with "allowing" adolescents to leave high school early. But in their absence, the recommendation is suspect. What are low-income adolescents going to do once they are allowed to leave, while their more affluent peers are sent to a school counselor when they ask to drop out (see Fine 1986)? They are merely extricated from the public's responsibility—off the public school register, with their mothers' public welfare subsidies reduced proportionately. The incentive seems likely to work precisely, and adversely, along class and race-stratified lines.

"Alternatives"

August 1987. Discussion among chief state school officers.

Chief I: Given that the comprehensive high schools, or equivalents, are going to remain inside urban areas, what we need to do is develop alternative settings for youths at risk, so that they have some choices.

Chief II: But not in the urban areas. We need to create as many opportunities as possible to get kids out of city schools and into suburban settings.

As I listen, I recall advocates from Boston arguing that the Medco program (which buses city kids from Boston schools to the suburbs) actually robs the city of some high-achieving and active students and their parents; and American advocates from Connecticut and elsewhere disputing the ostensible virtues of the New Haven experiment in which the black adolescents who "successfully" survived the desegregation busing program to neighboring suburbs proved ultimately to be *more* likely to live in integrated neighborhoods, work in integrated settings, and attend integrated colleges. "Alternatives" are often wonderfully successful internally. As a district policy, however, alternatives involve limited access, programmatic writing off of the majority of students who remain in comprehensive city schools, and, typically, psychological (often racial) assimilation in order to be considered a success.

The final controversy is one about which I am most ambivalent: the proliferation of [positive] *alternative schools* for "at-risk" youths. *All* adolescents deserve and desire small, intact, and personal spaces in which to engage their educations. And we know that the success of alternative schools is attributable, in part, to a smallness that enables personal contexts for empowered and empowering teachers (Foley and Crull 1984). But the proliferation of alternatives for at-risk students simply irrigates large (e.g., 3,200-5,000, in New York City) comprehensive high schools while, at the same time, preserving those schools. The bulk of urban students remain inside those buildings. The question we are left with is, How can we enable innovation and alternative models to do more than preserve and strengthen the mainstream.

To illustrate the problem: New York City has recently decided that adolescents who leave their public high schools to enroll in a board-certified and sponsored GED program will be counted no longer as dropouts, but as students/graduates instead. Individuals who have been GED instructors for years and have been asking the board for fiscal sponsorship for an equal length of time, report that they are now being solicited by the board:

> It works for everybody. Now they pay for us, so when we work with kids the dropout rates for the comprehensive high schools go down, and our retention rates go up! We get what are considered their better kids; they attend more regularly, and come in with higher skill levels because the schools can encourage more of their relatively on-grade kids to come to us. They can reduce their dropout rates, we increase our retention/graduation rates and the kids who really need get ever more buried. (Personal communication with GED Director, 1985)

As in any area of innovation, the creation of alternatives, even positive alternatives, may accommodate a few, but they more fundamentally buttress the mainstream.[2]

CONTROVERSIES OF STRUCTURAL INTERDEPENDENCE: SUBJUGATED, SILENCED, AND NOT FLOATING UP

Public obsessions with measurement, early intervention, promotion, suspension, minimum age of exit, and public alternatives (schools or degrees) for at-risk youth dominate public discourse on what can be done about high school dropouts. My own work suggests that while these issues clearly feel central to public education, a series of subjugated controversies, surrounding the interdependencies of "us" and "them," also deserve policy attention. The issues may suffer from a lack of vocal advocates or from constituencies of parents and advocates too tormented, disempowered, frightened, or alienated to persistently agitate for change inside public education. I raise these controversies to resurrect the arguments and to invite popular and policy debates on these issues.

Equal Opportunities versus Outcomes

The first unarticulated controversy concerns the historic, ideological, and legal distinction between equal opportunities and severely unequal outcomes (Apple 1982; Bowles and Gintis 1976; Ryan 1981). While public education in the United States has historically been differentially accessible, based on a youngster's social class, race/ethnicity, language, gender, or disability and on legal status of parents, it is fair to say that today all children inside the United States—even those of undocumented workers—have legal access to a public education. Questions of equity no longer sit at the doorways of public schools. But children, on the basis of social class, race/ethnicity, gender, and geography, receive substantially different educational experiences and reap sharply distinct outcomes. Questions of equity must be interrogated today inside schools and at their exits. The notion of equal opportunity rings hollow without analyses of outcomes. We must ask, again, what constitutes equality?

The Ideological Public/Private Split

The second subjugated controversy involves the artificial severing of the public sphere from the private sphere inside public education. Relatively undisputed among educators and policymakers lives an acceptance that public schools can't do it all. Students' private affairs therefore cannot be school business.

We survive in a culture in which this ideological public/private distinction is held to be precious and assumed to be universally understood and shared (Eisenstein 1989). But one need not spend a lot of time inside a low-income urban public school to notice the weighty presence of state and corporate interests and the attenuated interests of community, labor, advocacy, and social change organizations and families. This latter collection of interests, collapsed into the private sphere, are expelled from public education's purview, while AT&T representatives lecture students on the work ethic; Shearson Lehman opens an academy of finance; the military recruits (and denies it); Wilfred Academy of Beauty displays its promises on career day, and right-to-life advocates speak to hygiene classes. If we conceptualize public schools as a space for the practice and expression of critique and democracy and for the interrogation of social inequity, then we must admit that there is nothing wrong with the presence of these private and state bodies inside schools, except insofar as public interests are expelled. In this case, what is called "democracy" is in fact the hegemony of private and state interests, which thrive off of the "privatization" of public concerns.

School/Community Relations

The third subjugated controversy involves the relationship of low-income schools to low-income communities. My travels through a series of urban comprehensive middle and high schools in the Northeast convince me that while exceptions are obvious, public schools in low-income neighborhoods often represent themselves as the means for low-income students to escape their local communities; sometimes as a way to save "those students" from "those parents." Obviously problematic, insofar as it nurtures both racism and classism, this position is also patently ineffective pedagogy. It undermines that which adolescents bring to their schools and classes and that which their parents/guardians could. Fundamental to a strong school/community relationship are beliefs that schooling is a vehicle for activating individual enhancement as well as social critique and community and social change; that school/parent/community collaboration will strengthen adolescents' commitment to schooling; and—a moral belief—that low-income parents and communities are precisely the "public" and the constituency to whom public schools are accountable.

With some important exceptions,[3] little (outside of Chicago) is being said or done by policymakers or educators that truly incites parental participation, empowerment, and critique (Epstein 1988). To the extent that parent involvement is noted as essential to school improvement, the typical strategy is one in which parents are trained as homework monitors or coreaders, not as collaborators, sources of critical information, innovators, or critics. Even many one-time liberals have given up on "those parents"—perhaps now that "those parents" [inside cities] are disproportionately African-American, Latino, and low-income. Unless this power differential that marks relations between schools and the low-income community is addressed *as controversial* inside public policy debates, the relationship will continue to be frivolous and bankrupt.

Postsecondary "Alternatives"

The fourth subjugated controversy involves the structural ring of "post-high-school alternatives" for dropouts: proprietary schools, GED programs and the military (and, more recently, job-readiness programs). In my ethnographic work at Comprehensive High School (CHS) and since, these four alternatives have popped out as most frequently sought after by high school dropouts. Emerging from comprehensive high schools as "discharges," seventeen-year-old adolescents are for the most part alive, energetic, creative, and motivated and trying to figure out how to create a life for themselves, for their existing (or planned) children, and sometimes for their mothers as well. Intrigued by all that they hear about GEDs, proprietary schools, and the military, they are never educated to the realities. The folklore furnished and fueled by peers and educators in the NYC school obfuscated the facts that

- in New York State, only 48 percent of GED test takers passed the examination in 1985-86;
- in New York State, the department of education released a report on proprietary schools in which they documented 70 percent dropout rates; the fact that these schools earn significantly more from students who enroll and do not complete, than from those who do complete, their educations; and evidence of unethical and unrealistic promises and abysmal post-program placement rates in what are often temporary or probationary positions; and
- nationally, many high school dropouts may get into the military (although it is unlikely that they will pass the entrance examination) but have substantially greater than average chances of being less than honorably discharged within six months and that female dropouts will not be allowed into the military (at least during "peacetime").

Public schools inside urban areas fundamentally and uncritically bolster these alternatives as "second chances." Public schools provide no evidence of their problematic aspects; public schools in fact volunteer bodies to these institutions by enabling recruitment, advertising, and the solicitation of names; and the public sector substantially subsidizes all three efforts— most particularly proprietary schools.

Given the dismal consequences of these three alternatives for most low-income adolescents,[4] why do we not feel compelled to inform students, to investigate recruitment, advertising, and financing, and to hold public schools accountable for the numbers of their students who are allowed or encouraged to flee to these alternative institutions?

The generic issue of the collapsing economy for low-income workers remains fundamentally suppressed. The proprietary schools and the military continue to represent themselves as the last institutions willing to serve low-income black and Latino adolescents. And no counterevidence emerges publicly. The wealth earned by the proprietary schools, the questionable exchange rate of the GED, and the automatic waiving of civil rights of those who enter the military seeking jobs, training, glamour, and travel are realities about which public discourse is silent.

REFLECTIONS ON YOUTH AT RISK

[Social ideology is] *real* in that it is the way in which people really live their relationship to the social relations which govern their conditions of existence, but *imaginary* in that it discourages a full understanding of these conditions of existence and the ways in which people are socially constituted within them. (Belsey 1980, 46, emphasis added)

We find ourselves faced with the fundamentally suppressed question, Who benefits from the ideological and material construction "youth at risk"? In recent debates over public education, the term has gained not only popularity but promiscuity. An adolescent may be "at risk" if she exhibits high absenteeism, has been retained, performs poorly in class, indicates a "previolent" disposition, is pregnant, lives in a low-income single-mother household, or simply arrives from Puerto Rico.

To position these students as being at risk potentially bears two very distinct sets of consequences. The benevolent consequence is that their needs could in fact be attended to. But the notion of being at risk, in the dropout literature, also offers a deceptive image of an isolatable and identifiable group of students who, by virtue of some personal characteristic, are not likely to graduate. As Foucault would argue, the image betrays more than it reveals. Diverted away from an economy that is inhospitable to low-income adolescents and adults, particularly U.S.-born African-Americans and Latinos, and away from the collapsing manufacturing sectors of the country, housing stock, and impoverished urban schools, our attention floats to the individual child, to his or her family, and to those small-scale interventions that would "fix" the child as though her or his life were fully separable from ours.

This essay has elaborated the range of controversies surrounding what is popularly represented as "the dropout problem." Those controversies publicly constructed divert social attention to individual children and adolescents, their families, and their communities. As Catherine Belsey would argue, these controversies indeed represent "real" issues (Belsey, 1980). More dangerously, however, they are imaginary, reproducing existing ideologies, shaving off alternative frames, and recommending as "natural" programs of reform that serve only to exacerbate class, race, and gender stratifications.

Controversies that have been *subjugated* and *silenced*, in contrast, turn our critical concern onto the very ideological and material distinctions that privilege those already privileged and disadvantage those already disadvantaged. They force our attention to the existing tapestry of social inequities woven through structural *interdependencies* of class, race, and gender and ask us to interrogate long-privileged distinctions between "public" and "private" spheres; between the liberal rhetoric of equal opportunity and radical demands for equal outcomes; between what we permit "our children" to do and where we send "those children" in the name of helpful alternatives.

Simply said, "youth at risk" is an ideological and historic construction. While the numbers of youth, their class, and their unbalanced racial distributions are intolerable, and the academic and economic consequences incurred by them are severe, we must remember that in the late 1980s more students graduated from high school than was true fifteen years ago. Today, however, they will not as easily find work, housing, community, or support, particularly if they are low income and/or of color. The

U.S. Department of Labor documents the differential consequences of dropping out for white males and females and black
males and females. For dropouts age 22-34, 15 percent of white
males live in poverty compared to 28 percent of white females,
37 percent of black males, and 62 percent of black females. While
31 percent of black female *graduates* live below the poverty line—
half the proportion of black female dropouts—this is still twice
the rate of white male *dropouts*. The absence or presence of a
high school diploma does not disrupt the much more encrusted
structural interdependencies of class, race/ethnicity, and gender inequities.

The dropout problem is a real issue, but more profoundly it
too has been appropriated as an ideological diversion. We can
and must improve public schools to retain and critically educate a greater percentage of students, particularly low-income
students. But at the same time, the diploma must have exchange
value across class, race, and gender lines; the economy must be
rich for all; housing, child care, health care, and social services
must be designed to accommodate *all* urban dwellers. While
these conditions remain as they are, the urban dropout problem continues to be exploited and cast, deceptively, as the central
cause of the erosion of city, state, and national strength. In such
contexts, the construction of the "at risk" adolescent distracts.
And far more fundamentally, it keeps us from being broadly,
radically, and structurally creative about transforming schools
for today's, and tomorrow's, youths.

NOTES

1. This work derives from research I have conducted across the
growing terrain of urban high school dropouts, from 1980 through the
present. This research program, if I can offer it some *post-hoc* coher-
ence, has involved quantitative evaluation research comparing dropouts
and stay-ins at an alternative high school in the South Bronx (Fine
1985); a year-long ethnographic analysis of a comprehensive high school
(CHS) in upper Manhattan (Fine 1986); consultation with diverse urban
school districts sprinkled across the Northeast corridor, legal testimony
I have delivered before the New York City Council, the New York State
Legislature, and the legislature's minority caucus; extensive involvement with advocacy groups nationally, and participation in a series of
policy-making sessions including the 1987 Summer Institute of the
Council of Chief State School Officers (Fine 1988).

2. Perhaps the best publicized "scare" statistics come from Chicago, which recently estimated a 43 percent dropout rate, and Boston, where it is reported that fewer than half of public high school entrants graduate on schedule. Hence the conventional view: one in four of our young people is failing to get through high school, and that ratio is far higher in cities, with the problem especially severe among minority youngsters. This is a shame, a scandal, and an outrage. Surely something must be done.

Finn, relying upon the Census Bureau Survey data, which reveal that 86 percent of the adult population (aged 25 to 29) have completed at least four years of high school by 1985, explained that most high school dropouts ultimately return to school within a few years and some even earn a GED. Finn concluded that the gap was explained by an alternative—earned GEDs.

Chester Finn is far more optimistic than others about educational rebound of high school dropouts. Andrew Kolstad and Jeffrey Ownings (1987), researchers from Finn's own department, conducted a longitudinal analysis of a sample of dropouts from the High School and Beyond data set. Of the twenty-eight thousand sophomores in the original cohort—which excluded all adolescents who dropped out prior to the tenth grade—Kolstad and Ownings' analysis draws on approximately two thousand dropouts included for follow-up. Of these, 40 percent had completed diploma or certificate requirements within two years of when they should have graduated from high school. Disproportionately, however, the returning dropouts were those who had dropped out as seniors (41 percent vs. 27 percent who were sophomores); were white (41 percent vs. 30 percent of Hispanics and 33 percent of blacks); of high income (53 percent of high income, compared to 37 percent of medium and 30 percent of low income), and from the suburbs (42 percent vs. 35 percent urban). Kolstad and Ownings report that in urban areas, 42 percent of males returned and graduated, but only 25 percent of female dropouts earned a diploma or certificate by the time of the follow-up. For blacks and Latinos— but not for whites—males return and graduate at rates approximately 10 percent higher than females. The race, class, and gender discrepancies, confounded by geography, demand attention for any analysis of "at risk" youth.

Former assistant secretary Finn also failed to acknowledge the differential financial consequences of a GED and a standard high school diploma. A report commissioned by the American Council on Education (Passmore 1987) concludes that while young adults with GEDs are economically better off than those with neither degree nor diploma—on outcomes including labor force participation rates, employment and wages, young adults with high school degrees are substantially better off than those with GEDs.

The typical GED recipient would have earned in 1985 about $780 more than a youth without at GED or diploma, but $1,340 less than a youth with a high school diploma.

In the absence of a discussion of differential rates and differential outcomes, Finn's argument obscures more than it enlightens about "at risk" youth. Relying on the GED "alternative" as solution, by the end of the essay Finn reveals his embedded assumptions, and priorities, about *us* and *them* (1989).

> To the degree that dropping out is caused by factors beyond the school's control, the symptom is not likely to be eradicated by school-based remedies. Insofar as it is a manifestation of linked social pathologies and inherited characteristics, it is more like "going on welfare" or "committing a crime" than like the commonplace problems of school effectiveness that are susceptible to alteration within the framework of education policy and practice. Moreover, if the dropout problem is more accurately seen as a symptom of the "underclass" phenomenon than as an educational issue, then school-based solutions are not apt to yield much more success than change in the delivery-room protocols of obstetricians are likely to alter the incidence of out-of-wedlock pregnancy" (15-16).

3. The Parent Empowerment project sponsored by the National Committee for Public Education in Baltimore, the Center for Responsive Education in Boston, the organizing initiated by Designs for Change in Chicago, and the activism sponsored by numerous individual advocacy organizations across the country.

4. There are many fabulous GED programs for adolescents and adults, but most GED educators agree that a standard diploma has greater exchange value than a GED and may be easier to acquire (Passmore 1987).

REFERENCES

Apple, M. W. 1982. Curricular form and the logic of technical control: Building the possessive individual. In *Cultural and economic reproduction in education*, ed. M. Apple. Boston: Routledge & Kegan Paul.

Belsey, C. 1980. *Critical practice*. London, New York: Basic Books.

Bowles, S., and H. Gintis. 1976. *Schooling in capitalist America*. New York: Basic Books.

Children's Defense Fund. 1987. *Preventing children having children: A special conference report.* Washington, D.C.: Children's Defense Fund.

Committee on Economic Development, Research and Policy Committee. 1987. *Children in need: Investment strategies for the educationally disadvantaged.* Washington, D.C.: Committee for Economic Development.

Eisenstein, Z. 1989. *The female body and the law.* Berkeley: University of California Press.

Epstein, J. 1988. Schools in the center: School, family, peer, and community connections for more effective middle grades school and students. Mimeo prepared for the Carnegie Task Force on Education of Young Adolescents. Johns Hopkins University.

Fine, M. 1985. Dropping out of school: An inside look. *Social Policy* (Fall): 43-50.

———. 1986. Why urban adolescents drop into and out of public high school. *Teachers College Record* 87:393-409.

———. 1987. Silencing in the public schools. *Language Arts* 64(2): 157-74.

———. 1988. Deinstitutionalizing educational inequity. In *At-risk Youth: Policy and research,* ed. Council of Chief State Officers. New York: Harcourt Brace Jovanovich.

———. 1991. *Framing dropouts: Notes on the politics of an urban high school.* Albany: State University of New York Press.

Fine, M., and P. Rosenberg. 1983. Dropping out of high school: The ideology of school and work. *Journal of Education* 165:257-72.

Finn, C. E., Jr. 1989. The high school dropout puzzle. *The Public Interest* 87 (Spring).

Foley, E., and P. Crull. 1984. *Educating the at-risk adolescent: More lessons from alternative high school.* New York: Public Education Association.

Jackson, T. 1989. The high school dropout puzzle. *The Public Interest* 87 (Spring).

Kolstad, A., and J. A. Ownings. 1987. High school dropouts who change their minds about school. Mimeo. Washington, D.C.: U.S. Department of Education, Office of Educational Research and Improvement, Center for Statistics, Longitudinal Branch.

Labaree, D. F. 1983. *Setting the standard: The characteristics and consequences of alternative student promotional policies.* Philadelphia:

Citizens Committee on Public Education in Philadelphia.

Mann, D. 1986. Can we help drop-outs: Thinking about the undoable. *Teachers College Record* 87:307-23.

McDill, E., G. Natriello, and A. Pallas. 1985. Raising standards and retaining students: The impact of the reform recommendations on potential dropouts. *Review of Educational Research* 55 (4): 415-33.

Passmore, D. L. 1987. *Employment of young GED recipients*. GED Research Briefs 14. Washington, D.C.: American Council on Education.

Ryan, W. 1981. *Equality*. New York: Pantheon Books.

5

Children's Legal Rights?
A Historical Look at a
Legal Paradox

In February 1986, sixteen-year-old John Grundy won a $1 million Cincinnati radio station lottery. Grundy, who lived with his disabled, divorced mother, left school and filed a petition with the Hamilton County juvenile court asking to be emancipated—legally declared an adult—so he could spend his newfound riches. He pleaded parental poverty, provided proof of his mother's consent, and told the court of his dreams to move out, buy a car, and enter vocational school to become a disc jockey. Juvenile court judge John O'Connor said no. The judge told Grundy to wait until his eighteenth birthday. Substituting his assessment of Grundy's needs for that of the youth and his mother, O'Connor declared: "We have a sixteen year old boy who has dropped out of the seventh grade, who has no plans for accounting or investing. Granting him his adulthood would not be in his best interests." Grundy's lawyer counseled against an appeal, advising the youth to "bide his time, listen to rock 'n roll and get ready."[1]

In the words of this volume, Judge O'Connor decided that Grundy would be "at risk" if made an adult. In many ways Grundy's case is quite typical; and it ended for him when he passed his eighteenth birthday. But Grundy's encounter with the law can serve other purposes. It can help us consider how policies toward children at risk are conceptualized and how conceptualization dictates their resolution. Stepping back and examining the framing of policies is important, because it allows us to locate the basic assumptions embedded in them but too often overlooked in the policy-making rush to collect empirical data or negotiate conflicts among policymakers. Yet unexamined assumptions can be as critical in determining the outcome of children's policies as specific program goals or funding requests.

From this perspective, the Grundy case is significant not so much for its outcome as for the way in which the issues were presented and Judge O'Connor resolved them. The case can be reconsidered as a recent conversation in a long-running debate about children at risk. The law has provided a changing and varied vocabulary for that debate. It is a vocabulary used by all of those involved with children at risk—from teachers and parents to physicians and social workers. And it can be understood by turning to the recent work of legal literary analysts. They ask us to consider that the very way in which we use law to talk about problems determines their resolution. According to law professor James Boyd White, "It is the process of thought and conversation by which choices are made, the culture of legal argument, that is the law itself." White tells us that the "law establishes roles and relations and voices, positions from which and audiences to which one may speak, and it gives us as speakers the materials and methods of a discourse. It is this discourse, working in the social context of its own creation, this language in the fullest sense of the term, that *is* the law. It makes us members of a common world."[2]

The law has supplied a common language for talking about children at risk. Since the early nineteenth century one dialect in this language has dominated legal discussions of these children: "rights talk." That is, attempts to use the law to articulate the basic interests and needs of children have been expressed in terms of the legal rights of the young. Words like *capacity*, *responsibility*, and *welfare* have filled the vocabulary of children's rights. These words have had different meanings at various times and over time, but they have remained a primary way of talking about children at risk—in part because of the power of rights talk itself. Drawing on the recent work of cultural anthropologists, political scientist Neal Milner has identified the appeal of rights talk as "dominant criteria for people to interpret notions of fairness, justice, and general cultural norms. Rights language is part of everyday language and not something that has to be used or assessed primarily in the context of the formal legal process."[3]

However, rights talk for children has proven to be both attractive and troublesome.[4] Our dominant conception of rights is rooted in the individualistic biases of the law. It presumes individual autonomy and a direct relationship with the state. Conceptually and practically, children ill-fit these assumptions. Not only are children assumed to be relatively powerless and to have different needs than adults, they are double dependents: on their parents and on the state. Consequently, children have seemed to many to fall outside the sphere of rights. And yet, rights have become so wedded to our notions of individual entitlement and protection that denying children rights has also seemed to make them even more defenseless. So there have been persistent attempts to endow children with rights. These fundamental tensions have made the language, and thus the very idea, of children's rights a continuing legal paradox.

The implications of this paradox for contemporary children's policy is best understood by examining its historical development. Rights talk about children is the product of generational solutions to the persistent problem of defining the legal place of children. In three distinct eras of the past, specific legal conceptions of children were used to create and redefine the vocabulary of children's rights.[5] The changes were neither linear nor exactly dialectical. Rather, each era produced a dominant form of rights talk that reacted against, but did not entirely displace, the words of the previous period. Instead they combined to establish a linguistic framework—what White means by a "common discourse"—that influenced the discussions of succeeding generations.

By examining the history of rights talk for children, we can gain a sense of the basic assumptions embedded in the legal language we have inherited to frame policies toward children at risk. It is a vocabulary that can help explain our failure to make the United States the child-centered society we seem to think it ought to be but know it is not and fear it never has been.

CREATING A LANGUAGE, 1800-1870s

English philosopher Thomas Hobbes offered the stark traditional Anglo-American view of children and the law: "Over
naturall fooles, children, or madmen there is no law."[6] Despite
various caveats, there was much in the law to support Hobbes's
declaration. But twin transformations of the family and the law
in the late eighteenth and early nineteenth centuries led to a
basic reexamination of the place of the child in the law. During
the first three-quarters of the nineteenth century, judges took
the lead in creating a new legal language to articulate the results,
which included the first American rights talk about children.

As family historians have described in detail, new family
beliefs and practices treated children more than ever before as
distinct individuals with special needs.[7] Concurrently, there
arose what historian Elizabeth Pleck has called "The Family
Ideal": a set of ideological commitments that deified family privacy, made conjugal and parental rights sacrosanct, and promoted family preservation. The ideal assumed a fundamental
division between public and private realms of society, assign-
ing the family to the private realm. This division proved critical,
because it helped decree that children's problems were private
matters, not public ones. Public power only became relevant
when parents failed, and even then it remained suspect. A
changing but resilient set of beliefs, the family ideal has been a
powerful influence on all attempts to devise children's policies.[8]
Law became a primary means of translating this new family ideology into practice, including discussions of children in rights
talk.

A legal individualization of the household implicit in the
new family order created pressure to revise the Hobbesian view
of children and the law. More so than ever before in Anglo-American law, children came to be seen as distinct legal individuals.
Yet the exact place of children in the new legal order had to be
determined. In a society that used rights to debate the ends and
legitimacy of public policy, discussions of children's rights were
unavoidable. The postrevolutionary legal order assigned the
responsibility to state judges in the new federal system that had
placed the family in the states' jurisdiction.[9]

Three attempts by judges to articulate a legal language for
children illustrate the necessary yet problematic need to discuss
children's policy in terms of rights. First, judges confronted

attempts by youths to wrest economic freedom from their parents, much as John Grundy would many years later. These youths sought adult rights through judicial declarations of emancipation. In England and colonial America, emancipation had been a relatively unimportant doctrine tied to issues of poor relief. But nineteenth-century state judges transformed the doctrine in an effort to address the problems of what had become an uncertain stage of life. They added a greatly expanded conception of emancipation to the law's vocabulary.[10]

Embedded in the judicial debates over youthful independence were basic assumptions about the risks and rights of children. Most cases involved a young male wage earner and parental creditors who sought the youth's assets in payment for family debts. The courts balanced the dependence of sons on their families with a belief that the young should seek economic independence. Such balancing tests were typical ways courts translated complex disputes into the language of the law. By examining the changing factors weighed in the balance, this method of depicting and resolving conflict can be used to recover judicial assumptions. For example, the emancipation cases illustrate how judges had imbibed the family ideal to give primacy to private family decision making. At the same time, in the most difficult cases, where family agreement was unclear or parent and child were in conflict, they felt compelled to balance family sovereignty against the fear that parental poverty risked blighting the future of the child. In such cases, judges used emancipation to protect youths from bearing the burden of family economic failure, one of the judiciary's first and most persistent definitions of risks for children. In returning two steers to a sixteen-year-old who had been contractually emancipated by his bankrupt father, the Vermont Supreme Court declared in 1829 that to decide otherwise would "virtually render children bondslaves to their father's creditors; and entail the poverty of the father in all of its discouraging and depressing circumstances."[11]

Case-by-case determinations ran the gamut from dogmatic endorsements of youthful independence to vigorous support for parental authority.[12] These first postrevolutionary discussions of children's legal claims voiced a uniform conception of rights. Rights were assertions of independent authority only adults could make. Youths seeking rights had to be made adults or remain children. Judges made this line clear. But they were flexible in their notions of maturity, even emancipating youths of thirteen and fourteen. For most judges, determinations of youthful maturity ought to be private matters that they merely policed. Emancipation by voluntary parental action could occur in a release of wages and also as a result of marriage, military enlistment, parental poverty, hospitalization, death, or even cruelty and abandonment. In each situation, judges drew a line separating childhood from adulthood, and thus rights holder from non-rights holder. Only in this way did the courts begin to create a language of juvenile rights as a way to use the conferral of adulthood as a protection against risk. The judicial vocabulary could not include children in its rights talk, it could only allow youths to bargain for full autonomy and thus individual protection. Children remained legal dependents.

The cases highlight the prominent role that youths caught in the uncertain years between childhood and adulthood played in discussions of children's rights. Decades before social scientists would invent the term *adolescence*, Judges struggled to describe this recognizable but ambiguous time of life. Drawing the line between adulthood and childhood would continue to bedevil debates over children's rights and risks.[13]

That point is particularly apparent in the judicial approach to a second issue, the status of unemancipated children. Judges struggled to find a way to talk about these younger children as somehow distinct legal actors, and yet not rights holders, in a legal system that tied legal power to autonomy. Their efforts echoed the declarations of theorists of the liberal state like John Locke, Henry Maine, and John Stuart Mill, all of whom assumed that children stood outside the sphere of liberty and legal rights.[14] The judicial answer, to be repeated over and over in the years ahead by others who confronted the problem, was to emphasize needs. This approach found its most effective expression in a phrase that would dominate the legal—and social welfare—discussion of children late into the twentieth century: *the best interests of the child.*

Though the exact origins of the phrase are not clear, judges translated the traditional state power of *parens patriae* and the newfound sense of children as having distinct legal interests into the new doctrinal expression. As a Georgia superior court judge put it in 1836, "All legal rights, even those of personal security and liberty, may be forfeited by improper conduct, and so this legal right of the father to the possession of his child must be made subservient to the true interests and safety of the child, and the duty of the State to protect its citizens of whatever age."[15] The ambiguous phrase assumed separate children's needs yet expressed the conviction that others, most appropriately parents, and when they failed, judges, must determine them. It sanctioned broad judicial discretion to determine the interests of children when family conflicts or failure forced them into the legal arena. By defining children's concerns as interests, judges gave the young recognition, not rights. And by doing so, they expressed a tension between custody and liberty that would frame subsequent debates over children and the law.[16]

The ambiguous language of rights and risks found some clarity in a third set of disputes: those involving children thought to be at greatest risk, the neglected and delinquent. The most influential declaration of public responsibility for children at risk came in the 1838 case of *Ex parte Crouse*. The Pennsylvania Supreme Court rejected a father's claim that his daughter had due process rights and thus her placement in a house of refuge without a trial was illegal. The judges responded with a declaration that would remain a first principle of the law: "The basic right of children is not to liberty but to custody." As in other cases, these judges asserted that children had needs, not rights: "We know of no natural right exemption from the restraints which conduce to an infant's welfare." In this way, they equated the legal status of children at risk with their physical and social dependency. They went on to argue that placement in the house of refuge was treatment, not punishment, and that the public had the right to act when parents failed.[17]

The judges in the *Crouse* case coined phrases and articulated assumptions that would remain a vital part of the law and language of children's rights. The opinion gave legal expression to the underside of the family ideal: while the state must respect family sovereignty, failed families lost their rights. And children in failed families needed therapeutic treatment to integrate them into society, not legal rights or adversarial proceedings. And, as in the emancipation rulings, the decision voiced a clear distinction between adults and juveniles. On the other hand, it blurred the many differences among children by lumping together all juveniles deemed at risk. As a result, childhood became a clearer legal category of American law, and one that tended to disregard the immense diversity of the nation's young. At the same time, the meaning for children's rights of the division of the world into public and private realms became apparent. The judges assumed an intervention/nonintervention distinction that would become a fundamental starting point for talking about children's risks. This assumption ignored the reality that the state always "intervenes" in the sense that noninvolvement in family matters expresses approval or at least lack of disapproval of what goes on in the supposedly private realm. The ideological commitment to the public/private distinction clouded—and would long continue to cloud—direct discussion of children's policies behind a haze of rhetoric about the proper role of the state in family life. And the distinction opened a linguistic doorway for what lawyer Jacobus tenBroek would call the "dual system" of American family law: a liberationist set of policies for the middle and upper classes and a repressive set for the lower classes and racial and ethnic groups.[18] Ambiguous words in the *Crouse* case, such as *treatment, welfare,* and *interests,* were to be repeated over and over again in the years to come and to be given class, racial, and gendered meanings that sanctioned this dual system.

The new language of children and the law expressed the rules and assumptions of a legal system that had become more explicitly stratified by age. The language did not dictate the results of individual cases involving children at risk; it created a legal vocabulary that framed the way their problems would be presented and resolved. It did so because rights talk was simply unavoidable in the new republic. It was so pervasive that even the exclusion of children from rights had to be explained and legitimated. In the process, the problematic character of rights talk for children began to emerge as judges struggled to use the law to balance the humanity and the dependency of the young. In this era, the primary division between childhood and adulthood also came to represent the legal line between rights and needs, between autonomy and dependence. In the era's newly minted vocabulary, rights for children primarily meant flexible claims to adulthood. Beyond that, the law offered doctrinal expressions of protection dependent on state and parental actions that could have quite varied results. Children, like other dependent groups in a society fundamentally divided by class, race, and gender, were determined to be special legal individuals, and the judiciary created a special language for them, as it did for others.[19] And yet in the very act of its creation, rights talk for children at risk suggested the instability of these initial phrasings.

THE LANGUAGE OF PATERNALISM, 1870s-1940s

The language of children's rights became more precise late in the nineteenth century. In an era overwhelmed by economic and social upheaval, panic over children renewed the discussion of children's rights. For the first time, explicit use of children's rights became part of the public-policy vocabulary. Fears about the risks children faced amid industrial capitalism, urbanization, and massive immigration—particularly the ability of families to rear children in a way deemed proper—led to repeated studies and reports on existing laws and policies about children at risk. They also spawned a new sense of the role of the state in family life and new forms of litigation. The unsettling changes of the era thus led to new definitions of risks and altered the way children were discussed in relation to both their parents and the larger society. The inherited language of children's rights helped frame these discussions. In the process, though, it was altered by a paternalistic strain of rights talk expressly for children.[20]

Beginning in the 1870s, fears of disorder in the nation's families stirred intense public debate about children. As evidence of child abuse, delinquency, and neglect mounted, reformers turned to the state. Emphasizing the differences between children and adults, they and their legislative allies filled state codes with new regulations that substantially enlarged the legal definition of children at risk and focused on the newly labeled years of adolescence. Each addition, from bans on entering dance halls or skating rinks to prohibitions against joining the circus or purchasing alcohol, represented a risk to be proscribed. Each was premised on the assumption not only that childhood was a distinctive and vulnerable stage of life, but that public regulation of childrearing had to be expanded. Protective legislation challenged an earlier faith in parental supervision of children by circumscribing youthful social and legal independence and by mandating cultural homogeneity in the nation's homes. It thus also challenged the existing allocation of rights among parents, children, and the state.[21]

Child saving culminated in three major institutional changes: the juvenile court, the prohibition of child labor, and compulsory school laws. Each expressed the central assumption of the age, that childhood must be prolonged through adolescence by keeping the young in their families to gain more extensive preparation of children for adult roles. Proclaimed as supports for the private family, the intent, if not the full result of these changes, was to strengthen children's dependence on adults and to legally remove the young from the adult spheres of the marketplace and the civic community.[22]

Reformers felt compelled to advance their claims with the rhetoric of rights. Rights talk had become a necessary method of justifying state activism in the antistatist republic. Policy goals were not enough; child protection had to be explained and legitimated. Equally important, unlike in the previous era, children's rights also became an explicit means for enhancing the stature of policies. Reformers used rights as a "trump" to win privileged status for their policies. But constrained as it was by previous usages and persistent uncertainties about the legal place of the young, rights talk continued to be a very difficult language to use for talking about children.

Reformers had to create a new paternalistic vocabulary that defined rights in terms of children's needs and parental failure. Child savers like Miriam Van Waters argued that parental failure deprived children of the "right to life, liberty, and the pursuit of happiness."[23] The neglected or delinquent child became a waif who had "lost or has never known the fundamental rights of childhood to parental shelter, guidance, and control."[24] Prolonged childhood, especially, was proclaimed as the natural right of every youth that the state must protect. Education, socialization, nurture, and other fundamental needs of children were rephrased as rights; child-saving legislation and institutions were proclaimed as necessary means to protect those rights.[25]

Attorney Elbridge Gerry, founder of the New York Society for the Prevention of Cruelty to Children, declared in 1882 that it had become a fundamental "axiom that at the present day in this country, children have some rights which even parents are bound to respect."[26] By 1918, child advocates had formulated a "New Bill of Rights of Childhood": a right to life, a right to a mother, a right to a home, a right to liberty, a right to play, and a right to the pursuit of happiness.[27] Steeped in a revised natural rights theory, reformers spoke of the child as having "inalienable rights with which the Creator has endowed all children by virtue of their very birth into the human family."[28] Like others before and since, child savers hoped to make these needs inviolate by turning them into rights.

Legitimizing paternalism through rights talk was both necessary and difficult. It was a significant addition to the inherited libertarian tradition and embedded in children's rights talk a fundamental contradiction. Paternalistic rights represented an enlarged use of state power that ran against the long-standing aversion to public regulation of childrearing. And yet state activism also grew out of the reconceptualization of the family in individualistic terms and more specific definitions of children's risks that encouraged greater regulation.

These contradictory impulses helped make children's rights a peculiar form of rights talk. Unlike that about adults' rights, discourse about children's rights was not conducted through individual claims of autonomy or choice. The talk went quite the other way to emphasize custody, not liberty, and the distinctiveness of children, not their commonalty with their elders. Compulsory education, child labor laws, and the like were justified by the duty to prevent children from asserting their independence, or being left independent, before they were deemed ready. The intent of children's rights in this era was to authorize official supervision when parents failed, not to deny the appropriateness of state control or to grant children themselves the power to choose. The problems of using rights language in this fashion were swept away by the need to present expanded public supervision of the young in the most palatable terms possible in a society resistant to direct expressions of state power. Rights talk proved too attractive to ignore.[29]

Judges, in particular, struggled with the inconsistencies and contradictions of the new paternalistic children's rights talk. Judicial interpretations made it clear that children's rights continued to be a blend of parental claims and state protections that the new strain of paternalistic rights talk altered but did not fundamentally revise.[30] The very way judges entered the dialogue explains much of the legal meaning of the new children's rights. It was not children, but parents, reformers, and bureaucrats, who asserted these rights. Primarily courts faced parents' protests that state actions had violated *their* constitutional rights. The litigation phrased the legal debate over protective legislation as an adversarial struggle over parental rights and interests of the state.

Generally, judges sustained the constitutionality of protective legislation. They narrowed parental authority and argued that children at risk had needs that could countermand parental rights. Yet the new language of children's rights rested uneasily within the existing legal vocabulary. Judges were reluctant to talk of the new protections as rights.

The most suggestive judicial statements came in endorsements of the juvenile court. In a new balance of procedural rights and therapy, judges rejected arguments that the informal tribunals violated children's rights by denying them the counsel, self-incrimination protections, jury trials, and other due process rights accorded adult criminal defendants. The Pennsylvania Supreme Court upheld the constitutionality of the state's juvenile court in 1905: "Every statute which is designed to give protection, care, and training to children, as a needed substitute for parental authority, and performance of parental duty, is but a recognition of the duty of the state, as the legitimate guardian and protector of children where other guardianship fails. No constitutional right is violated."[31] A year earlier a federal appeals court was even more direct. It ruled that a seventeen-year-old girl who had been committed to a reform school without notice or opportunity for a hearing "had no legal right to be heard in [the] proceedings."[32]

For the courts, needs and rights remained distinguishable categories despite reformers' attempts to collapse the two. Perpetuating the earlier distinction between punishment and treatment, judges denied that juveniles had due process rights separate from those of their parents. And parental rights could be forfeited, as the Supreme Court of Idaho explained in 1908: "It would be carrying the protection of 'inalienable right,' guaranteed by the Constitution, a long ways to say that the guaranty extends to a free and unlimited exercise of the whims, caprices, or proclivities of either a child or its parents or guardians for idleness, ignorance, crime, indigence, or any kindred dispositions or inclinations."[33]

The range of rights talk was evident as well in the way that the family ideal continued to influence legal language as judges policed the boundaries between the private family and the state. Parental rights, though more restricted, retained primacy. In schooling disputes, for example, judges balanced state and parental authority by endorsing the compulsory education laws but reserving a large domain for parental control of education. In 1901 the Indiana Supreme Court turned back a parental challenge to the state school law by arguing that children had a basic right to education:

The natural rights of a parent to the custody and control of his infant child are subordinate to the state and may be restricted and regulated by municipal laws. One of the most important natural duties of the parent is his obligation to educate his child and this duty is owed not to the child only, but to the commonwealth. If he neglects to perform it, or willfully refuses to do so he may be coerced by law to execute such a civil obligation. The welfare of the child, and the best interests of society require that the State shall exert its sovereign authority to secure to the child the opportunity to acquire an education.[34]

On the other hand, a California appellate court in 1921 supported the right of a couple to keep their child out of mandatory dancing exercises instituted as part of a physical education program. The court ruled that the decision of whether to allow the child to have dancing instructions was "a question of morals and the liberty of conscience" and therefore a parental right.[35] Contradictory decisions in disputes between parents and state authorities filled the case reports, as judges struggled to draw lines between parental rights and state interests.[36]

In this manner, *best interests of the child* acquired a new meaning. This inherently subjective policy-guiding phrase was used to authorize vastly increased judicial discretion. As always, it granted free play to judges' personal biases and beliefs. Juvenile court judges could, and did, use the phrase to sanction the application of policies drawn from racial, ethnic, and gender beliefs, particularly in regard to status offenses such as sexual precocity, incorrigibility, and truancy. The best *interests* phrase remained, in the words of a later critic, "an empty vessel into which adult perceptions and prejudices are poured."[37] But the doctrinal ambiguity did not eliminate the confusion of rights and needs so prominent in the era's debate over children's policies. Instead, the revised use of the doctrine as a way to address children at risk highlights the range of meanings rights had already acquired.

The new rights language entered national constitutional discourse in a series of United States Supreme Court decisions beginning in the 1920s. Fittingly it did so by establishing a constitutional basis for parental authority. *Meyer v. Nebraska* (1923) declared unconstitutional a Nebraska statute that prohibited the teaching of foreign languages to children below the eighth grade.

The justices termed the act an invasion of parents' right to select their children's teachers.[38] Two years later in *Pierce v. Society of Sisters* the court sustained a challenge to an Oregon law requiring that students attend only public school until they reached sixteen. The justices condemned the act because it "unreasonably interfered with the liberty of parents and guardians to direct the upbringing and education of children under their control."[39] The court continued the dialogue in the 1944 *Prince v. Massachusetts* decision when it acknowledged "a private realm of family life which the state cannot enter." Even so, a parent could go too far when she allowed her daughter to violate a ban on street solicitation by children. The girl passed out the Jehovah Witnesses' *Watchtower* tract. In such a situation, the state could regulate the family "in the public interest" because it had "a wide range of powers for limiting parental freedom and authority in things affecting the child's welfare."[40]

In these cases, the justices assumed either that the interests of the parent and child were congruent or only the parent's voice had to be heard. Their decisions placed a constitutional foundation under the common-law rights of parents and state officials to direct children's education and other life choices. They did so in language that encouraged litigation as the way to solve disputes between the two. Equally important, children did not bring these cases. In the era that invented paternalistic rights for children, it was parents, social workers, judges, and other protectors who spoke for the young and fought over them.

Decisions like these suggest why the paternalistic strain of rights talk was, and would largely remain, a dialect of non-lawyers, particularly of professional social workers and other child advocates. Many of those trained in the law resisted demands that children's needs be transformed into legally enforceable rights. They spoke of rights in traditional adult, adversarial, and antistatist terms. In a 1914 evaluation of the juvenile court from a "lawyer's standpoint," Pennsylvania attorney Edward Lindsey argued that the statutory reform promoted a "socialistic tendency," which he contrasted with the "individualistic tendency" of the courts. Decrying the "socialistic idea that the abstract political entity we call the state is a sort of artificial parent of all minors with rights over them superior to any rights of the natural parents or of the minors themselves," he asserted that misguided judicial acceptance had meant that "constitutional safeguards as far as minors and the relations of parent and child is concerned have completely broken down." Lindsey defended parental rights and called for common-law individualism to triumph over state socialism.[41] Lawyers like Lindsey retained a skepticism toward paternalistic rights that complicated the debate over children's policies by fostering professional conflicts.

In 1915, social gospel leader Walter Rauschenbusch identified the contradictory character of the new children's rights talk. He too wanted health, nutrition, play, education, loving parents, and "a strong and joyous life" for children. But he expressed uneasiness at calling these "rights." Maintaining that children were essentially defenseless, he contended that they only had rights "on human love and solidarity." Using traditional rights talk, he argued that rights were not gifts of love:

> Rights have to be fought for and won. They have to be wrested by political agitation, by political organization, and often by physical force, from hostile classes and interests. "They have no rights who dare not maintain them." The child can maintain nothing, not even itself. . . . The child has no weapon of defense except the cry of pain.[42]

Rauschenbusch voiced a common concern. Defining children's needs as rights masked the nature and complexity of what was at stake and shifted the debate to the issue of rights themselves.[43]

And yet a new strain of rights talk had entered the law. A distinctive age-based conception of rights, steeped in paternalism, had expanded the rights vocabulary. The new rights talk did so quite awkwardly by translating children's needs into rights without jettisoning the young's dependence. These rights were unusual, because they could not be exercised or waived by their holder. Their intent was social integration, not individual independence, prolonged custody, not liberty. They clashed with the traditional conception of legal rights as assertions of personal autonomy and thus added a second strain to children's rights. Autonomous legal rights, like emancipation or marriage, continued to exist for youths who secured the status of adults. Yet even these became more circumscribed by the new policy of prolonging childhood that undercut juvenile claims of economic independence and led to higher statutory marriage ages.[44]

Paternalistic rights talk helped institutionalize the irresolvable tension between treating the young as family dependents and treating them as autonomous individuals. The changes of the era reinforced the tension and perpetuated the language and, thus, deepened the paradox of children's rights.

LIBERATIONIST TALK, 1950s-1970s

Rights talk about children has taken a dramatic turn in the last few decades. In an era dominated by rights struggles, children's rights became a movement. For the first time, children's problems were explained as a consequence of children's lack of adult rights. Lack of rights itself became a risk for children. The result was the addition of a liberationist strain to the already paradoxical language of children's rights.

Reexaminations of the paternalistic legislation of the previous period sparked a new campaign for children's rights. Separate, paternalistic protections for children came under fire. Beginning in the mid 1950s, critics attacked the creation of adolescence in particular for stigmatizing and excluding the young from adult worlds and responsibilities. They demanded that recognition of children's similarity to adults replace the policy emphasis on differences. In a line of reasoning similar to that used in the civil rights movements that extended rights to African-Americans and women, children's rights advocates fought to include children in the era's vision of self-determining persons who could make claims recognized by law. They sought to make children's rights a new kind of trump by making them more like traditional adult rights.[45]

The United States Supreme Court and other federal tribunals contributed mightily to the liberationist talk of children's rights. The language of autonomous legal rights for children proved more congenial to judges than had the earlier paternalistic rights talk of child savers like Gerry to lawyers of his day like Lindsey. Since the late 1930s, federal judges had become increasingly receptive to claims of individual liberty and due process rights. They devised a new discourse on rights that retained the adversarial and legalistic assumptions of traditional rights talk. The implications for children became evident in the seminal 1954 *Brown* decision. Not only did the court ban segregated schools, it voiced its decision in the rhetoric of children's rights: "In these days it is doubtful that any child may reasonably be expected to succeed in life if he is denied the opportunity of an education. Such an opportunity, where the state has undertaken to provide it, is a right which must be made available to all children."[46]

The court's most dramatic discussion of children's rights came in the 1967 case of *In re Gault*. The justices accepted a major argument advanced by a new generation of child welfare reformers: the juvenile court had failed to fulfill its therapeutic promises, and thus its exchange of procedural protection for treatment unfairly denied constitutional rights to minors. They altered the balance of interests weighed in juvenile justice cases by declaring that children faced with delinquency proceedings were entitled to the right to counsel, notice of charges, confrontation of witnesses, and the privilege against self-incrimination. In a critical contribution to the language of children's rights, the court asserted: "Neither the Fourteenth Amendment nor the Bill of Rights is for adults alone." The justices rejected the argument launched in the 1838 *Crouse* decision that institutionalization should be considered treatment, not punishment. They announced that children were to be treated as rights-bearing persons, not just objects of paternalism. The result was to make rights an even more central part of the debate over the definition and treatment of children at risk.[47]

A series of subsequent decisions expanded the liberationist language of children's rights. *Tinker v. Des Moines* classified high school students as persons under the constitution and asserted that they had fundamental constitutional rights: "First Amendment rights, applied in light of the special characteristics of the school environment, are available to teachers and students. It can hardly be argued that either students or teachers shed their constitutional rights to freedom of speech or expression at the schoolhouse gate."[48] *Goss v. Lopez* gave clearer meaning to the right to education by requiring hearings before the imposition of severe disciplinary punishments such as suspensions.[49] Unlike earlier decisions, these cases and those involving student privacy, search and seizure, and dress talked of children's educational rights independent of correlative parental rights.[50] Equally significant, many of them involved claims made by youths themselves.[51]

The court even began to speak of children's rights against their parents. *Planned Parenthood of Central Missouri v. Danforth* rejected a statute requiring parental consent to a minor's abortion. The court ruled that a minor had a right, as did an adult, to determine whether to terminate her pregnancy independent of the state, parents, or other parties. Justice Harry Blackmun argued that "constitutional rights do not mature and come into being magically only when ones attains the state-defined age of majority. Minors, as well as adults, are protected by the Constitution and possess constitutional rights."[52] Similar assertions came in cases dealing with contraception and even growing long hair.[53]

Decisions like these added a liberationist strain to discussions of children's rights. They recast the definition of children at risk by applying an adult model of rights to children. Corresponding statutory initiatives, such as medical emancipation laws and lowered drinking ages, spoke in the same liberationist language as did the Twenty-sixth Amendment in lowering the voting age to eighteen.[54] The lure of rights talk was evident in the renewed tendency to issue children's "bills of rights." In this era, unlike the previous one, due process, not paternalism, was the emphasis. Lawyers Henry Foster and Doris Freed, for instance, included in their charter a child's right to emancipation from a troubled home and called for the abolition of minority status, which they likened to slavery and coverture. Rights talk for the young rephrased the entire discussion of children at risk.[55]

Child rights advocate John Holt observed in 1974, "Much is said and written these days about children's 'rights.' Many use the word to mean something that we all agree it would be good for every child to have: 'the right to a good home' or 'the right to a good education.'" But Holt discounted these paternalistic rights of a previous generation in favor of autonomous rights: "I mean what we mean when we speak of the rights of adults. I urge that the law grant and guarantee to the young the freedom that it now grants to adults to make certain kinds of choices, do certain kinds of things, and accept certain kinds of responsibilities."[56] Declarations like this underscored the anti-interventionist, antistatist strain that ran through much of the children's rights movement and its use of rights as trumps to challenge special public protections for the young. The emphasis was liberty, not custody. For the liberationists the denial of legal autonomy itself was a fundamental risk to children; consequently, in the words of Richard Farson, "we are not likely to err in the direction of too much freedom."[57]

But the new liberationist talk of children's rights added

words to the law, it did not create a new language. On the contrary, despite dismissals like Holt's, the legal language of independence coexisted uneasily with that of dependence. Even in the seminal rights decisions just discussed, dissenters often urged the retention of language recognizing children's special needs and special risks. In *Tinker,* Justice Potter Stewart insisted that the rights of children were not "co-extensive with those of adults."[58]

Other decisions perpetuated the language of parental authority and the unity of family interests in opposition to the new assertions of youthful autonomy. In *Wisconsin v. Yoder,* the court upheld the right of Amish parents to withdraw their children from public schools in violation of state compulsory school laws. Despite a dissent from Justice William O. Douglas, asking whether the children had been heard, the majority resorted to the established judicial policy of endorsing parental authority over childrearing as the best protection for children.[59] And in *Ginsberg v. New York* the court accepted age-graded standards of risk. It upheld regulations limiting access to obscene materials for those under seventeen. Justice Stewart asserted: "I think that a State may permissibly determine that, at least in some precisely delineated areas, a child—like someone in a captive audience—is not possessed of that full capacity for individual choice which is the presupposition of First Amendment guarantees."[60] Similarly the court ruled that children's due process rights in juvenile court proceedings did not include that of a jury trial.[61] In the same vein, the National Council of Juvenile Court Judges advocated a new balancing test for the young by resolving in 1974 that "the basic premise of juvenile court jurisdiction [is] that children are different from adults and deserve not only due process protection but also benefit of individualized dispositions based on the needs of the child which are and have been the hallmark of the juvenile court."[62] Such decisions and declarations underscored the longevity of language expressing dependent notions of children's rights and the *parens patriae* authority of the states under the best interest of the child doctrine. They illustrated the persistence of a legal discourse of children's rights as expressions of needs.

And amidst fears of mounting risks for the young—parental abuse, teenage pregnancy, suicide, and drug addiction—the children's rights movement itself faced growing opposition. During the 1970s and 1980s critics reversed the terms of debate and argued that liberation put children at risk. A growing number of opponents charged that talk of rights had undermined child welfare by fostering adversarial relations and undermining necessary parental and school authority.

Law professor Bruce Hafen warned in 1976 that "serious risks are involved in an uncritical transfer of egalitarian concepts from the contexts in which they developed to the unique context of family life and children." He argued that "the most harmful of the potential consequences is that the long-range interests of children themselves may be irreparably damaged as the state and parents abandon children to their rights." In a declaration that revealed how expansive, yet illusive, rights talk had become, Hafen even asserted that the right not to be abandoned to rights may well be the young's most basic right.[63] A few years later, Edward Wynne resuscitated paternalistic rights. He charged lawyers and courts with harming children by fostering legalistic relationships in the home and school that destroyed the adult authority and sense of community children required. Returning to the language of the child savers, he insisted that children needed "other rights which are not so subject to judicial enforcement: the right to have others care for us; the right to have some authority over, and responsibility to, others; and finally the right to live, work, and learn in a community instead of an impersonal environment." Wynne linked these paternalistic rights to greater public regulation of the young by demanding the restoration of custodial policies that "subjected young persons to certain forms of more intense protection, scrutiny, and constraint."[64]

Critics like these challenged the fundamental liberationist premise that courts and the adversarial process were effective means of raising and resolving the problems of children at risk. For them, the dangers outweighed the benefits. Indeed, the continued incongruity of the words *children* and *rights* even took the form of cartoons and other derisive dismissals, such as a poem by Shel Silverstein:

> Strike! Strike! For Children's Rights
> Longer weekends
> Shorter school hours
> Higher allowances
> Less baths and showers
> No Brussels sprouts

More root beer
And seventeen summer vacations a year
If you're ready to strike—line up right here[65]

Opposition to liberationist rights for children illustrated the continuing difficulties of fitting children into the American language of rights.

The examples also indicate the persistence of the family ideal as a check on the exertion of autonomous children's rights. Despite the obvious expansion of state regulation of the family, the assumption of separate public and private spheres and the language of intervention/nonintervention still dominated the debate over children's rights and the framing of policies toward children at risk. And class, gender, and racial distinctions remained as well. In a revision of tenBroek's original distinction between the family law of the poor and that of other classes, Carol Stack now pointed out the emergence of a "dual system of children's rights—a system that creates differences in the rights of poor and non-poor children and families."[66] These divisions were most visible in the bitter debates over abortion in which both age and class differentiated rights.[67]

Rights talk remained complicated and contradictory because even at the height of liberationist claims—as at the peak of previous debates—other voices continued to be heard. That reality reminds us that conversations about children's rights have never taken place in a single voice. They have always been filled with conflict and contradictions. But recent discussions also tell us that debates over children's rights and risks have always been bounded in time, as the cultural blinders of an era encourage certain rights talk and stifle others.

As a result of these debates, children's rights talk had become a very complex and confusing language. It contained three major strains: claims that children had rights of their own; claims that parents had a broad range of rights over children; and claims that the state had the right to treat children differently than adults when they needed special protections.[68] These clashing claims produced a rights rhetoric that could be, and was, used to argue that children must be treated like adults and that they must be treated differently than adults. In short, it incorporated the fundamental disagreements over children at risk without resolving them. As a result, rights talk included a broad range of expressions to articulate clashing views of the powers of children, parents, and the state. Consequently, rights talk remained an irresistible vocabulary for all participants in debates over children at risk.

A 1988 clash at a meeting of the Cleveland, Ohio school board exemplified the results. The city council asked the board to ban student beepers and pagers. A council member argued that the devices were used to facilitate drug deals. The school superintendent responded by questioning the effectiveness of the tactic as an antidrug measure and insisting that the board respect student rights: "It is not illegal to have beepers in this society, there is no city ordinance that makes it illegal." The councilperson replied angrily: "What about the rights of the students who are there to get an education? What about the rights of the taxpayers who are footing the bill? Beepers and pagers do not belong in the hands of the students. I am really getting sick and tired of students' rights. We have given them control of the system and look at what we've got. The emphasis must be on an undisruptive environment."[69] The paradox continues.

CONCLUSION

In a 1977 report, the Carnegie Council on Children voiced a new orthodoxy: "The right of children to be viewed as legal persons capable of interests and deserving representation independent of their parents has emerged only recently."[70] Attributing these changes to the liberation movements of the era, eroding faith in parents and other figures of authority, and a greater belief in the capacity of children to govern themselves, the council insisted: "In recent years the legal trends have been decidedly in the direction of granting children greater legal rights and responsibilities both by statute and by court decisions." And yet the council feared that "the balance of legal power among parents, the state, and children will continue shifting, which is healthy; but we are concerned that too much if not most of the law affecting children has been hammered out on a case-by-case basis." It called for a comprehensive look at the legal principles affecting children and for the enactment of an integrated, comprehensive children's code.

The contradictions and incoherence of children's rights that the council bemoaned were quite real. Like other critics, its members could point out the inconsistent lines drawn between adulthood and childhood in various states and in various contexts ranging from voting and drinking to marriage and abortion. And yet the very rights language that the report championed illustrated just how elusive such a code would be. The likelihood of using rights talk to resolve these contradictions ignored the way in which they were embedded in the language of the law itself.

By the 1990s, rights talk about children expressed, without resolving, the fundamental ambiguities about the place of the young in American law and society. It had proven to be a troublesome yet attractive language for debating children's policies dealing with independence and dependence, powers and risks. One the one hand, it failed to express the intense hopes and fears inspired by children, and thus the very humanity of the young. Historian and social critic Michael Ignatieff's critique of rights talk was particularly appropriate for children's rights: "Rights language offers a rich vernacular for the claims an individual may make on or against the collectivity, but it is relatively impoverished as a means of expressing individuals' needs *for* the collectivity."[71] On the other hand, rights talk for children had proven to be resilient, changeable, and alluring. It persisted as one of the few ways to carry on a common discussion about children and public policy aimed at establishing humane treatment of the young. Rights for children, as for others, law professor Martha Minnow argues, "can be understood as a kind of communal discourse that reconfirms the difficult commitment to live together while engaging in conflict."[72] Equally important, rights for children retained their appeal as trumps for all of those involved in devising policies for children at risk; that is, as ways to give privileged status to policies by making them seem permanent and important. In the final analysis, rights talk about children persisted despite its contradictions because it "encourages a common language and a vague but common and powerful set of values about the ways to frame and handle conflict."[73]

These realities are not likely to change. Even a cursory glance backward like this one underscores that point. Our conversations about children at risk will continue to find expression in rights talk in the future as they have in the past. And so in many ways we are, as were our predecessors, captives of that language. Much as John Grundy was told by his lawyer to wait and plan, this excursion into the past suggests that before we rush to make policy, perhaps we should contemplate just how our inherited language of children's rights dictates the way we discuss children at risk.[74]

NOTES

1. "Boy Denied Access to $1 Million Prize," *The Cleveland Plain Dealer*, February 12, 1986, p. 20-A.

2. "Law as Language: Reading Law and Reading Literature," *Texas Law Review*, 60 (1982), 436, emphasis in original; and see *When Words Loose Their Meaning* (Chicago: University of Chicago Press, 1984), 266; "Law as Rhetoric and Rhetoric as Law," *University of Chicago Law Review*, 52 (1985), 688-89. For a critique see Robin West, "Communities, Texts, and the Law: Reflecting on the Law and Literature Movement," *Yale Journal of Law and the Humanities*, 1 (1988), 129-56.

3. "The Denigration of Rights and the Persistence of Rights Talk: A Cultural Portrait," *Law and Social Inquiry*, 14 (1989), 648, and see generally 631-53.

4. For a valuable discussion of the notion of rights talk and its use in addressing historical issues see Hendrik Hartog, "The Constitution of Aspiration and 'The Rights that Belong to Us All,'" *Journal of American History*, 74 (1987), 1013-34. In approaching the issue of children and public policy in this fashion I have been influenced by the work of Martha Minnow, especially "Interpreting Rights: An Essay for Robert Cover," *Yale Law Journal*, 96 (1987), 1860-1915.

5. In adopting a periodized analysis I want to voice my agreement with Peter Stearn's argument that periodization is one of the major contributions of historians to public policy debates, "History and Policy Analysis: Toward Maturity," *The Public Historian*, 4 (1982), 14.

6. Thomas Hobbes, *Leviathan*, Richard Tuck, ed. (Cambridge: Cambridge University Press, 1991), 187.

7. For the most recent synthesis of family history see Steven Mintz and Susan Kellogg, *Domestic Revolutions, A Social History of American Family Life* (New York: Free Press, 1988), chaps. 1-3.

8. *Domestic Tyranny, The Making of American Social Policy Against Family Violence From Colonial Times to the Present* (New York: Oxford University Press, 1987), esp. chap. 1.

9. For a typical description of parent-child relations from the period see James Kent, *Commentaries on American Law*, O.W. Holmes, Jr.,

ed. (Boston: 12th ed., Little, Brown, 1873), vol. 2: 190-218; for an analysis of the changes in the era see Michael Grossberg, *Governing the Hearth, Law and the Family in Nineteenth Century America* (Chapel Hill: University of North Carolina Press, 1985), esp. chap. 1.

10. For a general discussion of emancipation in nineteenth century America see Tapping Reeve, *The Law of Baron and Femme* (Albany, N.Y.: Gould, 3rd. ed., 1854), 422-25; Kent, *Commentaries*, 2:194; "Parent and Child," *The Central Law Journal*, 15 (1882), 24-26. For an historical assessment of these issues see F. Raymond Marks, "Detours on the Road to Maturity: A View of the Legal Conception of Growing Up and Letting Go," *Law and Contemporary Problems*, 39 (1975), 78-92.

11. *Chase v. Elkins*, 2 Vt. 290, 291 (1929).

12. This analysis is based on a reading of approximately 225 appellate cases drawn from jurisdictions around the country from 1790 to 1920. See for example, *Gordon v. Potter*, 17 Vt. 348 (1845); *Weeks v. Morrow*, 40 Me. 151 (1855); *Atwood v. Holcomb*, 39 Conn. 270 (1872).

13. Judges were also more reluctant to emancipate daughters, an example of the use of gender to differentiate rights that formed a pervasive part of the judicial approach to parent and child relations and to their vocabulary.

14. See for example John Locke, *The Two Treatises of Government* (New York: Cambridge University Press, 1960), 346-54; Henry Maine, *Ancient Law* (New York: Dutton Publishing Company, 1870), 163-64; John Stuart Mill, *On Liberty* (Boston: Tricknor and Fields, 1863) 13, 14; and for a general discussion of the problems of granting children liberty interests see Catherine J. Ross, "Of Children and Liberty: An Historian's View," *American Journal of Orthopsychiatry*, 52 (1982), 470-79.

15. *In the Matter of Mitchell*, 3 Charlton Reps. 489, 495 (Ga. 1836); and for a full discussion of the rise of the best interests of the child doctrine see Grossberg, *Governing the Hearth*, chap. 7.

16. For the relationship of the doctrine and the particular approach of judges to cases involving children see Michael Grossberg, "Who Gets the Child? Custody, Guardianship, and the Rise of a Judicial Patriarchy in Nineteenth Century America," *Feminist Studies*, 9 (1983), 235-60.

17. 4 Wharton 9, 10, 11 (Pa. 1838).

18. For tenBroek's argument see Joel F. Handler, ed., *Family Law and the Poor: Essays by Jacobus tenBroek* (Westport: Greenwood Press., 1971); and see Steven Schlossman, *Love and the American Delinquent, The Theory and Practice of Progressive Juvenile Justice, 1825-1920* (Chicago: University of Chicago Press, 1977); Lee E. Teitelbaum, "Family History

and Family Law," *Wisconsin Law Review*, (1985), 1135-81; Frances E. Olsen, "The Myth of State Intervention in the Family," *Journal of Law Reform*, 18 (1985), 835-64.

19. For a related discussion of slave law in terms of balances between property and humanity see Mark Tushnet, *The American Law of Slavery* (Princeton: Princeton University Press, 1981).

20. For the general context of these changes see Mintz and Kellogg, *Domestic Revolutions*, chaps. 4-6; and for a compelling account of the transition from viewing children as productive assets to valuable emotional necessities see Viviana Zelizer, *Pricing the Child, The Changing Social Value of Children* (New York: Basic Books, 1985).

21. United Board of Education, "The Legal Rights of Children," U.S. Bureau of Education Circulars of Information, No. 3 (Washington, D.C., 1880); Florence Kelley, "On Some Changes in the Legal Status of Children Since Blackstone," *The International Review*, 13 (1882), 83-98; Thomas C. Carrigan, "The Law and the American Child," *The Pedagogical Seminary*, 18 (1911), 121-83; Marks, "Growing Up and Letting Go," 85-88; Ross, "Of Children and Liberty," 473-75; and for the general institutional context of these changes see Morton Keller, *Affairs of State, Public Life in Late Nineteenth Century America* (Cambridge: Harvard University Press, 1977), chaps. 12-13.

22. David B. Tyack, "Ways of Seeing: An Essay on the History of Compulsory Schooling," *Harvard Educational Review*, 46 (1976), 355-89; Tyack, Thomas James, Aaron Benavot, *Law and the Shaping of Public Education, 1785-1954* (Madison: University of Wisconsin Press, 1987); Schlossman, *Love and the American Delinquent*, Part II; David Rothman, *Conscience and Convenience, The Asylum and Its Alternatives in Progressive America* (Boston: Little, Brown, 1980), Part III; Stephen Wood, *Constitutional Politics in the Progressive Era: Child Labor and the Law* (Chicago: University of Chicago Press, 1968).

23. "The Juvenile Court from the Child's Point of View," in Jane Addams, ed. *The Child, The Clinic, and The Court* (New York: New Republic, 1925), 218.

24. Ibid.

25. Lee E. Teitlebaum and Leslie J. Harris, "Some Historical Perspectives on Government Regulation of Children and Parents," in Teitlebaum and Adrian R. Gough, eds., *Beyond Control, Status Offenders in Juvenile Court* (Cambridge: Harvard University Press, 1977), 28-31; N. Ray Hiner, "Children's Rights, Corporal Punishment, and Child Abuse, Changing American Attitudes, 1870-1920," *Bulletin of the Menninger Clinic*, 43 (1979), 239-41.

26. Elbridge Gerry, "The Relation of Societies for the Prevention of Cruelty to Children to Child-Saving Work," *Proceedings of the National Conference of Charities and Corrections* (1882), 9:129.

27. Cited in Hiner, "Children's Rights," 239-40.

28. Henry D. Chapin quoted in Hiner, "Children's Rights," 238.

29. Lee E. Teitelbaum makes a useful distinction between "integrative" rights and "autonomous" rights that helps clarify the emergence of different strains of rights talk in this era, see "Foreword: The Meaning of Rights of Children," *New Mexico Law Review*, 10 (1980), 235-53.

30. For a recent example questioning the usefulness of general paternalistic claims as opposed to legal ones see Hillary Rodman, "Children Under the Law," *Harvard Educational Review*, 43 (1973), 495-97.

31. *Commonwealth v. Fisher*, 213 Pa. 48 (1905).

32. *Rule v. Geddes*, 23 App. D.C. 31, 50 (1904).

33. *Ex parte Sharpe*, 15 Id. 120 (1909).

34. *State v. Bailey*, 157 Ind. 324, 329-30 (1901).

35. *Hardwick v. Board of School Trustees*, 54 Cal. App. 696, 708, 205 Pacific 49, 54 (1921); and see similar rulings on bookkeeping, *Rulison v. Post*, 79 Ill. 567 (1875), and geography, *Morrow v. Wood*, 35 Wis. 59, 65 (1874).

36. For a full discussion of the education cases see Tyack et al., *Law and the Shaping of Public Education*; Bruce R. Stewart, "Reconciling the Competing Interests of Parents and Children," *School Law Bulletin*, 13 (1982), 1-9.

37. Rodman, "Children Under the Law," 513.

38. 262 U.S. 390 (1923).

39. 268 U.S. 510 (1925).

40. 321 U.S. 159 (1944).

41. "The Juvenile Court Movement from a Lawyer's Standpoint," *Annals*, 52 (1914), 142, 143. Similarly, Harvard Law School Dean Roscoe Pound likened the juvenile court to the oppressive English star chamber and expressed his doubts that such institutions would ever "take the place of the old-time interview between father and son in the family woodshed by means of which the intangible duties involved in that relation were formally enforced." Pound, "The Limits of Effective Legal

Action," *International Journal of Ethics*, 27 (1917), 163.

42. Quoted in Ross, "Of Children and Liberty," 478; and for a compelling historical analysis of the new paternalistic approach, see David J. Rothman, "The State as Parent: Social Policy in the Progressive Era," in Willard Gaylin, David Rothman, Steven Marcus, and Ira Glasser, *Doing Good: The Limits of Benevolence* (New York: Pantheon Books, 1978), 67-96.

43. For a discussion of this concern see Carl Schneider, "Rights Discourse and Neonatal Euthanasia," *California Law Review*, 76 (1988), 151-76.

44. See for example, Michael Grossberg, "Guarding the Altar: Physiological Restrictions and the Rise of State Intervention in Matrimony," *American Journal of Legal History*, 26 (1982), 206-11.

45. For a general collection of pieces by children's rights advocates that offers a survey of the movement see Beatrice Gross and Ronald Gross, eds., *The Children's Rights Movement, Overcoming the Oppression of Young People* (Garden City, N.Y.: Anchor Books, 1977); for the general historical context of the era see Mintz and Kellogg, *Domestic Revolutions*, chaps . 7-10 .

46. 347 U.S. 483, 493 (1954).

47. 387 U.S. 1, 13 (1967).

48. 393 U.S. 503, 506 (1969).

49. 419 U.S. 565 (1975).

50. For surveys of the relevant cases see Robert Burt, "Developing Constitutional Rights Of, In, and For Children," *Law and Contemporary Problems*, 39 (175), 118-50; Eva R. Rubin, *The Supreme Court and the American Family* (Westport: Greenwood Press, 1986).

51. Perhaps the most emblematic of such cases were those involving school bans on males wearing long hair. In a series of decisions, teenagers won the right to challenge school dress codes. For the judicial debate over long-hair see *Leonard v. School Committee*, 349 Mass. 704 (1965); *Breen v. Kahl*, 419 Fed. 2nd. 1034 (1969); *Dawson v. Hillsborough County*, 322 Fed. Supp. 286 (1971); *Freeman v. Flake*, 448 Fed. 2nd. 258 (1971); *McAlpine v. Reese*, 309 Fed. Supp. 136 (1970); "Public Schools, Long Hair, and the Constitution," *Iowa Law Review*, 55 (1970), 707-14; "The Long-Haired Student: A Constitutionally Protected Right of Personal Taste," *Idaho Law Review*, 8 (1971), 164-204.

52. 428 U.S. 52 (1976).

53. See for example *Carey v. Population Services International*, 431 U.S. 678 (1977); *Buckholz v. Leville*, 37 Mich App. 166 (1972).

54. Marks, "Detours on the Road to Maturity," 87-92; Stewart, "Reconciling the Competing Interests of Parent and Child," 8-9; for general overviews of legal changes in the period see Sanford Katz, ed., *The Youngest Minority: Lawyers in Defense of Children* (Chicago: American Bar Association, 1974); Ibid., *The Youngest Minority: Lawyers in Defense of Children, Part II* (Chicago: American Bar Association, 1977).

55. "A Bill of Rights for Children," in Katz, ed., *Lawyers in Defense of Children*, 318-50.

56. Quoted in Gross and Gross, *The Children's Rights Movement*, 321.

57. Richard Farson, *Birthrights* (New York: Macmillan, 1974), 153.

58. 393 U.S. 515.

59. 406 U.S. 205 (1972).

60. 390 U.S. 629 (1968).

61. *McKeiver v. Pennsylvania*, 403 U.S. 526 (1971).

62. Quoted in Sanford J. Fox, "Philosophy and the Principles of Punishment," in Katz, ed., *Lawyers in Defense of Children, Part II*, 373.

63. "Children's Liberation and the New Egalitarianism: Some Reservations about Abandoning Children to their 'Rights,'" *Brigham Young University Law Review*, (1976), 607, 656.

64. Edward A. Wynne, "What Are We Doing to Our Children?" *The Public Interest* (Fall, 1981), 13-14, 18; and see Gerald Grant, "Children's Rights and Adult Confusions," Ibid., (Fall, 1982), 83-99. For similar reservations phrased in a less polemical tone, see [Judge] Abner J. Mikva, "Judges and other People's Children," in Rebecca S. Cohen, *Parenthood, A Psychodynamic Perspective* (New York: Guilford Press, 1984), 220-26.

65. *A Light in the Attic* (New York: Harper Collins, 1981), 128-29.

66. Quoted in Ross, "Of Children and Liberty," 479.

67. Rubin, *The Supreme Court and the American Family*, chap. 3.

68. For valuable discussions of the current controversies over children, law, and rights see Robert H. Mnookin, et al., *In the Interests of Children, Advocacy, Law Reform, and Public Policy* (New York: Freeman Press, 1985); Martha Minnow, "Rights for the Next Generation: A Feminist Approach to Children's Rights," *Harvard Women's Law Journal*, 9 (1986), 1-24.

69. *The Cleveland Plain Dealer*, Thursday, December 22, 1988, 1-B.

70. The Cargnegie Commission's report was published as a separate volume; see Kenneth Keniston, *All Our Children, The American Family Under Pressure* (New York: Harcourt, Brace, Janovich, 1977), 184.

71. *The Needs of Strangers, An Essay on Privacy, Solidarity, and the Politics of Being Human* (New York: Penguin, 1985), 14, emphasis in the original.

72. "Interpreting Rights," 1911.

73. Milner, "The Denigration of Rights," 671.

74. Toward that end, James Boyd White tells us that "habits of thought and language have tendencies, pressures of their own than can perhaps be checked or controlled, but ought certainly be reckoned with: . . . language has real power over the mind that uses it, even the mind that contributes to its reformulation." White, "Thinking About Language," *Yale Law Journal*, 96 (1986), 1968.

6

Inventing the Problem Child: "At Risk" Children in the Child Guidance Movement of the 1920s and 1930s

My subject is the definition of the "at-risk child" by the child guidance movement of the 1920s and 1930s. Child guidance, originally launched and sponsored by the Commonwealth Fund, was a systematic effort to provide community mental health services for children across the country. My contention is that, constrained by larger social processes, notably the need to bolster the middle-class family through its early-twentieth-century transition and the demands of a "professionalization" process, designers of the child guidance movement defined an at-risk population so as to entirely miss the children in greatest need of help.

The child guidance movement of the early 1920s was a far

cry from what it became by 1930. Early child guidance embodied the optimism and vigorous outreach of the mental hygiene movement—psychiatry's broad, educational push into the community. When it first emerged from the Commonwealth Fund's Program for the Prevention of Delinquency, child guidance was an enthusiastic, broad-based effort to muster all of the resources of the adult community on behalf of the psychological and emotional well-being of children. Its goal was as much raising normal children as it was preventing pathology.[1] The very term *guidance* suggests something between education and nurture, on the one hand, and medical models of treatment and cure, on the other, revealing the message the early movement wished to convey.

Child guidance clinics were greeted with enthusiasm by many who saw them as panaceas for popular anxiety about social change and the deterioration of family life. Misbehaving or maladjusted youngsters who disobeyed their parents or failed in school were part of more general concern about children and youth in the 1920s. Earlier in the century Progressive reformers and parents focused on juvenile crime and problems associated with poor youth living in urban slums, but now middle-class parents found their own children and adolescents straying from family values and control. Teenagers in cities were feared to be under the corrupting influence of movies and dance halls, and youths in smaller towns found new independence in the keys to automobiles. College youth developed a separate, eroticized culture of their own, including women with bobbed hair and short skirts, men who smoked and drank, and parties for necking and petting.[1] At the same time, professional attention was lavished on so-called problem children, and parents were deluged with advice aimed at stopping maladjustment in young children as a way of preventing the development of delinquent or disturbed youth and adults.

Child guidance clinics, employing clinical teams of psychiatrists, psychologists, and psychiatric social workers, attempted to be truly novel institutions, outside of the conventional rubrics of education and medicine, but drawing on both. The new facilities caught on rapidly: From the eight original demonstration clinics introduced by the foundation between 1922 and 1925, a network of some forty-two clinics emerged across the country by 1933. Seeking broad integration into the local community, a host of institutions including schools, child welfare agencies, recreation departments, and medical facilities were enlisted in service of the clinics' aims.

By 1930, however, child guidance was a clearly delineated medical endeavor, aimed at treating a population of children with mild behavioral and emotional problems within the confines of clinic offices. Lost was the rhetorical bravado of protecting the community's mental health and preventing a range of social problems through early intervention. Gone too was the broad local outreach through which the clinics were connected to networks of child-helping services, and problems were identified by a range of child-care workers in children appearing in a variety of locations throughout the community.

In spite of this dramatic change of purpose and narrowing of institutional scope, child guidance continued to direct itself toward the same at-risk population, the treatment of what was called "the problem child." But the social meaning of the problem child *did change* over the years, and looking closely at who the problem child was, and how he or she was perceived, explains a good deal about how notions of children at risk for mental illness were constructed in the early part of this century.

Child guidance defined the problem child as a child of normal intelligence who exhibited a range of behavior and psychological problems, which were lumped together in a category called "maladjustment." The problem child was of elementary school age, that is, roughly between five and thirteen years old. Thus, these were children surfacing in society for the first time, appearing outside of their families in institutions designed for their education and care. Maladjustment was defined in relation to the expectations of those in the child's immediate environment, the demands of the adults responsible for her or his care.[2] Indications of such maladjustment ranged from undesirable habits in younger children, including thumb sucking, nail biting, enuresis, masturbation, peculiar food fads, and night terrors, to personality traits such as sensitiveness, seclusiveness, apathy, excessive imagination, and fanciful lying. Also included was a category of undesirable behavior in older children such as disobedience, teasing, bullying, temper tantrums, bragging or showing off, defiance of authority, seeking bad companions, keeping late hours, and sex activities.

By thus defining the problem child, leaders of the movement specifically excluded another group of children: "Cases where mental defect (feeblemindedness) is the central problem, psychopathic status of years standing, and cases of mental disorder such as epilepsy, dementia praecox etc., are not handled by a child guidance clinic, since usually they are provided for by the community's other facilities."[3] The next sentence in this 1928 statement by psychiatrist Ralph Truitt, who served from 1925 to 1927 as director of the Commonwealth Fund's Division on the Prevention of Delinquency, revealed the more important rationale for excluding this other group of children: "[They] do not permit of the concrete, constructive and continuous treatment in the community which the clinic is especially interested in providing and securing."[4] The leaders of the child guidance movement—both the professionals in the field and the administrators at the Commonwealth Fund—sought a group of children for whom they could make a difference, whom they could help. They identified a range of mild problems amenable to their "concrete, constructive and continuous treatment" and worthy of their optimism. In the process, they left out more serious problems that persist as intractable today.

In the early 1920s the purpose of the new clinics included both insuring that normal children developed normally and preventing individual mental illness and "social ills"—such as delinquency, crime, dependency, and prostitution—that were believed to be the results of the constellation of symptoms described above. In this slippery way, the problem child could also be a normal child, so that, paradoxically, while the movement explicitly excluded organically damaged or mentally defective children, it cast a rather wide net when it came to the "healthy" end of the spectrum.

This concern that the normal child might be temporarily in need of therapeutic guidance reflected a range of contemporary assumptions about children. First, the theoretical literature on childhood, from Sigmund Freud's psychoanalytic studies to G. Stanley Hall's research on child development, all emphasized the malleability and vulnerability of children and the emotional complexity of childhood as a stage of life.[5] In addition, and perhaps most important, this view of childhood reflected contemporary anxiety about children derived from the early-twentieth-century middle-class family's smaller size and exclusive focus on the proper rearing of children, as well as the perceived impact of life in growing cities, which were feared to be sources of corruption to youth. These phenomena made parents and "experts" on children deeply concerned that the family execute its one remaining function, nurture, effectively.

The mental hygiene literature both blamed families for causing problems in their children and enlisted parents in the effort to treat and prevent the problem child. A careful reading of the child guidance literature of the 1920s reveals that it incorporated two opposing views of parents. Alongside the well-cited parent- and mother-blaming view, which saw parental mishandling of children as the cause of maladjustments in children, was another, far more respectful and supportive view of parents. This position recognized that the family was the only effective setting for childrearing and argued that reinforcing and preserving stable family life was a matter of great importance for the future of society.[6]

Thus, the child guidance movement identified the problem parent as it discovered the problem child and insisted that parents be treated along with children. A 1929 report from the Philadelphia clinic voiced the balanced view of the interrelationship between the child's problems and the parents' problems that came to characterize treatment at the clinics: "Our real philosophy is that both the parents and the child are reacting to the given situation and that it is the interaction of each with the situation and with each other that is causing the difficulty."[7]

Once the mental hygiene movement applied its already zealous concern with preventing mental illness to children, it conveyed an extraordinarily broad notion of what constituted the at-risk child, finding signs of incipient psychosis and pathology in the everyday behaviors of the normal child. The mental hygiene movement coined the terms *predelinquent personality* and *prepsychotic personality*, revealing its dismal view of hazards of growing up. Again in the words of Ralph Truitt: "Considerable study has . . . [revealed] some of the early causes of mental diseases to show the connection between the so-called insanities and such apparently benign symptoms as those we see in what is called the problem child. . . . The child may out grow these [early] difficulties, . . . but nevertheless these incipient personality disorders have to be considered seriously as the possible beginning of disease trends."[8]

Thus, the early movement's mandate of prevention incorporated several dimensions. On the one hand, it implied that children (or at least *certain* children) were easy to work with and amenable to change. Children were therefore "good investments," since catching emotional problems in childhood would prevent more serious and costly difficulties in the adult. But on the other hand, it implied that all children were in some danger of either maladjustment or incipient insanity. This view of children reflected theoretical views of the psychological stage of childhood, contemporary changes in family and urban life, and the imperatives of a series of professional groups whose new professional roles and services were in part justified by this broad view of the at-risk child.

The problem child in the early movement was thus a social problem. Maladjustment meant maladjustment to the environment and by implication to the larger society. Preventing maladjustment was a matter of profound social significance, since it involved preventing social deviance—preventing a child from growing into a criminal or a dependent, mentally ill adult. On the positive side, preventing maladjustment meant raising individuals to become productive members of society and responsible citizens.

The definition of the problem child thus signified nonconformity to socially constructed norms for behavior. The role of the movement in the enforcement of norms was all the more explicit because of the conscious inclusion of so-called normal children in the definition of the problem child. In this early stage of child guidance, the clinics were invested with profound social importance, because they were responsible for preventing social deviance.

By roughly 1930, child guidance changed: Both the social mission of the movement and the social meaning of the problem child were lost. The rhetoric of improving society by preventing deviance and mental illness, all predicated on directly linking the individual and society, dropped from the literature. Child guidance became a more narrow, medical endeavor of helping individual children whose problems were seen as important only to themselves and their families. Without the ambitious purpose of preventing social problems, child guidance directed itself at helping children and families *feel better* about their place in the social order.

While the problem child lost his or her social meaning once she or he no longer threatened to become social problems, the individual characteristics of the problem child remained the primarily the same: The target population of the clinic continued to be children of normal intelligence experiencing temporary behavioral or emotional difficulties—still, in effect, normal children. After 1930, however, the problem child changed subtly and tended to be more introverted, while in the earlier years she or he was characterized by more aggressive, acting-out sorts of behavior. This change is consistent with the loss of social threat and social significance of the problem child in the later period of the movement. But the retreat from the program's social agenda did bring a significant change in the *social* characteristics of the problem child: Through the 1930s, child guidance reached an increasingly middle-class, native-born population. This shift in the social composition of clients underscores the modesty of child guidance's goals by the 1930s. The clinics steered away from poorer and immigrant children and essentially reinforced a status quo by supporting the middle-class family in effectively doing its job.[9]

The nature of child guidance practice and this dramatic shift in its goals are best appreciated through descriptions of case examples. The case of twelve-year-old Mildred, published in 1925, illustrates early child guidance practice. Mildred was referred to the Bureau of Children's Guidance in New York for school failure. She was described as being in a "profound state of intimidation, embitterment, and withdrawal from contact with others, . . . apathetic, unsocial and sullen." The visiting teacher (a school social worker) involved in the case made a home visit and explained that Mildred's father was a "drinking man, bad tempered and unemployed." Her mother worked as a janitor and did washing, and though "sober and industrious" she had to accept aid from relief agencies. Mildred had enuresis and was under treatment for syphilis, but the record explained that this condition was "not responsible for the school problem." Hereditary factors were carefully considered, and the staff concluded that in Mildred's case there was "no special hereditary burden. . . . [But] there is reason to believe that both drunkenness and syphilis in a parent may so affect the offspring as to hinder normal development before and after birth."[10]

Since Mildred tested "normal" on IQ tests, the staff "felt that with assistance in the fundamentals of education she would advance rapidly." Testing normally on intelligence examinations was a key to a child's being perceived as amenable to treatment. The general policy was for clinics to screen out children of "defective intelligence," but a small percentage of these children (roughly 5 percent in the late 1920s) were accepted when the staff felt that the child's adjustment would benefit through

"manipulating factors . . . which are subject to change."[11]
The staff then offered the following diagnosis:

> Thus although Mildred's inaccessibility, lack of interest, emotional dullness, and general withdrawn, subjective attitude were strongly suggestive . . . [of] the early stages of dementia praecox, this diagnosis was not taken seriously enough to determine the procedure in the case. . . . The physicians of the Bureau were inclined to view the entire situation as a deep emotional difficulty which might well be understood as in the nature of reaction to various harassing and intimidating influences that came to the child from the home, the school, and the general environment.[12]

This conceptualization of Mildred's problem and its causes reveals that categories of serious mental illness loomed large in minds of the clinic staff as possible long-term results of such early symptoms. However, the serious diagnosis of dementia praecox—which would have disqualified Mildred from treatment—was eliminated in favor of a conceptualization of her problem as an emotional reaction to troublesome factors in her environment.

Mildred's central problem and the task of treatment were framed as "restoring hope, self-confidence, and self-esteem, while at the same time every possible external lever was being applied to lightening the load."[13] Treatment consisted of psychiatric interviews with Mildred, attempts to work with the family, and changes in her environment. Mildred responded favorably to the psychiatrist because "here was a grown-up [the psychiatrist] who didn't try to teach her anything or to correct her, who seemed to understand things even when all the words needed to express them wouldn't come, who talked a language she could understand, someone who made the whole business of life seem a little less desperate and hopeless."[14] This flattering portrait of the psychiatrist's role captured some of the psychiatrist's contribution to helping the problem child: The psychiatrist offered the child an alternative kind of relationship with an adult; a sympathetic, understanding, and uncritical relationship, which provided comfort and hope because of the different perspective it gave the child.

Mildred responded well to treatment. Her treatment included allowing her to come to the clinic alone, instead of requiring an escort, and arranging for her to sleep "with another sister," since she wet her bed because she "hated the [sister] she slept with." Her enuresis vanished as a result. Mildred was also encouraged to develop outside interests and joined the Girl Scouts. The social worker "enlisted the family's awareness of [her] sensitivity to school problems, [and] asked for their encouragement."[15] A year after she first came to the clinic, Mildred was "alert, interested and keen, and [making] good progress in school."[16]

While the published histories of clinic cases in the early years tended to present favorable accounts of the impact of staff interventions and the outcome of treatment, Mildred's case illustrates the essential features of treatment in the early stage of the movement. First, Mildred came from a poor, working-class family. There was initial concern that her symptoms might be the early signs of serious mental illness, and although this diagnosis was abandoned, treatment was construed as preventing adult maladjustment or dependency . The social-study and social-treatment aspects of the case were extensive, including involvement by a visiting teacher (a school social worker), home and school visits, and the encouragement of recreational activities. Finally, the psychotherapeutic dimension of the treatment is best characterized as "support," which led to enhanced self-confidence and self-esteem in the child. All of these features distinguished child guidance practice in the 1920s.

The case of Cynthia, who was referred to the Philadelphia Child Guidance Clinic by her father in 1937, provides an example of the later model of child guidance. Cynthia's father described her as "withdrawn, does not get along with other children, nervous, sensitive." Cynthia's father was a "custom tailor" who felt that his wife was "psychotic" and "feared that his daughter [will become] schizophrenic." The father's awareness of these psychiatric symptoms and terms came from reading a psychiatric text because of his concern about his wife's behavior, and he learned about the work of the clinic from friends.[17]

Cynthia and her father were seen at the clinic for four months, the father by a psychiatrist and Cynthia by a psychologist. The father was initially reassured that Cynthia was not psychotic or schizophrenic, and his treatment centered around his marital relationship, although his wife never came in to the clinic. Cynthia's treatment was described to the father as consisting of the psychologist's "playing and friendly sort of talking, not a great many questions." The case was closed with a status of "improved, according to father's report of [Cynthia's] outside behavior." While the precise nature of Cynthia's problem is not clear from the description in the records, it was clearly not serious mental illness. The salient features of this later type of case and treatment are these: First, the case was referred by the parent, based on his awareness of psychological problems. Second, the description of the problem was entirely about emotions, or psychological states, all of which were stated in terms of introversion. The outcome, however, was described in terms of improved behavior, suggesting that Cynthia may have felt better and made a better "adjustment." Finally, all of the contact between the clinic staff and the family was restricted to the clinic itself, with no home or school visits. All of these points underscore the narrowing of the child guidance enterprise and its increasing focus on the internal, emotional well-being of the individual child.[18]

Why did the child guidance movement define the at-risk population in this way, and what is the significance of this screening process? The two most compelling explanations are the interests of the professionals involved in the movement and the movement's overall relationship to the middle-class family. The new child guidance clinics provided tremendous opportunities for the advancement of the three professional groups employed in the child guidance clinical team. In the years around 1920, when child guidance was designed by administrators at the Commonwealth Fund, these groups—psychiatrists, clinical psychologists, and psychiatric social workers—already existed, but each was in a process of professional transition. Each agressively sought enhanced professional status by establishing new functions and roles and modeling themselves against developments in the medical profession.

Psychiatry sought social relevance and a viable outpatient role for itself, and each group sought specialized clinical functions through which they could demonstrate effectiveness. Child guidance clinics were fashioned—to some extent by these professionals—to provide precisely these sorts of professional opportunities, but these professional interests could only be served if they could have an impact on the population they reached.

Hence the screening out of children whom they did not know how to help and the inclusion of children who worried parents and the public and for whom they could make a difference. The early definition of the problem child meshed the public need to apply science and medicine to childrearing, and to problems of delinquency and crime, with psychiatry's interest in steering away from chronic problems and ministering to the needs of community mental health. Psychologists and social workers rode along on the coattails of psychiatrists, applying their own skills and perspectives on the clinical team, which both advanced their status and created a tense internal struggle to preserve the psychiatrist's dominance on the clinical team.

The later, individually based definition of the quieter problem child also fit professional interests. Psychiatrists pressed hard to demonstrate the specifically medical nature of their practice in an effort to identify with the larger medical profession. This necessity steered them away from interventions that resembled the work of educators or other child servers, leading them toward the esoteric internal terrain of the unconscious. But this point must be qualified. First, it is certainly not the case that psychoanalysis dominated child guidance; psychoanalysis takes too long, and is too time-consuming, to have been a practical method of treatment. And second, psychoanalysis is the least medical of psychiatric approaches, so it is ironic that it could have enhanced child psychiatrists' claims to be medical. My point is that the shift around 1930 does represent the influence of psychoanalytic ideas on psychiatrists: the new belief that enduring psychological change could come only from investigating unconscious, psychodynamic processes and the professional prestige that such one-to-one explorations of the child's psyche gave to psychiatrists.

If defining the at-risk population this way served the interests of three advancing professional groups by enabling them to have an impact, it also reflected the positioning of the efforts of the Commonwealth Fund, and the professionals it supported, in relation to the overall structure of American society. By working with misbehaving normal children and their parents, child guidance did not endeavor to alter the alignment of groups in the population—either by helping to ensure a productive role for a more seriously disturbed child or by helping poorer or immigrant "maladjusted" children with their particular difficulties. The specific focus on middle-class children and families meant that the program's efforts were placed behind the status quo and not in the interest of social change. In this the foundation responded to public anxiety about the family, the Commonwealth Fund, like all foundations, wanted to show results from its investments, and the public in the 1920s wanted to feel better about its youth and the family. The modest definition of the problem child served both of these needs.

NOTES

1. This description of middle-class youth in the 1920s is based on Paula S. Fass, *The Damned and the Beautiful: American Youth in the 1920s* (New York: Oxford University Press, 1977), ch. 2. See also Robert S. Lynd and Helen Merrell Lynd, *Middletown: A Study in Contemporary American Culture* (New York: Harcourt, Brace and World, 1929).

2. George S. Stevenson and Geddes Smith, *Child Guidance Clinics: A Quarter Century of Development* (New York: Commonwealth Fund, 1934), 11.

3. Stevenson and Smith, *Child Guidance Clinics*, 55.

4. Ralph Truitt, Lawson G. Lowrey, Charles W. Hoffman, William L. Connor, Ethel Taylor, Fanny Robson Kendel, *The Child Guidance Clinic and the Community* (New York: Commonwealth Fund, 1928), 11.

5. Ralph Truitt, *Clinic and Community*, 13.

6. Marc Ventresca has noted the emphasis on the vulnerability of children and the broad conception of the at-risk child in the mental hygiene movement in "Notes Toward a Discourse of At-Risk Children: The Mental Hygiene Movement and the Schools," unpublished paper, Stanford University Department of History, 1986. For the Freudian view of childhood, see, for example, Sigmund Freud, "Three Essays on Sexuality," *Standard Edition of the Complete Psychological Works of Sigmund Freud*, vol. 7, ed. James Strachey (London: Hogarth Press, 1953). See also G. Stanley Hall, *Youth: Its Education, Regimen, and Hygiene* (New York: Appleton, 1912).

7. This conceptualization of the mental hygiene movement's attitudes toward parents appeared in Margo Horn, "The Moral Message of Child Guidance, 1925-1945," *Journal of Social History* 18 (September 1984), 27.

8. Quoted in Dorothy Hankins, "An Incomplete History of the Philadelphia Child Guidance Clinic," unpublished typescript, Philadelphia Child Guidance Clinic (1969), 138.

9. Truitt, *Clinic and Community*, 138.

10. Stevenson and Smith, *Child Guidance Clinics*, 102.

11. *Three Problem Children: Narratives from the Case Records of a Child Guidance Clinic* (New York: Joint Committee on Methods of Preventing Delinquency, 1925), 11.

12. Stevenson and Smith, *Child Guidance Clinics*, 72-73.

13. *Three Problem Children*, 28.

14. *Three Problem Children*, 30.

15. *Three Problem Children*, 30.

16. *Three Problem Children*, 31.

17. "Cynthia," 1937, case records of the Philadelphia Child Guidance Clinic. Client names have been changed, and details of the family situation altered, to ensure confidentiality, but the problem and treatment were as reported.

18. Case of "Cynthia," 1937.

Part III

Contemporary Public Discourse

ALAN GARTNER
DOROTHY KERZNER LIPSKY

7

Children at Risk: Students in Special Education

INTRODUCTION

Children labeled "handicapped" and placed in special education are "at risk" in several ways: (1) from the inappropriateness of this designation, (2) from the stigmatization that is a consequence of such labeling, (3) from the inadequacy of the education they receive, and (4) from separation from their peers. The current special education system has been aptly described as being characterized by "conceptual pathology" (Algozzine, Morsenik, and Algozzine n.d., 18). All this in addition to the consequence(s) of whatever impairment they may have and the societal limits that too often transform an impairment into a handicap.

In the following pages we describe the current special education arrangements (with a brief word of history), the processes by which students are evaluated and placed, the outcomes of the current arrangements, various alternatives, and public policy issues.[1]

THE SPECIAL EDUCATION SYSTEM: THE LAW

Education for students with handicapping conditions dates back more than a century. Currently, such education is within the framework of P.L. 94-142, the Education of All Handicapped Children Act, which became law in 1975. During the prior decade, a series of court suits brought by parent groups challenged the exclusion of students with handicapping conditions from public education or, when they were included, their limited participation.

Parent groups followed the precedent of *Brown* in its assertion of the essential importance of education. Two key decisions, *Pennsylvania Association of Retarded Citizens (PARC) v. Commonwealth* (334 F. Supp. 1257) and *Mills v. Board of Education* (348 F. Supp. 866), in 1971 and 1972, respectively, rejected reasons school districts had given for excluding students with handicapping conditions. In *PARC*, the federal district court overturned a Pennsylvania law that had relieved schools of the responsibility of enrolling "uneducable" or "untrainable" children. Basing its opinion on extensive expert testimony, the court ruled that mentally retarded children could benefit from education. In *Mills*, the federal district court ruled that a district's financial exigencies could not be the basis for excluding students with handicaps; these students could not be made to take last place in the queue for funds.

P.L. 94-142 incorporates six basic principles: (1) the right of access to public education programs; (2) the individualization of services; (3) the principle of "least restrictive environment"; (4) the scope of broadened services to be provided by the schools and a set of procedures for determining them; (5) the general guidelines for identification of disability; and (6) the principles of primary state and local responsibilities (Walker 1987).

In the previous decade, federal law, state statutes, and court decisions had begun to reduce the exclusion of children with disabilities from public education programs or the charging of their parents for services otherwise provided at no cost to nondisabled children. Often, exclusions were based on categorical statements about classes of "uneducable" children or in deference to professional judgments on a child's educability. The law eliminated this exclusion of children with disabilities: it stated in the unambiguous language of its title that all handicapped children were to be provided with a free public education. Henceforth, no child was to be rejected as uneducable.

Once students with handicaps were included in public education, Congress wanted to assure that all students, particularly ones with severe handicaps, would receive services based upon individual need, not upon categories of handicap or preexisting service offerings. The law explicitly required a multidisciplinary individual evaluation that was nondiscriminatory and the development of an individualized education plan (IEP).

While each student's placement was to be individually determined, the law, in keeping with its philosophic acceptance of the concepts of "normalization," expressed a strong presumption that students with disabilities would be placed in regular classes whenever possible, where they could receive specialized services as necessary. Only when regular classroom placements did not meet individual students' needs would students be placed in separate classes or settings. This was expressed in the law's requirement that students be educated in the "least restrictive environment" (LRE).

The law, while rejecting the traditional medical model of disability, recognized that some of these students needed more than educational services alone to be successful in school. Hence the concept of "related services" was developed, incorporating services—including counseling, physical and occupational therapy, and some medical services—necessary to enable students to take advantage of and benefit from the educational program. In addition to describing the scope of services to be provided, the law established a process for determining a student's handicapping condition, educational placement, and related services, which incorporated parental involvement and required substantial due process procedures and appeal rights.

During the course of the congressional debate, there was considerable dispute about the total number of students who would be eligible for services and, foreshadowing a continuing issue, the number, out of that total, defined as having specific learning disabilities. For funding purposes, caps of 12 and 2 percent of the total school population, respectively, were set. Procedural guidelines were set for identification, assessment, and placement of students, with particular emphasis on nondiscrimination and procedural due process.

As was to be expected, the respective roles of the state and local educational agencies and the flow of money were key issues in the congressional deliberations The House bill required that funds go directly to local educational agencies (LEAs), but the Council of Chief State School Officers argued in favor of state responsibility for monitoring local school districts and gained a victory for the state educational agencies (SEAs). Funds were to flow through SEAs, with requirements that annual increasing percentages be passed on to the local level. Also, while recognizing that other state agencies might provide services to the students, particularly those with severe impairments, the SEA had responsibility for assuring that the educational services were provided, regardless of who provided or paid for them or where the student received them.

THE SPECIAL EDUCATION SYSTEM:
THE CURRENT SITUATION

Although there was considerable concern about the feasibility of implementing P.L. 94-142, and some difficulty in doing so, by and large it has been accomplished. Indeed, its achievement is one of the great accomplishments of recent public sector action.

Some 750,000 more students are being served than when the law was enacted. According to the most recent U.S. Department of Education report, some 4.59 million students received special education services during the 1988-89 school year. After several years of enrollment stabilization, there was a 2.1 percent increase in 1988-89. The current total represents nearly 12 percent of all students enrolled in public education. As we will note below, there are significant variations among states.

There has been a substantial increase in the federal funds devoted to special education. However, the promised federal contribution (40 percent of the average per-pupil cost by FY 1982) has never been met. Current figures are about 7 percent federal contribution, 58 percent from the states, and 34 percent from local districts. Again, there are considerable variations among the states as to the balance between state and local funds.

While there are some exceptions, such as students in prisons, from migrant families, and in some institutional settings, for the most part location of the student does not seem to be a factor in the availability of services. The overall responsibility of SEAs has been achieved, perhaps more so in special education than in other areas of SEA-LEA joint responsibility. With New

Mexico's submission of a state plan in August 1984, all fifty states are presently participating under P.L. 94-142.

Referral, Assessment, and Placement

Perhaps no area in special education has received as much concern as have procedures used for the referral, assessment, and, as necessary, eventual placement of students. Together, these activities raise substantive issues, such as (1) cost, a key factor in the congressional capping (at 12 percent of total school population) of the number of students who could be counted for funding purposes; (2) professional judgment, particularly with regard to identification of students with learning disabilities; (3) discrimination, as seen in the disproportionate number of minority and limited-English-proficient students referred for evaluation and placed in certain categories; and (4) quality of service.

Aside from students with obvious physical handicaps who are identified before entering a classroom, referral occurs, for the most part, "when student behavior and academic progress varies from the school norm" (Walker 1987, 105). The assumption in such cases is that there is something wrong with the student. In particular, referral is more likely to occur in cases where the student is a member of a minority group or from a family whose socioeconomic status varies from the district's norm (Ysseldyke 1987). Further,

> decisions about special education classification are not only functions of child characteristics but rather involve powerful organizational influences. The number of programs, availability of space, incentives for identification, range and kind of competing programs and services, number of professionals, and federal, state, and community pressures all affect classification decisions. (Keogh 1988, 22)

Referral rates vary widely. As a percentage of total student enrollment, referral rates in twenty-eight large cities range from 6 to 11 percent. The figures for assessment vary even more widely. For the same twenty-eight cities, the percentage of students who are referred and then placed in special education ranges from 7.8 percent to 91.8 percent (*Special Education* 1986, tables 8 and 9).

The most extensive study of the evaluation process reports

that results are barely more accurate than a flip of the coin, with the evaluation process often providing a psychological justification for the referral. The leading researchers conclude that current classification procedures are plagued with major conceptual and practical problems (for an extensive review of this literature, see Ysseldyke 1987).

While P.L. 94-142 includes eleven different classifications of handicapping conditions, "most diagnoses of students placed in special education programs are based on social and psychological criteria. These include measured intelligence, achievement, social behavior and adjustment, and communication and language problems. Furthermore, many of the measuring criteria used in classification lack reliability or validity" (Wang, Reynolds, and Walberg 1987a, 27). Indeed, few of the most frequently used evaluation instruments have been appropriately normed for this population (Fuchs et al. 1987).

The major classification problems concern students labeled "learning disabled." The number of students classified as learning disabled rose over 120 percent between 1976-77 and 1988-89, at a time when the overall special education population rose 18 percent. In 1988-89, students labeled "learning disabled" (aged three through twenty-one) accounted for 48 percent of the students receiving special education services. The percentage of special education students labeled "learning disabled" varied from 30 to 67 percent among the fifty states and from 0 to 73 percent among thirty large cities.

In what can be called a form of "classification plea bargaining," the increase in students labeled "learning disabled" has been accompanied by a decline in those labeled "mentally retarded." The mentally retarded now account for some 15 percent of special education students.

The problem is not only the excessive numbers of students classified as learning disabled; there are even more troubling issues as to the accuracy of the label: more than 80 percent of the student population could be classified as learning disabled by one or more definitions presently in use (Ysseldyke, 1987). Based solely upon the records of those already certified as learning disabled and those not, experienced evaluators could not tell the difference (Davis and Shepard 1983). Students identified as learning disabled cannot be shown to differ from other low achievers with regard to a wide variety of school-related characteristics (Ysseldyke et al. 1982).

Summarizing national data on the subject, the authors of one study remarked, "At least half of the learning disabled population could be more accurately described as slow learners, as children with second-language backgrounds, as children who are naughty in class, as those who are absent more often or move from school to school, or as average learners in above-average school systems (Shepard, Smith, and Vojir 1983).

Such results are not surprising, given reports concerning the inadequacy and inappropriateness of the measuring instruments, the disregard of results in decision making, and, often, the evaluators' incompetence and biases (Davis and Shepard 1980; Ysseldyke and Algozzine 1983; Ysseldyke, Algozzine, Richey, and Graden 1982). These problems in practice have now been mirrored by a powerful critique of the very fundamentals of the learning disability concept (Coles 1987).

Faced with charges of racial discrimination in special education evaluations and placement,[2] in the late 1970s the National Academy of Sciences commissioned a series of studies, a major conclusion of which was this: We can find little empirical justification for categorical labelling that discriminates mildly retarded children from other children receiving compensatory education" (Heller, Holtzman, and Messick 1982, 87). The academy's study reiterated points made by Hobbs (1975), and an ever growing number of studies has reinforced and expanded upon this point—namely, that there is little educational basis to distinguish students placed in remedial or special programs for the "mildly handicapped," that is, those called "learning disabled," some of those called "mentally retarded," and some of those called "emotionally disturbed" (Algozzine and Ysseldyke 1981; Allington 1983; Allington and Johnston 1986; Jenkins, Pious, and Peterson 1987; McGill-Franzen 1987; Wang, Reynolds, and Walberg 1987a; and Ysseldyke 1987). Articles in a special issue of the *Journal of Learning Disabilities* (Kauffman 1988), while sharply critical of reform proposals, offer little to defend the present evaluation and placement practices.

In 1976-77, when the first data on the implementation of P.L. 94-142 were collected, 67 percent of the students were served in general classes (that is full-time or with resource-room services), 25 percent in special classes, and 8 percent in separate schools or other environments (Walker 1987, 104). A decade later, with an increase of over half a million students served in special education programs, the placement figures for the 1986-87 school year are uncannily similar: 67 percent in general classes, 24 percent in special classes, and 9 percent in separate schools or other environments (Viadero 1988). Further, to a considerable degree these figures overstate the extent to which students receiving special education services do so in integrated settings.

These overall figures mask a great deal of variation—among states, among categories of handicapping conditions, and over time. These variations in the overall numbers of students labeled "handicapped," in the distribution among categories and in placement arrangements, are a function of a number of factors. Overall national policy changes have had their effects. McGill-Franzen (1987) points out that the increase in students identified as learning disabled nearly matches the decline in Chapter I participants over the past decade. As a report prepared by the directors of special education in large cities notes, the pressure for school excellence has led to dumping of students into special education, where their scores on standardized tests are often excluded from overall district totals (*Special Education* 1986). A 1987 study cited by the Department of Education confirms this point, concluding that "higher standards in the name of educational reform seem to be exaggerating the tendency to refer difficult children to special education" (Viadero 1988).

Such results indicate that students with seemingly identical characteristics qualify for different programs, depending on where they reside and how individuals on school staff evaluate them. Most often, these are pull-out programs, despite evidence about their lack of efficacy, as we discuss in the following section.

Patterns of service often appear to relate more to systems of funding than to indices of pupil benefit. For example, each of the states with the highest percentages of students in these four categories placed in regular classes used the same type of funding formula ("cost" basis), while in all but one case the states with the lowest percentage of students in the four categories in regular classes used another type of formula ("unit" basis).

Program Effects

The basic premise of special education is that students with deficits will benefit from a unique body of knowledge and from smaller classes staffed by specially trained teachers using special materials. There is no compelling evidence that the current organization and conduct of special education programs has significant benefits for students.

Indeed, careful review of the literature on effective instruction demonstrates that the general practice of special education runs counter to the basic effectiveness tenets in terms of teaching behaviors, organization of instruction, and instructional support (Bickel and Bickel 1986). Furthermore,

> there appear to be at least three discrepancies between the suggestions for best practice and the observation of actual teaching practice for mildly handicapped students: a) there is almost no instruction presented to these students that might be classified as involving high level cognitive skills, b) there is a small amount of time spent in activities that could be considered direct instruction with active learner response and teacher feedback, and c) students receive a low frequency of contingent teacher attention. (Morsink et al. 1986, 38)

In making the case for reform, described as the "general education initiative," U.S. Department of Education Assistant Secretary for Special Education and Rehabilitative Services Madeleine C. Will noted that present program designs suffer from

1. fragmented approaches ("Many students who require help and are not learning effectively fall 'through the cracks' of a program structure based on preconceived definitions of eligibility");
2. a dual system ("The separate administrative arrangements for special programs contribute to a lack of coordination, raise questions about leadership, cloud areas of responsibility, and obscure lines of accountability within schools");
3. stigmatization of students (producing in students "low expectations of success, failure to persist on tasks, the belief that failures are caused by personal inadequacies, and a continued failure to learn effectively"); and
4. placement decisions becoming a battleground between parents and schools. (*Educating Students* 1986, 7-9)

The problem of the current system of delivery of special education to students labeled "handicapped" is not in its implementation, but in its basic conceptualization. The problems are systemic, not a matter of the failure or inadequacies of the persons who work in special education programs. Indeed, persons working in the current system have worked very hard, and, overall, access to public education has been achieved for nearly all students with handicapping conditions. In this regard, P.L. 94-142 is a major achievement on the input side.

The basic issue facing education today is the absence of satisfactory outcomes for students. Unfortunately, the overall results of the current special education system do not indicate significant academic, social, or behavioral success for students. Outcome measures include student learning, graduation rates, return to general education, and postschool education, employment, or community living.

Although more than a third of school districts excuse students labeled "handicapped" from the standardized tests that all other pupils take—a telling comment in itself—the results available indicate the schools' failure in terms of academic knowledge acquired by these students. According to the National Longitudinal Transition Study, almost one in four students with disabilities failed to pass any part of the minimum competency tests they were required to take, a third of the students passed some of the test, and four in ten passed the entire test (Wagner and Shaver 1989, table 9).

Although there are no systematic national data collected regarding dropout rates, the information available from the latest report of the Department of Education to the Congress on the implementation of P.L. 94-142 shows dropout rates a fifth or more greater than those for students in general education. Among students labeled "learning disabled, "who are generally the least impaired, the dropout rate was 47 percent of all those over age sixteen (*Tenth Annual Report* 1988, table 18.)

As for graduation rates, the National Longitudinal Transition Study reports that in a two-year period, 56 percent of special education exiters left secondary school by graduation (Wagner and Shaver 1989, table 10). Of this group, 79 percent received a regular diploma (Wagner 1989). Thus, of 3,045 special education school exiters in the study's sample, 1,347 (44 percent) graduated with a regular diploma.

Data concerning the return to general education for students who have been "in" special education and then declassified are not available. The federal government collects voluminous amounts of data, but it does not collect this essential information. Even though collecting such information would be difficult, it would be no harder than for other data collected by the government. Are the data missing because they would show low rates, perhaps in the low single figures?[3] Or is it because students in special education are not expected to achieve, to compete, to succeed?

In terms of life after school, while the schools alone are not at fault, studies indicate that a substantial percentage of students labeled "handicapped" are unemployed, live at home, and have few friends. For example, according to a recent study funded by the Department of Education, fewer than half of the students with disabilities who had been out of school for one year had found paid employment. And among those employed, less than 30 percent had full-time jobs. And while 56 percent of nonhandicapped youth enroll in postsecondary courses in their first year out of high school, fewer than 15 percent of the youth with disabilities do so (Wagner and Shaver 1989).

Even more troubling is the report that 31 percent of the youth with disabilities who had been out of school for more than a year had not been engaged "in any productive activity in that year" (Wagner 1989, 11). This is particularly troublesome given the broad definition of not being engaged in a "productive activity" as including not taking any courses from any postsecondary educational institution; not working for pay, full- or part-time, either competitively or in a sheltered environment; not engaging in a volunteer job or unpaid work; not receiving job skills training from other than a family member; or, not being married or reported to be involved in childraising. In short, not engaged in a "productive activity" means doing nothing, and this was true of nearly a third of the youth with disabilities. This, of course, is the reality that many parents are coming to face as their children "age out" of their P.L. 94-142 entitlement.

TOWARD A NEW PARADIGM: NEW CONCEPTIONS

The paradigm that undergirds the current organization and conduct of special education is defective.

[It] operates to identify among persons with disabilities areas of deficits and "deviancies," as determined by the consensus of those persons who assume responsibility (and control) over their behavior, and buttressed by an array of diagnostic instruments and surveys that depict either expected "normal" development or assumed community standards for behavior and conduct. The assumption is, of course, that once having identified the problems associated with the disability, the environment can be arranged, controlled, or otherwise manipulated to bring about the desired change in the student. This orientation, variously referred to as "prescriptive-teaching," "remedial," "let's fix it," and so on always carried with it the (at least) implicit assumption that persons with disabilities are somehow less than normal or, at its worst, "deviant." (Guess and Thompson n.d.)

A dual system continues to operate despite the data that indicate its ineffectiveness. Ysseldyke (1987) summarizes that data as follows:

1) There is currently no defensible psychometric methodology for differentiating students into categories. . . .
2) There is no evidence to support the contention that specific categories of students learn differently. . . .
4) The current system used by public schools to classify exceptional children does not meet the criteria of reliability, coverage, logical consistency, utility, and acceptance to users. (265)

The basic assumptions underlying the present special education programs are summarized by Bogdan and Kugelmass (1984).

1) Disability is a condition that individuals have;
2) disabled/typical is a useful and objective distinction;
3) special education is a rationally conceived and coordinated system of services that help children labelled disabled; and
4) progress in the field is made by improving diagnosis, intervention, and technology. (173)

Skrtic (1986) argues that the first two assumptions are challenged by different understandings of disability, ones that are less rooted in biology and psychology "and derive more from sociological, political, and cultural theories of deviance, and which provide many different perspectives on virtually every aspect of special education and 'disability'" (6).

While much of the criticism of the current organization of special education comes from actual practice, increasingly there are more fundamental challenges to its basic conceptualization (Berres and Knoblock 1987; Biklen 1985, 1987; Biklen et al. 1987; Bogdan and Kugelmass 1984; Gartner and Lipsky 1987; Lipsky and Gartner 1987, 1989; Skrtic 1986, 1987; Stainback and Stainback 1984; Stainback, Stainback, and Forest 1989). Some of these formulations focus on the characteristics of students, while others emphasize the conceptualization of special education.

Stainback and Stainback (1984) emphasize the shared characteristics of students. They argue (1) that there are not two distinct groups of students, regular or normal students and others who deviate from the norm, but rather that all students vary across a range of physical, intellectual, psychological, and social characteristics; and (2) that it is not only special education students who can benefit from (or indeed need) individualized services, but that all students can benefit.

The current models reflect disdain for persons with disabilities. It is a reflection, as well as a part, of the larger societal disdain for persons with disabilities. As Goffman (1963) wrote, "By definition, of course, we believe the person with a stigma is not quite human." Only when we see persons with disabilities, including students, as "capable of achievement and worthy of respect" (Lipsky and Gartner 1987, 69) will new, more appropriate school designs be developed. The role of persons with disabilities and the disabilities rights movement is central in both this conceptualization and its incorporation in the education of students labeled "handicapped."

These new models reject the "cascade," or continuum, concept (i.e., a range of services through which students were to progress) basic to current special education practice. An advance when introduced in the 1960s this concept has, in practice, resulted in too many students placed inappropriately at the restricted end of the continuum and too few moving upward, that is, from more to less segregated settings.

The "most restrictive" placement did not prepare students for the "least restrictive" placements. Parents of children in institutions and special schools were often told that their children "weren't ready" to live in the community or to attend regular neighborhood schools. The irony of this situation was that segregated settings did not prepare students with disabilities to function in integrated settings. That is to say, the skills necessary to function in integrated settings, whether in a public school, a grocery store, or a restaurant, are different from those that can be taught in a segregated environment. Many students spent their entire lives "getting ready" only to leave the segregated school without the skills they really needed to make it in the general society. (Biklen et al. 1987, 10)

Taylor (1988) sharpens this critique, suggesting that the very concept of least restrictive environment needs to be reconsidered. He argues for an unrestricted commitment to integration, with the intensity of services varying according to the students' needs. This formulation is in sharp contrast to the variation of the extent of mainstreaming in the traditional continuum model.

ALTERNATIVES FOR ORGANIZING SERVICES

Given the variety of criticisms of the current organization of special education services, it is not surprising that current reform activities range across a broad spectrum. Some proposals seek to bridge the gap between the two parallel systems, others attempt to blend aspects of each together, and yet others call for an end to dual systems.

Bridging Parallel Systems

The current organization of special education has developed an elaborate system to assess and classify students for the purpose of placing them in appropriate programs, broadly organized in a bimodal design of special and general education systems. Within this basic dual system approach, there have been various efforts to bridge the gap between them.

Mainstreaming is a term used a great deal, although it does not appear in P.L. 94-142. It slides together two concepts worth keeping separate: (1) the general stricture for placement in the least restrictive environment, and (2) activities involving a student whose basic placement is in a special education setting and who spends a portion of the day in a general education (mainstream) setting. A recent ERIC search identified over 120 studies involving the latter concept. The data as to the effectiveness of this type of mainstreaming are mixed, some showing positive social benefits, others showing both social and academic benefits, and still others showing no benefits (*Research* 1987). Basically, the studies identify two sets of factors that determine the effectiveness of mainstreaming: (1) the adequacy of the preparation, and the appropriateness of the identification, of the students to be mainstreamed; and (2) the activities in the mainstreamed class, including organization of the environment, adaptation of the curriculum, and teaching strategies.

The limits in the quality of the instruction students receive in separate special education programs has been noted above (see also Gartner and Lipsky 1987; Wang, Reynolds, and Walberg 1987a). The inadequacies of the arrangements made in the general education setting are equally consequential. Zigmond and colleagues have conducted some of the few studies that examine the actual conditions of mainstreaming, both at the lower grades and in high schools. Their study of mainstreaming in the thirty-eight elementary schools in Pittsburgh found that "over 90 percent of the mildly handicapped elementary students . . . were *never* assigned to regular education academic classes" (Sansone and Zigmond 1986, 455, emphasis in the original). Not only were few students involved, but for those who were, their participation was limited in three ways: they were scheduled for fewer than the full number of periods in the week, they attended several different general education classes for the same subject, and they were assigned to inappropriate (by age or level) general education classes. The opportunity "to provide preparation periods for special education teachers . . . seems to be the decisive factor in these assignments" (Sansone and Zigmond 1986, 453).

Four studies of the mainstreaming, in twelve high schools, of students labeled "learning disabled" found very little that was different instructionally when these students were mainstreamed (Zigmond, Levin, and Laurie 1985). The major adjustment they found was the lowering of grading standards so that the students had a better opportunity to pass the courses. Given the inadequacies of the adjustments made, it is not surprising that only 1.4 percent of the special education students in Pittsburgh returned to general education (*Special Education* 1986, table 13).

Blending at the Margin

Increasingly, there are efforts under way to break down the wall between the special and general education systems. That is, there are educational programs designed to serve students now in special education and variously called "mild" or "moderately" handicapped, in a common setting with other students with learning problems and students at risk. Among the various efforts are those under the rubric of the general education initiative launched by U.S. Department of Education Assistant Secretary Madeleine Will. Among the components of the initiative are increased instructional time, support systems for teachers, empowerment of principals to control all programs and resources at the building level, and new instructional approaches that involve shared responsibility between general and special education (*Educating Students* 1986, 7-9).

At the same time as there are increasing questions about services for students with mild or moderate handicaps, concerns are being expressed about other students in "pull-out" programs, such as Chapter I and other remedial efforts. Indeed, some of the same people are involved in what has been called, unfelicitiously, "repairing the second system" (Wang, Reynolds, and Walberg 1987b). This formulation addresses the unmet needs of a broader group of students. The basis of these efforts is the recognition that a wide variety of school programs have been created to provide special, compensatory, and/or remedial education services for students not well served in the general education system. And whatever the improvements of such efforts— and in many instances they are real—they nonetheless have created large, separate, costly, and overall ineffective systems. Furthermore, they have left the mainstream largely unaffected, except for having extruded an ever growing group of students who do not fit an ever narrowing standard of normalcy.

A Single System

Although it does not quite fully give up a dual system approach, the "rights without labels" concept put forward by the National Coalition of Advocates for Students (Boston), National Association of School Psychologists (Washington, D.C.), and the National Association of School Social Workers (Washington, D.C.) moves in that direction. While affirming that access to special education must be assured for all significantly handicapped children who need and can benefit from it, they point out that it is not a benign act to label as "handicapped" a child who is not. They state that such labels are often irrelevant to instructional needs and lead to reduced expectations for children so labeled; that the process of assessment to assign such labels depletes scarce resources; and, finally, that this all leads to a decreased willingness on the part of general education to meet the diverse needs of all students.

There is now a growing body of practice that builds upon these new conceptualizations. In part they borrow from the school effectiveness work in general education (Edmonds 1979a, 1979b; Rutter et al. 1975) and its adaptation to special education (Bickel and Bickel 1986; Goodman 1985; Jewell 1985; Peterson et al. 1985). Knoll and Meyer (n.d.) summarize these principles as follows:

Principals in effective schools are instructional leaders, who pose high expectations for students and teachers.

The climate in an effective school is orderly, disciplined, and comfortable. A commitment to excellence is evident and there are high expectations for student achievement.

Students' goals and objectives are meaningful, clearly written, sequenced, and reviewed and updated periodically based on student progress data which are collected on a regular basis.

Student achievement is recognized and rewarded frequently.

Student progress is monitored using a criterion-referenced approach: the measures used are directly related to the instructional objectives.

Within effective classrooms, "down time" is kept to a minimum. Students spend a high percentage of their time actively engaged in learning tasks.

Effective teachers spend a high percentage of their time involved in active instruction.

Effective teachers adapt, modify, and create curricular units for their own class which are sequenced and integrated into the long range educational goals of the school.

Effective schools tend to have a low teacher/student ratio.

Administrators, teachers, support personnel, students, and parents in effective schools describe an atmosphere of cooperation and open communication.

Parents support and are actively involved in effective schools. (2, f)

They conclude "that these same principles are outlined in virtually every special education text as the hallmarks of a good 'special' education program" (3).

Programs of full (or nearly full) integration are being carried out in a few states, such as Vermont and Washington, and in individual schools within some school districts, including those of Johnson City and Syracuse, in New York, and Riverview, Pennsylvania. In Vermont, for example, the "homecoming model" brings students from regional special education centers to their local school, and in individual districts, such as Winooski, there are no full-time, self-contained classes.

In Washington, the focus has been on integrating students with mild handicaps, as well as sustaining youngsters in general education—in Johnson City, New York, mastery learning principles have long been a critical feature of district activities (Vickery 1988), and this has served to hold down the percentage of students referred to special education. Except for a few older students whose parents wanted them to stay out of district schools, all students are served in the district, and all those with mild and moderate handicapping conditions are served in integrated classes. The use of teacher teams, specialists coming into the classroom, and teacher control over time and pace of learning are key features.

In Syracuse, New York, at the Ed Smith Elementary School (and to a lesser extent at the Levy Middle School), a full range of students labeled "handicapped" are integrated, including several autistic children. (The impetus for the effort here came from

Peter Knoblick, who had set up a private school for autistic children.) Again, team teaching is a key resource.

The Verner School, in the Riverview school district, Pennsylvania, is the fullest implementation of the Adaptive Learning Environments Model (ALEM). All fifty students labeled "handicapped" are taught in integrated classes full time. Classes are taught by a general education teacher, with two special education teachers circulating to provide assistance as necessary to teachers and direct services to students.

There are limits to the evaluation data (for example, random assignments of pupils to control groups would seem to violate P.L. 94-142), but in each of these programs there seems to be sound basis to conclude that student learning is enhanced. And after initial start-up costs, the programs operate at costs equal to or less than those of the previous segregated models.

A central feature of each of these programs is that while they provide integrated settings, they do not ignore the individual needs of students, be they labeled "handicapped" or not. Attention to individual needs may include the use of aides and support staff in the classroom; teaming between general and special education teachers; consultation and technical assistance to teachers; adaptation of curricula; and the use of specific learning strategies, such as cooperative learning designs and peer instruction. By providing for the individual needs of each student, a unitary system is not a "dumping" ground, but rather, a refashioned mainstream.

The examples cited here are not the only ones available, but they do represent some of the major current efforts. What presently exist are some integrated programs and some integrated schools, but no whole districts that are integrated. Indeed, it is not dissimilar to the situation in the reform of general education a few years ago. In that effort, the late Ron Edmonds argued that if some schools could be effective in the education of low-income and minority students, then others, with commitment, could do so also (Edmonds 1979b). The same holds true for special education.

PUBLIC POLICY INITIATIVES

As we have noted earlier, the achievements of P.L. 94-142 have been considerable. In barely a dozen years, major changes have occurred in the education of students with handicapping conditions. Their education is now seen as the appropriate responsibility of public education; increasingly they are being served in the public schools; the due process rights of parents are honored in most schools; and there has been little in the way of backlash over the costs of such services. To argue for a new level of understanding, a new paradigm, is not to gainsay these achievements.

The present period is one of heightened scrutiny and concern about special education. Conferences, proposals, special journal issues, and books all are looking at the future of special education. Although it is not often included in the debate about educational reform, the education of students with handicapping conditions is likely to be a major agenda item in the coming years. Let us suggest some specific, and other more general, steps.

First, the quality of education provided to students in current special education programs must be scrutinized with greater care. The focus of the scrutiny must be on outcomes for students. This must be done despite the fears of some that the findings will be dismal and may threaten hard-won current programs. Indeed, this is all the more reason to undertake such scrutiny. The scarce resources of public funds and trust, and most importantly student needs, demand no less.

Second, the interests of students labeled "handicapped" must be incorporated into the broad debate on educational reform. A part of this is to examine the extent to which the labeling and consequent separation of these students is warranted. More broadly, it is to challenge the premise of much of that debate, that the purpose of such reform is to pick and promote winners rather than to nurture and educate well all students.

Third, building upon the "rights without labels" formulation described above, the yoking of funding and program services to categorization of students must be ended. So, too, the debate needs to be shifted from one about placement to a concern for quality—academic and social learning, preparation for work, participation in community life, and citizenship. A part of this involves identifying and promoting effective practices. Given the knowledge base being developed, there is little continuing justification for the perpetuation of practices that are not effective, especially those that offer limited opportunities based upon pernicious notions of limited capacity of students labeled "handicapped" (Goodlad and Oakes 1988; Lipsky and Gartner 1987).

Fourth, given the development of successful (although not, as yet, widespread) models of effective unitary designs, serious thought must be given to a new formulation of what a "free, appropriate public education" means. Tom Gilhool, a former lawyer at the Public Interest Law Center of Philadelphia (and later secretary of education for the Commonwealth of Pennsylvania), put forward what he called the "developmental twin" argument: "If a child with a particular type of disability can be successfully integrated, with special services in a regular class or school, then why can't all children with the same type and level of disability also be integrated?" (Gilhool and Stutman 1978). There are now, more than a decade after Gilhool posed this question, enough examples of quality and integration for the full range of students for his challenge to be answered with commitment and action. Indeed, it may be time to consider the shape of a "new" P.L. 94-142, one that focuses less on procedures and more on outcomes, one that challenges—and rejects—the dual system approach, one that requires a unitary system, special for all students.

NOTES

Alan Gartner is professor and director, Office of Sponsored Research, Graduate School and University Center, City University of New York. Dorothy Kerzner Lipsky is superintendent, Riverhead Central School District, and senior research scientist, Graduate School and University Center, City University of New York. Both served in the Division of Special Education, New York City Public Schools, he as executive director and she as chief administrator, Office of Program Development. They are coauthors of "Beyond Special Education" (*Harvard Educational Review*) and "Capable of Achievement and Worthy of Respect: Education of the Handicapped As If They Were Full-Fledged Human Beings" (*Exceptional Children*, 1987) and coeditors of *Beyond Separate Education: Quality Education for All* (Brookes, 1989). In 1987-88, Dr. Lipsky was Mary E. Switzer Distinguished Fellow, National Institute on Disability and Rehabilitation Research.

The order of authorship does not imply seniority.

1. We draw upon several recently published papers (Gartner and Lipsky 1987, 1989a, 1989b, 1989c; Lipsky and Gartner 1987, 1989). Material from these sources is not cited.

2. Office of Civil Rights data show a continuing overrepresentation of minority students referred to and placed in special education. For example, while black students represent 16 percent of the public school population, they comprise 35 percent of those labeled "educably mentally retarded" (EMR), 27 percent of those labeled "trainably mentally retarded" (TMR), and 27 percent of those labeled "seriously emotionally disturbed" (Hume 1988). While the overlap between poverty and race would account for some of this disparity, cultural bias and discrimination are present as well.

3. A report from the National Longitudinal Transition Study indicates that about 5 percent of secondary youth enrolled in special education programs were declassified from special education annually (Wagner and Shaver 1989, table 2). This challenges reports from a four-city study of significantly higher declassification rates (Singer 1988); it is about the same as the report of the Council of Great City Schools (*Special Education* 1986).

REFERENCES

Algozzine, B., C. V. Morsink, and K. M. Algozzine. What's special about self-contained special education? Manuscript.

Algozzine, B., J. E. Ysseldyke. 1981. Special education services for normal students: Better safe than sorry? *Exceptional Children* 48:238-43.

Allington, R. L. 1983. The reading instruction provided readers of differing ability. *Elementary School Journal* 83:548-59.

Allington, R. L. and P. Johnson. 1986. The coordination among regular classroom reading programs and targeted support programs. In B. J. Williams, P. A. Richmond, and B. J. Muson (eds.) *Designs for Compensatory Education: Conference Proceedings and Papers*. Washington, D.C.: Research and Evaluation Associates, Inc.

Berres, M. S., and P. Knoblock, eds. 1987. *Program models for mainstreaming: Integrating students with moderate to severe disabilities*. Rockville, Md.: Aspen.

Bickel, W. E. and D. D. Bickel. 1986. Effective schools, classrooms, and institutions: Implications for special education. *Exceptional Children* 52 (5): 489-500.

Biklen, D. 1985. *Achieving the complete school: Strategies for effective mainstreaming*. New York: Teachers College Press.

Biklen, D. 1987. In pursuit of integration. In *Program models for mainstreaming: Integrating students with moderate to severe disabilities*, ed. M. S. Berres and P. Knoblock. Rockville, Md.: Aspen.

Biklen, D., S. Lehr, S. J. Searl, and S. J. Taylor. 1987. *Purposeful Integration . . . Inherently Equal.* Boston: Technical Assistance for Parent Programs.

Bogdan, R., and J. Kugelmass. 1984. Case studies of mainstreaming: A symbolic interactionist approach to special schooling. In *Special Education and Social Interests*, ed. L. Barton and S. Tomlinson. London: Croom-Helm.

Coles, J. 1987. *The Learning Mystique.* New York: Pantheon.

Davis, W. A., and L. A. Shepard. 1983. Specialists' use of test and clinical judgment in the diagnosis of learning disabilities. *Learning Disabilities Quarterly* 19:128-38.

Edmonds, R. R. 1979a. Effective schools for the urban poor. *Educational Leadership* 40 (3): 15-27.

——— . 1979b. Some schools work and more can. *Social Policy* 9 (5): 28-32.

Educating students with learning problems—a school responsibility. A report to the secretary. 1986. Washington, D.C.: U.S. Department of Education.

Fuchs, D., L. S. Fuchs, S. Benowitz, and K. Barringer. 1987. Norm-referenced tests: Are they valid for use with handicapped students? *Exceptional Children* 54 (3): 263-71.

Gartner, A., and D. K. Lipsky. 1987. Beyond special education: Toward a quality system for all students. *Harvard Educational Review* 57 (4): 367-95.

Gartner, A., and D. K. Lipsky. 1989b. School administration and financial arrangements. In *Educating all students in the mainstream of regular education*, ed. S. Stainback, W. Stainback, and M. Forest. Baltimore, Md.: Brookes.

——— . 1989c. *The yoke of special education: How to break it.* Rochester, N.Y.: National Council on Education and the Economy.

Gilhool, T., and E. Stutman. 1978. Integration of severely handicapped students: Toward criteria for implementing and enforcing the integration imperative of P.L. 94-142 and Section 504. In *Criteria for evaluation of least restrictive environment provision.* Washington, D.C.: U.S. Department of Health, Education, and Welfare.

Goodlad, J. I., and J. Oakes. 1988. We must offer equal access to knowledge. *Educational Leadership* 45 (5): 16-22.

Goodman, L. 1985. The effective schools movement and special education. *Teaching Exceptional Children* 17:102-5.

Guess, D., and B. Thomson. n.d. Preparation of personnel to educate students with severe and multiple disabilities: A time for change? In *Critical issues in the lives of people with severe disabilities*, ed. L. Meyer, C. Peck, and L. Brown. Baltimore, Md.: Brookes. In press.

Heller, K. A., W. H. Holtzman, and S. Messick, eds. 1982. *Placing children in special education: A strategy for equity*. Washington, D.C.: National Academy Press.

Hobbs, N. 1975. *The future of children*. San Francisco: Jossey-Bass.

Hume, M. 1988. OCR data show minorities overrepresented among disability groups. *Education Daily*, 17 February, 5-6.

Jenkins, J. R., C. Pious, and D. Peterson. 1987. Exploring the validity of a unified learning program for remedial and handicapped students. Unpublished manuscript.

Jewell, J. 1985. One school's search for excellence. *Teaching Exceptional Children* 17:140-44.

Kauffman, J. M., J. W. Lloyd, and J. D. McKinney, eds. 1988. *Journal of Learning Disabilities* Special Issue. 21 (1).

Keogh, B. K. 1988. Learning disabilities: Diversity in search of order. In *The handbook of special education: Research and practice*, ed. M. C. Wang, M. C. Reynolds, and H. J. Walberg. Vol. 2, *Mildly handicapped conditions*. New York: Pergamon Press.

Knoll, J. and L. Meyer. n.d. *Principles and Practices for School Integration of Students with Severe Disabilities: An Overview of the Literature*. Syracuse, N.Y.: Center on Human Policy.

Lipsky, D. K., and A. Gartner. 1987. Capable of achievement and worthy of respect: Education for the handicapped as if they were full-fledged human beings. *Exceptional Children* 54 (1): 69-74.

——, eds. 1989. *Beyond separate education: Quality education for all*. Baltimore, Md.: Brookes.

McGill-Franzen, A. 1987. Failure to learn to read: Formulating a problem. *Reading Research Quarterly* 22:475-90.

Morsink, C. V., R. S. Soar, R. M. Soar, and R. Thomas. 1986. Research on teaching: Opening the door to special education classrooms. *Exceptional Children* 53 (1): 32-40.

Peterson, D., S. S. Albert, A. M. Foxworth, L. S. Cox, and B.K. Tilley.

1985. Effective schools for all students: Current efforts and future directions. *Teaching Exceptional Children* 17:106-10.

Research on the effectiveness of mainstreaming. 1987. Reston, Va.: ERIC Clearinghouse on Handicapped and Gifted Children.

Rutter, M., B. Maugham, P. Mortimore, J. Ouston, and A. Smith. 1975. *Fifteen thousand hours: Secondary schools and their effects on children.* New York: Wiley.

Sansone, J., and N. Zigmond. 1986. Evaluating mainstreaming through an evaluation of students' schedules. *Exceptional Children* 51 (5): 452-58.

Shepard, L. A., L. A. Smith, and C. P. Vojir. 1983. Characteristics of pupils identified as learning disabled. *Journal of Special Education* 16:73-85.

Singer, J. D. 1988. Should special education merge with regular education? *Educational Policy* 2 (4): 409-424.

Skrtic, T. 1986. The crisis in special education knowledge: A perspective on perspective. *Focus on Exceptional Children* 18 (7): 1-16.

Special education: Views from America's cities. 1986. Washington, D.C.: Council of Great City Schools.

Stainback, W., and S. Stainback. 1984. A rationale for the merger of special and regular education. *Exceptional Children* 51 (2): 102-11.

Stainback, S., W. Stainback, and M. Forest. 1989. *Educating all students in the mainstream of regular education.* Baltimore, Md.: Brookes.

Taylor, S. J. 1988. Caught in the continuum: A critical analysis of the principle of the least restrictive environment. *Journal of the Association for Persons with Severe Handicaps* 13 (1): 41-53.

Tenth annual report to the Congress on the implementation of the Education of the Handicapped Act. 1988. Washington, D.C.: U.S. Department of Education.

Viadero, D. 1988. Study documents jumps in special education enrollments. *Education Week*, 2 March, 17.

Vickery, T. R. 1988. Learning from an outcomes-driven school district. *Educational Leadership* 50 (2): 52-56.

Wagner, M. 1989. Personal communication, 24 May.

Wagner, M., and D. M. Shaver. 1989. *Education programs and achievement of secondary special education students: A report from the*

National Longitudinal Transition Study. Menlo Park, Calif.: SRI International.

Walker, L. 1987. Procedural rights in the wrong system: Special education is not enough. In *Images of the disabled/disabling images*, ed. A. Gartner and T. Joe. New York: Praeger.

Wang, M. C., M. C. Reynolds, and H. J. Walberg, eds. 1987a. *Handbook of special education research and practice.* Vol. 1, *Learning characteristics and adaptive education.* New York: Pergamon Press.

———. 1987b. Repairing the second system for students with special needs. A paper presented at the 1987 Wingspread Conference on the Education of Children with Special Needs, January 29, 1987.

Ysseldyke, J. E. 1987. Classification of handicapped students. In *Handbook of special education: Research and practice*, ed. M. C. Wang, M. C. Reynolds, and H. J. Walberg. Vol. 1, *Learner characteristics and adaptive education.* New York: Pergamon Press.

Ysseldyke, J. E., and B. Algozzine. 1983. LD or not LD: That's not the question! *Journal of Learning Disabilities* 16:29-31.

Ysseldyke, J. E., B. Algozzine, L. Richey, and J. L. Graden. 1982. Similarities and differences between low achievers and students classified as learning disabled. *Journal of Special Education* 16:73-85.

Zigmond, N., E. Levin, and T. E. Laurie. 1985. Managing the mainstream: An analysis of teacher attitudes and student performance in mainstream high school programs. *Journal of Learning Disabilities* 18 (9): 535-41.

8

Language and Ethnicity as Factors in School Failure: The Case of Mexican-Americans

INTRODUCTION

Making a transition to a new culture is almost always stressful, and when, in addition, a new language must be acquired, the adjustment process can be particularly challenging. Hence, it should come as no surprise that a child who is unfamiliar with the cultural demands of an American classroom might have difficulty meeting those demands; or that a child who does not understand the language of the classroom might fail to achieve in that setting. Hence, such children come to be "at risk" in the American school system. And because of recent and dramatic demographic shifts, an increasingly larger percentage of the U.S. school-age population falls into this category. In fact, in some states, such as California and Texas, up to half of the children in the public schools could be considered at risk for school failure because of ethnic and linguistic differences.

The experience of many generations of immigrant children has provided us with some insights into the special challenge that schooling represents for ethnically and linguistically diverse students. Immigrant students tend to score lower on standardized measures of achievement, leave school earlier, and be overage for their grade level (Olneck and Lazerson 1974; Olsen 1988). However, in spite of substantial variability in the amount of difficulty that different immigrant groups have experienced in school and the rate at which these difficulties have been overcome (Olneck and Lazerson 1974, 1980), broad patterns of assimilation can be discerned. Many studies have shown that the greatest adjustment problems for immigrant children are experienced during the first (foreign-born) generation, when the effects on families of both ethnic discrimination and economic exploitation are most evident. The second generation usually profits from the sacrifices of the first and makes substantial advances with respect to socioeconomic status variables, such as education, occupation, and earnings. And by the third generation, the process of structural assimilation is well established, as the group approximates parity with the American norm on educational and occupational indicators (Glazer and Moynihan 1963; Gordon 1964; Chiswick 1979, 1980; McCarthy and Valdez 1986). (These findings, of course, make no assumptions about the degree to which language and cultural practices persist within these ethnic communities.)

This pattern of assimilation, common to several waves of European immigrants, has come to shape our way of thinking about the education of all children who are ethnically and/or linguistically different from the American norm. This way of thinking about the education of minorities has consequently contributed to a belief in the inevitability of cultural and educational assimilation—a sense that no special intervention is required, because (ethnic minority) immigrants manage to survive and eventually prosper in this land of opportunity. Evidence of this widespread belief is found in the common refrain: *My grandparents came here from the old country, poor and without the ability to speak the language, and they managed to send their children onto college. Why can't others do the same?* We have come to believe that assimilation is simply and matter of time and a willingness to be assimilated. We have come to believe that assimilation is simply a matter of time and a willingness to be assimilated. Yet this model of the immigrant experience may be wholly unsatisfactory to explain the patterns of schooling for some ethnic groups.

For the purposes of this chapter, I have chosen to focus on one ethnic group, Mexican Americans, for whom the model of immigrant assimilation into American institutions appears to be a poor tool of analysis. Mexican Americans, whose numbers have been swelled by immigration in recent years, were already well established in the Southwest when it was annexed by the United States in the midnineteenth century (Grebler, Moore, and Guzman 1970; Nava 1972). They became an ethnic minority, not by any desire to leave their land of origin and begin anew, but as an accident of history, events not of their own doing..

I argue that Mexican Americans are not following the typical experience of U.S. immigrants and that a false perception that they are may, in itself, be helping to impede their assimilation process. I will then briefly review the literature on language and ethnicity as risk-inducing factors in the education of Mexican Americans. The chapter will conclude with an attempt to explain why factors that have not been perceived as insurmountable by other ethnic groups are so chronically troublesome for Mexican Americans and why their pattern of assimilation has differed so markedly from that of past immigrants.

The emphasis on Mexican Americans is defensible on a number of grounds: They number almost 14 million, making them the nation's second-largest minority, and they have been the largest ethnic minority in the Southwest for most of this century (Grebler, Moore, and Guzman 1970; Schwartz 1988; Hoffman, 1991). Their failure to enter the educational mainstream in anything but minuscule numbers poses a serious threat to the economy of the entire Southwest. And Mexican Americans represent an ethnic group for whom language, as well as culture, has been perceived as a serious risk factor in school achievement.

FAILURE TO ASSIMILATE

What is the evidence that Mexican Americans are not assimilating in the same way or at the same rate as other immigrant groups? Mexican Americans represent more than a quarter of all people living in the highly populated states of California and Texas (Hoffman, 1991). And even more to the point, up to 40 percent of the children entering the public schools in these states are Mexican American (Marshall and Bouvier 1986; California Department of Finance 1990; Bean and Tienda 1987). Yet by any standard, Mexican Americans are faring poorly in school. By the end of elementary school, the typical Mexican American child in California or Texas lags two years behind his or her non-Hispanic white counterparts, and by high school's end, up to 50 percent will have dropped out (compared to a dropout rate of about 25 percent for non-Hispanic whites) (Carter and Segura 1979; Stern 1985; Rumberger, 1991). In any given high school class, only about 2 percent of the Mexican American students will have completed a college degree within five years of high school graduation (Gandara 1986). The result is that while between 18 and 21 percent of non-Hispanic whites in these states had completed four or more years of college in 1987, only five to six percent of Mexican Americans were similarly well educated (Western Interstate Commission on Higher Education [WICHE], 1988). Moreover, indications are that the situation is deteriorating.

University of California researcher Jorge Chapa (1988) has reported on occupational status indicators for a sample of males third-generation and beyond in California, comparing various ethnic groups. He found that while Chicanos have increased their representation among the ranks of the middle class—as have all ethnic groups—their progress has been much slower than for either blacks or whites. Furthermore, although Anglo Americans have declined substantially among the ranks of blue-collar workers in recent years, Chicanos have been increasing their representation at this level dramatically. Even for the second generation, 70 percent of Chicanos are found in the ten lowest job categories.

In another analysis of the same data, Chapa (1988) used the Duncan Socio-Economic Index to compare occupational status attainment for the same groups in California between 1940 and 1979. During this period Anglo males gained fifteen points, while Chicanos gained only 5, with the result that *third-generation* and beyond Chicano males held only 69 percent of the status attainment of Anglo males, *down* from a high of 83 percent in 1940. Census bureau data from 1987 lend further support to the argument that Mexican Americans are losing ground socioeco-nomically. Although median family income rose 10 percent for non-Hispanic whites between 1981 and 1986, it dropped 6 per-cent in the same period for Mexican Americans (Schwartz 1988). This is consistent with the findings of Phillips (1990), that Amer-icans who are held at the lowest socio-economic levels in our society found it increasingly difficult to break the economic bar-riers into the middle class during the decade of the 1980s.

Gary Orfield of the University of Chicago reviewed the statis-tics available on school segregation, dropping out, and college-going behavior for Chicanos over a twelve-year period. In each of these categories, Mexican Americans were faring worse in 1988 than they were in 1976. Chicano students were more likely to be segregated in 1988 than they were twelve years prior, and they were more likely to be found in schools with low achievement and limited resources; Chicano dropout rates had increased, and more importantly, a smaller percentage of Chicano high school graduates were going on to college (Orfield, 1988). Declining lev-els of educational preparation help to explain the backward slide in the job sector for Chicanos. Because socioeconomic status and success in school are so highly correlated, these findings would suggest that the next generation of Mexican-American children will be at even greater risk for school failure.

But what are the specific factors associated with this popu-lation that impede their movement through the social strata of American society and place them at such great risk for school failure?

LANGUAGE AS A RISK FACTOR

The most common, and most persistent, explanation of edu-cational failure among Mexican Americans is language differ-ence (U.S. Commission on Civil Rights 1975). As a group, Chi-canos have been particularly tenacious in retaining their native language (Cortes 1980), and numerous studies have found a strong relationship between Spanish as the primary language of the home and low educational achievement in Hispanic chil-dren (cf. Carter 1970). These studies, however, tend to suffer from a particular methodological weakness: parents who speak Spanish at home are more likely to be non-English speakers and, as such, to have significantly lower education and income than

English speakers (Bean and Tienda, 1987). Additional research evidence undermining this assumed relationship between language of the home and academic achievement comes from two different studies conducted in the Los Angeles area. In these studies researchers found that Mexican immigrant students (who assumedly spoke Spanish at home) performed either as well or better than native-born Chicano students when grades were used as the criterion measure (Kimball, 1968; Lugo, 1970).

Ogbu and Matute-Bianchi (1986) provide further evidence against the hypothesis that home language might be the primary risk factor in school achievement. They cite several examples of immigrant groups who do extremely well in American schools in spite of language handicaps. There can be no doubt that language presents an initial barrier to education, but it is clear that for some children (Chinese and Japanese, as an example), the inability to speak English is only a temporary impediment that is quickly remedied and the adverse effects of which appear to be relatively short-lived.

James Cummins, of the Ontario Institute, and others have cautioned, however, that apparent communicative competence in English may mask deficits in verbal-conceptual competence in students for whom English is a new language. They claim that removing native-language instructional support too early can jeopardize the thinking skills of language-minority children (Cummins, 1984). Evidence from standardized achievement tests of large numbers of Asian students in California tends to support this contention. Although these students scored very high on quantitative tests, their reading and verbal scores are often quite low, approximating the level of Mexican American performance on these same tests (Olsen 1988).

Shedding further light on the language-achievement dilemma is a body of research on language issues in ethnic communities which suggests that the particular language that is spoken may have an effect on schooling outcomes. In a classic set of studies first conducted in Canada and then extended in the United States, identification with a language of lower prestige value was shown to affect negatively the perceptions of the academic competence of the speakers (Lambert, Hodgson, Gardner, and Fillenbaum 1960; Frender and Lambert 1972; Bikson 1974). Similarly, a review of the literature on learning handicaps among Mexican American children reveals a pervasive theme of blaming learning problems on bilingualism (Carter 1970).

This persists in spite of a significant literature on the cognitive benefits of bilingualism (Darcy 1953; Segalowitz 1977) and the prestige associated in many quarters with speaking more than one language. Nonetheless, being "bilingual" has become for many, in the Southwest, a euphemism for being Mexican American and therefore educationally handicapped.

Clearly, being a limited English speaker in an American school has an effect on educational outcomes for students. And being pushed too quickly to learn in English may negatively affect higher-order thinking skills. But importantly, the effects appear to vary among language groups, and the particular language a student speaks *does* seem to make a difference. Because there is so much variability among groups, and because some groups continue to achieve in spite of apparent deficits in learning, the argument that language difference alone could account for the underachievement of Mexican Americans is not compelling.

ETHNIC RISK FACTORS

Culture Conflict

Another common explanation for low school achievement among ethnic minorities is cultural differences. Emphasis on practical life skills rather than academic skills, cooperative rather than competitive problem-solving strategies, and intense familial loyalty are all well-documented as cultural traits believed to be shared by immigrants of Mexican origin (Grebler, Moore, and Guzman 1970; Kagan 1986; Bean and Tienda, 1987). To the extent that such traits aptly describe many Mexican Americans, they may be particularly functional in an agrarian society, but quite dysfunctional in American schools. Numerous studies have pointed out how Chicano children are adversely affected in the classroom by the "lack of fit" between their cultural patterns and the demands of American schooling (U.S. Commission on Civil Rights 1972; Carter and Segura 1979). Nonetheless, other ethnic groups, with similarly distinct and "traditional" cultural patterns (the Punjabi, as an example) have managed to straddle two cultures and successfully navigate the American educational system (Ogbu and Matute-Bianchi 1986). In fact, biculturalism appears to be a particularly effective response to meeting the competing demands of two cultures and may even promote educational and occupational achievement (Gandara in preparation). It is questionable, however, whether most Mexican Americans have acquired much of a knack for biculturalism.

Phenotype

Physical characteristics may also contribute to a condition of educational risk for some ethnic groups. American, as well as Mexican, culture has tended to favor lighter skinned and more European-looking people. Yet Mexicans, a mestizo people, span the spectrum from very dark to very fair-skinned, in color, and from very Indian to very European, in other physical characteristics. Some can pass as Anglo-Americans, but most are identifiably Mexican, with Mestizo features and darker than average hair and skin color. In this regard, some researchers have investigated the degree to which a typically Mexican appearance might reduce an individual's educational attainment and life chances. In one such study a significant relationship was found between darker complected skin and Indian features, on the one hand, and lower levels of educational and occupational attainment, on the other (Arce, Murgia, and Frisbie 1987). Still other researchers have concluded that identifiability as a Mexican American does, in fact, lead to discrimination in schooling and in the job market (Carter 1970; U.S. Commission on Civil Rights 1973).

No doubt a relationship does exist between one's skin color and one's life chances in the United States. However, Mexican society is also, at least partially, stratified along color lines, and the possibility exists that Indian appearance placed these individuals at an economic and social disadvantage in Mexico or within the Mexican American subculture. Such an initial disadvantage may have persisted in American society because of the strong relationship between socioeconomic status of parents and educational and occupational attainment of their children in this country. The fact that other dark-skinned minorities, specifically East Indians, have fared better in American schools may be at least partially explained by the fact that they immigrated more recently (post-Civil Rights period) and entered a country much more open to racial minorities than the country either blacks or Mexicans initially encountered. On the whole, the evidence suggests that identifiable ethnicity and phenotype have played a role in the undereducation of Mexican Americans, but this is probably not sufficient to explain all the differences that exist between them and other white ethnic groups.

Regeneration of Ethnic Culture

Unlike previous waves of European immigration, which spanned particular, and usually relatively narrow, time periods, Mexican immigration to the United States has always been a factor in the Southwest and has constituted a steady and increasing flow since the middle of this century (McCarthy and Valdez 1986). The constant influx of Mexican immigrants to the United States has been suggested as another specific factor in the schooling problems of Chicanos. Because of Mexico's seriously depressed economy and its porous border with the United States, thousands of new Mexican immigrants enter this country annually (Muller and Espenshade 1984; McCarthy and Valdez, 1986). A substantial number cross into Texas and Arizona, but the majority settle in southern California (McCarthy and Valdez 1986). Each new immigrant brings with her or him the seeds of revitalization of the traditional culture and language. The newcomers arrive like troop reinforcements in the battle for ethnic and linguistic integrity. Children growing up and becoming educated in these ethnic communities are faced with two distinct and competing cultural models: the safe and comfortable culture and language of the home and community, and the foreign and often alienating culture and language of the school. If they don't have compelling reasons to adopt the culture of the school, one has to wonder why children would subject themselves to the task of doing so. And given the omnipresence of the primary language in these communities, it cannot be surprising that Mexican Americans have displayed such tenacity in maintaining their cultural patterns and language. Yet the maintenance of one's language and culture does not preclude the adoption of other languages and cultural practices that may confer a higher status or provide particular benefits. This begs the question, to which I will return later, if Chicanos do indeed perceive any substantial benefit from acquiring Anglo cultural forms.

AN ALTERNATIVE HYPOTHESIS ABOUT EDUCATIONAL RISK AND MEXICAN AMERICANS

I suggested at the outset of this discussion that the experience of European immigrants and their subsequent assimilation into the American mainstream might not be an appropriate model by which to understand the educational experience of certain ethnic groups and of Mexican Americans in particular. This assertion is based on both theory and empirical observation. Existing data on the educational experiences of European immigrants to the United States suggest that these groups initially did, indeed, experience difficulty assimilating into the American educational system (Olneck and Lazerson 1974, 1980), but that "school was an avenue of success for many, especially second- and third-generation children of immigrants (Olneck and Lazerson 1980, 316)." And although educational assimilation was anything but uniform for all groups (for example, 1908 data record that Poles and Southern Italians lagged substantially behind other white immigrant groups in years of schooling), the socioeconomic differences that divided white ethnic groups before World War II have narrowed or disappeared, and today the only identifiable racial/ethnic groups that remain significantly behind nationwide means for years of schooling are those of color: blacks, Native Americans, and Hispanics (Baratz and Duran 1985). Moreover, some data suggest that for Mexican Americans the period of greatest educational mobility may be in the first generation rather than in succeeding generations (Lugo 1970; Kimball 1968).

Olneck and Lazerson (1980) suggest that variations in cultural characteristics that appeared to explain much of the difference, among European groups, in educational mobility may fail to account for the educational disparity for Mexican Americans:

Distinctive views of education go a long way toward explaining why some groups responded so differently to schooling. . . . This emphasis on cultural values however, should not obscure other processes of differentiation that had little to do with ethnic values and much to do with discrimination and exclusion in education and occupations. For Black Americans and Mexicans, school achievement was rarely translated into economic rewards commensurate with those gained by Whites with equivalent schooling. Studies through the 19th and 20th centuries revealed the same story: that school attainment had less to do with type of work later pursued than did race, and that student aspirations and educational attainments were not matched by significantly better jobs, save for the small number of college-educated middle-class Blacks and Hispanics who provided professional services within their own communities or the relatively few who found jobs in the civil service. (317)

There are two major problems with the European assimilation model: (1) Dramatic changes have occurred in the economic structure of American society since the last wave of European immigrants arrived, and (2) Mexican Americans are a semi-indigenous people of color who must deal with unique issues of identity and discrimination.

A Changing Economy

Mexican immigrants to this country have come here for the same reasons that all previous immigrants came—for a better opportunity and the chance to improve the living standard of their families. Yet Mexican immigrants are encountering a social and economic system that is not nearly so hospitable as it was for previous immigrants. The last major wave of immigration to this country occurred at a time when educational expectations and occupational opportunities were structured very differently. Lack of education did not pose the significant barrier that it does today. Evidence of this can be found in a recent study from the Urban Institute that concludes that recent immigrants are faring worse economically than past immigrant groups, even when differences in education are controlled for (Taylor 1986). Hence, when we read that Italian youth were less likely to attend high school than their Anglo American peers, at the beginning of this century, it is also noteworthy that most children, of whatever background, did not complete high school educations then (Olneck and Lazerson 1974). And though surely this limited occupational mobility, it by no means portended economic disaster for these children, since jobs and job mobility were much more loosely tied to formal education than they are today. School failure in this context had a very different meaning and very different consequences.

Today, young people without high school diplomas are at high risk for unemployment and underemployment (Stern 1985). Would-be workers without educational credentials who are fortunate enough to find jobs are almost certain to be confined to the secondary job market: low-skill, low-pay jobs, often in the service sector, that offer little or no possibility of upward mobility (Doeringer and Piore 1975). Qualifications inflation is another oft-documented fact of life in the latter part of the twentieth century. Jobs that formerly required nothing more than a desire to work now require a high school diploma. Jobs once open to high school graduates (e.g., entry-level management positions) now require two to four years of college (Berg 1970; Rumberger 1981). Some economists argue that the most important function of contemporary education is credentialing—the late twentieth century's method of ascribing status and opportunity in an otherwise anonymous world (Thurow 1972; Illich 1975).

For undereducated and low-skilled immigrants without credentials there are few opportunities, and there are fewer still for Mexican immigrants, who are likely to be undocumented and totally dependent upon one employer. Mexican Americans are the only ethnic group in this century to have been brought to the United States specifically as unskilled laborers, trapped in that role, not by slavery, but by a legal arrangement that disallowed them any other occupational recourse (Chapa 1988). To have left the fields meant deportation under the Bracero program, which brought significant numbers of Mexicans to the United States at mid century. The Immigration Reform and Control Act of 1986 renews this particular form of occupational confinement.

An Established Identity

Notwithstanding recent immigration, Mexican Americans have been in the United States for as long as the United States has existed, making them a semi-indigenous population (Cortes 1980). Hence, Mexican Americans and Anglo-Americans have a long history of interaction—much of it not very positive. They also have long-standing and well-formed ideas about each other. The particular characteristics ascribed to Mexican Americans are documented in a large body of literature (see, for example, Carter and Segura 1979). They are commonly described as passive, fatalistic, unable to delay gratification, and having low levels of aspiration. Through scholarly literature as well as social consensus, Mexican Americans have been assigned a "script": They are America's field-workers and urban shadows. They toil for low wages at menial jobs because they don't aspire to anything better. Their children don't perform well in school because the parents don't understand the importance of education. Low socioeconomic status is attributed to the family failing to provide the proper motivation; to the church, perpetuating the notions of obedience and fatalism; to the culture, being insulated and cliquish; and even to the language, because in its grammatical forms it releases the speaker from any responsibility for his or her actions (*se me hizo tarde*, "it got late for me," rather than the English form, "I am late"). It can be argued that the identity of the Mexican American is firmly fixed in the collective consciousness of the American communities in which Chicanos live and to varying degrees has been internalized in the minds of Mexican Americans. Although they may not agree with their role, they are well aware of it, and like actors who have been typecast, they may find it almost impossible to change the perception of who they are.

Vulnerability to Risk

Ogbu and Matute-Bianchi (1986) attribute the special vulnerability of Mexican Americans to linguistic and ethnic risk factors to what they call "a folk theory of success" (a way of conceptualizing success and how one achieves it) that is oppositional to the demands of American schooling and social structure. They contend that Chicanos, recognizing that the deck is stacked against them, have refused to play the game. The Chicano folk theory of success does not include examples of ethnic group members who, after generations in the fields and factories, meet with great social or economic success. Unlike the immigrants who come to this country with the idea that any achievement will surpass the conditions of their homeland and that hard work will conquer all, Chicanos, whether new to this country or not, look to the example of their people, who have been trapped in a cycle of poverty for generations, and conclude that there is really no way to win; the Anglo holds all the aces. Moreover, there is evidence that they may have assessed the situation accurately. In several studies of the returns on education for Hispanics, researchers have consistently found that, in contrast to non-Hispanic whites, Hispanics without a high school diploma earn relatively little less than those with a diploma (Stern 1985) and are only slightly more likely to be unemployed (Rumberger 1991). Furthermore, historical data suggest that the economic incentives for Hispanics to graduate from high school appear to be diminishing (Rumberger 1987).

In contrast to this folk theory of success postulated by Ogbu and Matute-Bianchi (1985), my own research on factors that contribute to educational success for Mexican Americans from low-income homes has uncovered a consistent theme of prior successes or prestige in the families of individuals who were academically successful (Gandara n.d.). As children, study subjects were often regaled with stories that can only be described as "legends of the golden past"—stories about how some member of the family had once held a prestigious position or how the family was once owners of its own lands. The message conveyed to the children seemed to be, "We are in difficult circumstances now, but this is only temporary, because we have a heritage of success." These family legends provide a competing and more functional folk theory of success—one of hope and possibilities.

Another finding of this research that sheds light on the issue of vulnerability to risk was the disproportionately large numbers of very successful Mexican Americans who came from border communities. Grebler, Moore, and Guzman (1970) also make passing reference to the fact that border towns tend to spawn particularly successful Chicanos. Speculation about why this may be comes from study subjects themselves. They hypothesized that because the border towns of the Southwest are so heavily populated with Mexicans, and hence the important roles in the community—mayor, police chief, and so on—are held by Mexicans, these children don't learn the "script" of underachievers. They grow up with possibilities.

In summary, the case of Mexican Americans serves to illustrate a number of points about educational risk, with implications for other ethnic groups: First, the classic model of cultural assimilation based on earlier European immigrants is an inadequate tool of analysis for groups immigrating to this country in the latter half of the twentieth century and/or semi-indigenous ethnic-groups. The power of the model has been compromised by changing economic circumstances and the unique histories of some groups. We cannot assume that the problems of all ethnic groups will be solved with enough time, and nothing else.

Second, when a minority group loses hope that it will be able to enter the main-stream, language and cultural differences may place them at serious risk of educational failure. Conversely, ethnic groups who view their situation as hopeful are likely to overcome the effects of language and cultural differences that might otherwise have put them at risk for educational failure.

Third, lack of hopefulness may also obscure for some students the true advantages of biculturalism. In a world that grows smaller every day, no country can afford to squander the cultural and linguistic capital that its immigrants and minority communities bring with them. Students who have been perceived as liabilities need to be reconceptualized as assets in the schools and in the society as a whole. Adopting the culture of the school should not require that they reject the culture and language of the home.

Finally, to break the cycle of failure for particular at-risk minorities, we may have to intervene in a timely fashion with more than vague words of encouragement. Hopefulness results from having seen the possibilities. Enfranchised groups *know* that education makes many things possible; they have seen it in their own homes and communities and it is a part of their history. We must teach *all* children to believe in the power of their own heritage. They need to know what is proud and noble about their own ancestry. One is reminded of the exhortations of Jaime Escalante, the barrio calculus teacher portrayed in the film *Stand and Deliver,* as he addresses a Chicano student plagued with self-doubt: "Do you know who invented the zero? Not the Greeks, not the Egyptians, the Mayans. Math is in your blood!"

NOTE

For purposes of this paper, the terms *Mexican American* and *Chicano* are used interchangeably. Likewise, *Anglo American* and *non-Hispanic white* both refer to majority-culture Americans.

REFERENCES

Arce, Carlos, Edward Murquia, and W. Parker Frisbie. 1987. Phenotype and life chances among Chicanos. *Hispanic Journal of Behavioral Sciences* 9:19-32.

Baratz, Joan C., and Richard Duran. 1985. *The educational progress of language minority students: Findings from the 1983-84 WACP reading survey.* Princeton, N.J.: National Assessment of Education Progress/ETS.

Bean, Frank D., and Marta Tienda. 1987. *The Hispanic population of the*

United States. New York: Russell Sage.

Berz, Ivar. 1970. *Education and jobs: The great training robbery.* New York: Praeger.

Bikson, Tora. 1974. *Do they talk the same language?* Santa Monica, Calif.: Rand Corp.

California Department of Finance. 1990. K-12 public school enrollments. Sacramento, Calif.: Populations Research Unit.

Carter, Thomas P. 1970. *Mexican Americans: A history of educational neglect.* New York: College Entrance Examination Board.

Carter, Thomas P., and Roberto Segura. 1979. *Mexican Americans in school: A decade of change.* New York: College Entrance Examination Board.

Chapa, Jorge. 1988. The question of Mexican American Assimilation: Socioeconomic parity or underclass formation? *Public Affairs Comment,* 35, 1-14.

Chiswick, Barry. 1979. The economic progress of immigrants: Some apparently universal patterns. In *Contemporary economic problems,* ed. William Fellner. Washington, D.C.: American Enterprise Institute.

Chiswick, Barry. 1980. Immigrant earning patterns by sex, race, and ethnic groupings. *Monthly Labor Review* 3:22-25.

Cortes, Carlos. 1980. Mexicans. In *Harvard encyclopedia of American ethnic groups,* 697-719. Cambridge: Harvard University Press.

Cummins, James. 1984. *Bilingualism and special education: Issues in assessment and pedagogy.* San Diego, Calif.: College Hill Press.

Darcy, N. T. 1953. A review of the literature on the effects of bilingualism upon the measurement of intelligence. *Journal of Genetic Psychology* 82:259-82.

Doeringer, P. B., and M. J. Piore. 1975. Unemployment and the dual labor market. *The Public Interest* 38:67-79.

Frender, Robert, and William E. Lambert. 1972. Speech style and scholastic success: The tentative relationships and possible implications for lower social class children. In *Monograph Series on Languages and Linguistics,* ed. R. Shuy, no. 25, 237-71. Washington, D.C.: Georgetown University Press.

Gandara, Patricia. 1986. Chicanos in higher education: The politics of self-interest. *American Journal of Education* 95:256-72.

————. n.d. *Through the eye of the needle: High achieving Chicanos from low income backgrounds*. Manuscript.

Glazer, N., and D. Moynihan. 1963. *Beyond the melting pot*. Cambridge: MIT Press.

Gordon, Milton. 1964. *Assimilation in American life: The role of race, religion, and national origins*. New York: Oxford University Press.

Grebler, Leo, Joan W. Moore, and Ralph C. Guzman. 1970. *The Mexican-American people: The nation's second largest minority*. New York: Free Press.

Hoffman, Mark, ed. 1991. *1992 World Almanac*. New York: St. Martin Press, 77.

Illich, Ivan. 1975. Why we must disestablish schools. In *Schooling in a Corporate Society*, ed. M. Carnoy, 2d ed., 340-61. New York: David McKay Co.

Kagan, Spencer. 1986. Cooperative learning and sociocultural factors in schooling. In California Bilingual Education Office, eds., *Beyond Language*. Los Angeles: Evaluation, Dissemination, and Assessment Center, California State University.

Kimball, William L. 1968. *Parent and family influences on academic achievement among Mexican-American Students*. Ph.D. diss., University of California, Los Angeles.

Lambert, William E., Richard Hodgson, R. C. Gardner, and Steven Fillenbaum. 1960. Evaluational reactions to spoken languages. *Journal of Abnormal and Social Psychology* 60:44-51.

Lugo, James O. 1970. *A comparison of degrees of bilingualism and measure of school achievement among Mexican American pupils*. Ph.D. diss. Los Angeles: University of Southern California.

Marshall, F. R., and L. F. Bouvier. 1986. *Population change and the future of Texas*. Washington, D.C.: Population Reference Bureau.

McCarthy, K. F., and R. B. Valdez. 1986. *Current and future effects of Mexican immigration in California* (R-3365-CR) Santa Monica, Calif.: Rand Corp.

Muller, Thomas, and T. J. Espenshade. 1984. *The fourth wave*. Washington, D.C.: Urban Institute Press.

Nava, J. 1972. *Los Mexicano-Americanos, pasado, presente, y futuro*. New York: American Book Co.

Ogbu, John, and Maria E. Matute-Bianchi. 1986. Understanding sociocultural factors: Knowledge and school adjustment. In *Beyond Language*, ed. Los Angeles: Evaluation, Dissemination, and Assessment Center, California State University.

Olneck, M., and M. Lazerson. 1974. The school achievement of immigrant children: 1900-1930. *History of Education Quarterly* 14:453-82.

──── . 1980. Education. In *Harvard encyclopedia of American ethnic groups*, 303-19. Cambridge: Harvard University Press.

Olsen, Laurie. 1988. *Crossing the schoolhouse border*. San Francisco: California Tomorrow.

Orfield, Gary. 1988. The growth and concentration of Hispanic enrollment and the future of American education. Paper presented at the National Council of La Raza Conference, Albuquerque, New Mexico, July.

Phillips, Kevin. 1990. *The politics of rich and poor*. New York: Random House.

Rumberger, Russell. 1981. The rising incidence of overeducation in the U.S. labor market. *Economics of Education Review* 1:293-314.

──── . 1987. High school dropouts: A review of issues and evidence. *Review of Educational Research*, 57:101-121.

──── . 1991. Chicano Dropouts: A Review of Research and Policy Issues. In *Chicano School Failure and Success*, ed. Valencia, R. New York: The Falmer Press.

Schwartz, Joe. 1988. Hispanics in the eighties. *American Demographics* 18:33-45.

Segalowitz, Norman. 1977. Psychological perspectives on bilingual education. In *Frontiers of bilingual education*, ed. B. Spolsky and R. Cooper. Rowley, Mass.: Newbury House.

Stern, David. 1985. Educational attainment and employment of major racial or ethnic groups in California. Paper presented at the Conference on Educational Underachievement of Linguistic Minorities, 30 May-1 June, University of California, Berkeley, California.

Taylor, J. Edward. 1986. *Schooling and economic adjustments of California's immigrants*. Washington, D.C.: Urban Institute.

Thurow, Lester C. 1972. Education and economic equality. *The Public Interest* 28:66-81.

U.S. Commission on Civil Rights. 1972. *The excluded student. Report 3: Educational practices affecting Mexican-Americans in the Southwest*.

Washington, D.C.: U.S. Government Printing Office.

———. 1973. *Teachers and students. Report 5: Mexican American education study, differences in teacher interaction with Mexican-American and Anglo students.* Washington, D.C.: U.S. Government Printing Office.

———. 1975. *A better chance to learn: Bilingual bicultural education* (Clearinghouse publication no. 51). Washington, D.C.: Government Printing Office.

Western Interstate Commission on Higher Education. 1988. *Demography and Higher Education in the Changing Southwest.* Boulder, Colo.

P. LINDSAY CHASE-LANSDALE
MARIS A. VINOVSKIS

9

Adolescent Pregnancy and Child Support

Sometimes seemingly closely intertwined social policy issues are discussed and dealt with separately. Such is the case with the issues of child support enforcement and adolescent pregnancy. The problems associated with adolescent pregnancies and inadequate child support payments by noncustodial fathers are receiving considerable attention, but until recently, few analysts or policymakers have examined these problems simultaneously. Given the increasing proportion and number of out-of-wedlock births among teenagers, questions about the financial role and responsibility of the absent father become more pressing.

This essay documents the recent trends in adolescent childbearing and out-of-wedlock births and the financial strains these place upon the young mother and the nation's welfare system. After a brief review of fathers' responsibility for out-of-wedlock births in the past, the current policies to increase child support payments by all absent fathers will be examined. In addition, the father's emotional role in the raising of young children will be discussed. Finally, specific problems involved in obtaining child support assistance from absent fathers for the offspring of adolescent mothers will be considered. By bringing together concerns about adolescent pregnancies and child support payments, perhaps we can expand and enrich the current policy discussions on each of these topics.

ADOLESCENT CHILDBEARING AND OUT-OF-WEDLOCK BIRTHS

Public concern about adolescent pregnancies and childbearing grew during the mid 1970s as the news media and policymakers emphasized the "epidemic" nature of this problem (Alan Guttmacher Institute, 1976). Although commentators acknowledged that some teenage pregnancies existed in the past, most focused on the current pregnancies and childbearing. To cope with this "epidemic" of teenage pregnancies, federal officials called for new programs to prevent unintended pregnancies and to alleviate the negative consequences of early childbearing (U.S. Congress 1978). Indeed, the Carter administration made the issue of adolescent pregnancy one of its highest domestic priorities when it proposed the Adolescent Health, Services, and Pregnancy Prevention Act of 1978 (Vinovskis 1986, 1988a).

Demographics of Adolescent Parenthood

A glance at the statistics on adolescent childbearing, however, suggests that the problem is not as recent and unprecedented as it has often been depicted as being. Adolescent childbearing increased sharply after World War II and reached a peak of 97.3 births per one thousand women ages fifteen to nineteen in 1957. Thereafter, the rate declined steadily during the 1960s and 1970s—in part because the Supreme Court's legalization of abortions in 1973 provided another option for pregnant teenagers. By 1986 the birthrate per one thousand women ages fifteen to nineteen had dropped from the peak of 97.3 to 50.6 (Hofferth and Hayes 1987; U.S. Bureau of the Census 1989, table 85).

Due to the increased number of teenagers during the 1960s and 1970s, the total number of births to women under age twenty did rise from 557,000 in 1957 to a high of 656,000 in

1970. Since then the total number of births to teenagers has also declined, and in 1986 there were 472,000 births to women under age twenty—15.3 percent less than even in 1957 (Hofferth and Hayes 1987; U.S. Bureau of the Census 1989, table 85).

While the rate or number of children born to adolescents may have peaked earlier, this does not mean that teenage pregnancy is not a serious, national problem. Forrest (cited in Hayes 1987, 51) estimated in 1981 that 43 percent of all adolescent girls would become pregnant by age twenty—a slightly higher figure than five years earlier. Significant differences were also evident between whites and blacks—40 percent of white teenage girls and 63 percent of black teenage girls would be pregnant before their twentieth birthday. The number of abortions among teenagers, just one indication of the undesirability of many of these adolescent pregnancies, rose dramatically from 244,070 in 1973 to 427,680 in 1983 (Moore 1987). Furthermore, numerous studies (Furstenberg, Brooks-Gunn, and Morgan 1987; Moore and Burt 1982; Furstenberg, Brooks-Gunn, and Chase-Lansdale 1989) have documented the adverse impact of teenage childbearing on the young mother and her child, such as truncated educational and occupational attainment for mothers and, for children, developmental delay, behavior problems, and school failure.

Nonmarital Childbearing

Although the total number of births to adolescents has decreased somewhat over time, the proportion of them occurring outside of marriage has risen dramatically. O'Connell and Rogers (1984) have estimated that the percentage of first births conceived out-of-wedlock, in adolescents ages fifteen to nineteen, rose from 30.1 percent in the period 1950-54 to 71.6 percent in 1980-81. At the same time, the proportion of premarital pregnancies followed by marriage declined from about one-half to less than one-third during this period. As a result, there has been a significant increase in the proportion and number of out-of-wedlock births to adolescent mothers.

Specifically, the proportion of out-of-wedlock teenage births has risen from 14.9 percent in 1955 to 58.7 percent in 1985. Again, there are significant racial differences. While 45.1 percent of white teen births are out-of-wedlock, 90.0 percent of black teen births are out-of-wedlock. The total number of teen births out-of-wedlock has increased from 72,800 in 1955 to 280,300 in 1985—a 285.0 percent increase in three decades (Hofferth and Hayes 1987; National Center for Health Statistics 1987).

Teenage parenting is not only difficult for the individuals involved, but it is expensive for society. Of all mothers under age twenty, one-third receive assistance from Aid to Families with Dependent Children (AFDC) (Moore 1987). Furthermore, those most likely to stay on AFDC for ten years or more are young unmarried women with children under three years of age (Bane and Ellwood 1983). The single-year cost in 1985 for AFDC, food stamps, and Medicaid for mothers who had a first birth as a teenager was $16.65 billion dollars (Burt 1986). Moreover, taxpayers will pay an additional $13,902 over the next twenty years for each new family created by a birth to an adolescent girl in 1985. Thus, the substantial welfare costs associated with early childbearing, especially to unmarried adolescent mothers, has led some to call for a reexamination of the financial responsibility of the absent fathers.

EFFORTS TO IMPROVE CHILD SUPPORT PAYMENTS

Historical Synthesis

Throughout our past, the assumption has been that both parents are responsible for raising and caring for their children (Hartley 1975). If a child was born out-of-wedlock, there was strong community pressure for the father to marry the mother or at least provide adequate financial support so that the child would not become a public burden (Demos 1982; Rothman 1984). Among the early New England Puritans, there was also a strong sense of moral outrage against nonmarital births, whereas among their Chesapeake counterparts the concern was only about the potential financial liability to the community of an out-of-wedlock birth (Karlsen 1987; Walsh 1979). Destitute young children, especially those who were orphans, usually were placed with relatives or neighbors and sometimes also received private or public charity from the local community. Older children were often apprenticed to someone in order to relieve the community of the cost of providing for them as well as to teach them an appropriate trade (Kulikoff 1986; Rutman and Rutman 1984).

Fathers were regarded as the primary financial providers,

and mothers were discouraged from entering the paid labor force unless dire economic circumstances necessitated it (Mason, Vinovskis, and Hareven 1978). Single women found it difficult, if not impossible, to provide adequately for their families without outside support (Lebsock 1984). Nevertheless, nineteenth-century widows were expected to reenter the paid labor force and to send their older children to work in order to reduce the need for any welfare (Grigg 1984). Public assistance usually was denied to children of never-married or divorced women who had offended community values (Katz 1986; Trattner 1989).

In the early twentieth century, reformers argued that children should be cared for by their own mothers at home. Several states enacted mothers' pensions so that poor, deserving widows could remain at home to raise their young children. Never-married or black mothers were frequently denied assistance by local authorities, and even those who received such support usually had to supplement it with their own earnings. Thus, while there was an increased willingness to provide public support for children whose fathers had died, less sympathy and assistance were provided for those whose fathers had abandoned them, and black mothers in particular experienced unfair discriminating treatment (Orloff 1988; Lehrer 1987).

As part of the Social Security reforms of the New Deal, Aid to Dependent Children (ADC) was established in 1935. This program broadened the definition of dependent children by explicitly providing for children of separated, divorced, and never-married mothers as well as widows. The level of benefits through ADC was also higher than hitherto available in the state mothers' pension programs—particularly for most widows under the provisions of the Survivor's Insurance law enacted in 1939, who now received higher benefits than were available under ADC (Lopata and Brehm 1986). Finally, states had to create statewide agencies to administer the ADC benefits, and appeals were now possible for those denied assistance. As a result, although there was still discrimination in providing assistance to never-married or black mothers, it was an improvement over the previous decades (Bell 1965).

Under Aid to Dependent Children, the absent father was financially responsible for supporting his own child, and state agencies were empowered to force him to contribute to the state ADC program to offset the benefits paid to his dependent child. In practice, however, most states did not devote much energy or resources to pursuing absent fathers, and only a small proportion of these fathers contributed assistance—a characteristic that would remain part of the welfare system even when Aid to Dependent Children was expanded in 1950 and became Aid to Families with Dependent Children (Garfinkel and McLanahan 1986).

As the number of divorces rose in the late nineteenth and early twentieth centuries, divorced wives were often granted alimony and child support through the judicial system (Griswold 1982; May 1980). The problem, however, was that many divorced mothers were denied court-awarded assistance from their former husbands, and others received only a token amount. The economic situation of the divorced mother often became more difficult as no-fault divorces in effect eliminated alimony payments and left only child support obligations. Furthermore, a sizable proportion of court-awarded alimony and child support payments was delinquent, and local and state authorities often did little to force the divorced father to comply (Weitzman 1985).

In colonial and nineteenth-century America, many children lived for a time in single-parent households due to the higher rates of adult mortality (Uhlenberg 1980; Vinovskis 1976). Today, fewer children under eighteen experience the death of a parent, but many more are affected by the sharp increases in out-of-wedlock births and divorces (Cherlin 1989; Rodgers 1986). Duncan and Rodgers (1987) estimate that 35.5 percent of children born between 1967 and 1969 spent some time in a one-parent family—30.3 percent of white children and 72.4 percent of black children. By age eighteen, white children had spent an average of 1.52 years in a one-parent family, while black children had spent 7.24 years.

Many of the early public assistance programs were primarily intended to help children whose parents had died rather than those whose parents had not married or had divorced (Bell 1965). In 1940 the death of a parent accounted for 42 percent of the caseloads in the ADC program, but by 1982 less than 1 percent of the children in the AFDC program were eligible because of the death of a parent (Lima and Harris 1988). In addition, the costs of welfare assistance have risen dramatically. Government expenditures per mother-only family rose from $2,568 in 1955 to $7,402 in 1975 (in constant 1983 dollars) (Garfinkel and McLanahan 1986). As a result, taxpayers are increasingly concerned about the seemingly high welfare expenditures going to families where the absent father is not living up to his historic responsibility for providing for the mother and his child (Vinovskis 1988b).

Recent Reforms in Child Support Enforcement

During the 1950s and 1960s, several efforts were made to use federal legislation to obtain more child support payments from absent fathers, but they were largely ineffective. On 4 January, 1975, however, President Gerald Ford signed Public Law 93-647, which established the Child Support Enforcement (CSE) Program as Part D of Title IV of the Social Security Act, which mandated that for both AFDC and non-AFDC cases, states were required to set up services to locate absent parents, establish paternity, establish support obligations, enforce support obligations, and assist in the collection of support payments (Katz 1983). Together with the Child Support Enforcement Amendments of 1984, which expanded and improved the process of establishing and enforcing support obligations, this legislation has helped to improve total child support collections from $1 million in 1978 to $2.7 million in 1985. The percentage of AFDC assistance payments recovered through child support collections has risen slightly, from 5.6 percent in 1979 to 7.3 percent in 1985 (Lima and Harris 1988).

Improvements have been made in child support payments during the past decade, but much remains to be done, as states have enforced these new federal regulations selectively. The ten states most successful in recovering AFDC payments recouped 15.7 percent of the expenses (with 25.0 percent of AFDC parents absent from the home paying some child support), while the worst ten only recovered 3.9 percent of AFDC expenses (with 4.1 percent of AFDC parents absent from the home paying some child support) (Kahn and Kamerman 1988). Furthermore, the administrative costs of the system remain high, with $3.34 total child support payments collected (AFDC and non-AFDC) per dollar of total administrative expenses of the program (Lima and Harris 1988).

Nationally, the problem of non-child-support by absent fathers continues despite the recent improvements in state and federal collection efforts. In 1985 only 61.3 percent of all women eighteen and over with children (under age twenty-one) and an absent father had been awarded any children support, and of these, only about three-fourths received any actual payments. Furthermore, among never-married mothers, only 18.4 percent were ever awarded any child support assistance from the father (U.S. Bureau of the Census 1989, table 609).

One very promising and innovative social welfare experiment is the Wisconsin Child Support Assurance Program, which was introduced in ten counties in 1984. A child support standard based upon a percentage of the noncustodial parents' income is established, and judges and family court commissioners are supposed to follow these guidelines. Children are assured of a certain minimum level of support regardless of the amount collected from the absent parent, and the state is allowed to withhold the wages of that parent to help finance the program (Garfinkel 1988).

Using national data from 1979, Oellerich and Garfinkel (1983) estimated that if a child insurance program were devised as an alternative to the current AFDC system, substantial improvements would be made in reducing the extent of poverty among mother-headed families. Based upon a minimum annual benefit of $2,500 for the first child and assuming an 80 percent effective collection system, 40 percent of the difference between the income of the eligible poor family and the income needed for that family to move above the poverty line would be reduced. There would also be a 49 percent reduction in AFDC caseloads and an overall savings of about half a billion dollars in federal and state welfare costs.

Family Support Act

The passage of the Family Support Act in 1988 ushered in a composite of changes in our nation's welfare system that do, in fact, highlight the poor economic prospects of never-married young mothers and thus strengthen the child support enforcement system even further (Chase-Lansdale and Vinovskis 1989). The overall goal of the reform inherent in the Family Support Act is to change our welfare system from one of income maintenance to one that assists impoverished families in becoming economically self-sufficient. Child support enforcement is one of a number of such changes, including mandatory education, job training, and employment for participants in AFDC.

The new child support enforcement policies in the Family

Support Act are a continuation and strengthening of the policy changes over the past fifteen years, as detailed above. The child support provisions focus on state guidelines for award amounts, the establishment of paternity, and the payment of awards (Garfinkel and McLanahan 1989). Guidelines for award sizes will be more uniform, as they must follow state-established formulas and not the discretion of individual judges. Of particular relevance to adolescent mothers is the new provision that states must establish fathers' identities for a minimum of one-half of AFDC children born out-of-wedlock, and Social Security numbers of both mothers and fathers are required in order for birth certificates to be issued. Furthermore, states must conduct genetic tests of paternity (usually blood tests) whenever there is disagreement between possible parents as to paternity, and the federal government will cover 90 percent of the costs of the test. Finally, wages are automatically withheld from absent fathers of children on AFDC, as opposed to the previous system, which mandated wage withholding only after fathers had failed to make payments. Garfinkel and McLanahan (1989) estimate that if all three new provisions are successfully implemented, the amount of child support paid by absent fathers will increase dramatically.

THE EMOTIONAL ROLE OF THE FATHER

So far in this essay we have documented the dramatic increase in the rate of out-of-wedlock births to adolescent girls, emphasizing the economic burdens upon the teen mother herself and society at large. Having continued an examination of the father's economic role in our discussion of U.S. policies toward child support enforcement, we now turn to a third issue that merits significant attention: What is the emotional role of the father in families?

Historical Perspective

Until very recently (i.e., within the last ten to fifteen years), the field of child development has largely ignored or minimized the role of the father in child development (Lamb 1976; Bloom-Feshbach 1981). The mother-child relationship has been viewed as central and unique to the child's healthy psychological growth. Currently there is heightened interest in the role of the father and acknowledgment of his importance in families, both in popular media and in scientific inquiry. Yet many of the recent discussions and investigations have focused narrowly upon the present without taking into account the varying role of the father in U.S. society in previous centuries (Vinovskis 1988a). We will first present a brief historical analysis of the changing role of the American father over time. This will be followed by a synthesis of what is known from current research about the father's impact on child development. It will immediately become evident that today's recognition of the importance of fathers' participation in family life is not new. At times in the past, fathers have been quite involved in the lives of their children (Moran and Vinovskis 1986).

This was particularly the case in seventeenth-century New England. The role of the Puritan father in the family was central and included far more than economic support. As the head of the household, the father had as his major responsibility the socialization and education of the children, with particular emphasis on religious training. Fathers taught their children to read and to study the Bible (Lockridge 1974). Fathers were also the primary disciplinarians of children. There is controversy, however, as to the nature of their emotional involvement with their children. Some scholars (Shorter 1975; Stone 1977) have concluded that seventeenth-century fathers were distant and aloof, while others (Demos 1982) contend that colonial fathers had affectionate, expressive relationships with their offspring. In contrast, mothers during this historical period were seen as assistants to the father, as socialization agents particularly responsible for physical care (Vinvoskis 1988a).

The eighteenth and nineteenth centuries witnessed a gradual diminution of the predominance of the father as socializer of the child. This was due to several major societal changes. In the eighteenth century, women became more active than men in the Puritan church and as a result competed effectively for the role of catechizing young children (Moran 1980). Consequently, women received support and tutelage from the community and church for their own education, with the goal of improving their abilities as spiritual teachers.

A second major factor in the decrease of paternal involvement in this period was the change in fathers' mode of economic support. In the late eighteenth and early nineteenth centuries, fathers' work changed from home-based to work outside the home, a pattern that was made widespread and permanent by the growth of a market economy and industrialization. Increasingly, the geographic separation of homes from the work place in nineteenth-century cities further reduced fathers' direct involvement in childrearing. The void left by fathers' withdrawal was replaced by mothers, who saw their roles enhanced by the beliefs of medical and educational experts that mothers were particularly suited for the care of young children (May and Vinovskis 1977).

In the nineteenth century, the doctrine of "separate spheres" and the "cult of domesticity" became firmly entrenched (Degler 1980), and by the end of the century the bond between mothers and children was the centerpiece of family life. An interesting indication of this was the change in the judicial decisions regarding child custody after divorce. Until the midnineteenth century, custody of the children had been awarded predominantly to the father. In the latter half of the nineteenth century, judges began awarding custody to women, reflecting the prevailing view that mothers were more important to the child's well-being and should not be separated from young children (Vinovskis 1988a). This practice became even more pronounced in the twentieth century and known as the "tender years doctrine" (Emery and Wyer 1987).

Thus, by the 1950s both scientists and the public came to see a diminished role of the father in raising children. The fifteen years immediately following World War II in particular were an unusual period of economic growth and marital stability, involving traditional roles for mothers and fathers (Cherlin 1981; Bloom-Feshbach 1981). Fathers were seen as "breadwinners" (Lamb 1986), and mothers were viewed as "naturally suited" for childrearing (Vinovskis 1988a).

Since 1960, a number of major demographic changes have altered the structure and functioning of American families. These are familiar statistics, involving dramatic increases in divorce and maternal employment as well as decreases in fertility. The labor force participation of married women with children under age six has soared from 18.6 percent in 1960 to 57.1 percent in 1988. Similarly, the divorce rate has significantly increased, from 9.2 divorces per one thousand married women ages fifteen and above, in 1960, to a rate of 21.7 in 1985. The total fertility rate has declined from 3.7 children per woman in 1955 to 1.8 children per woman in 1986 (U.S. Bureau of the Census 1989, tables 639, 127, and 87).

In part because of changes in family structures and in women's roles in the past two decades, the father's role in family life has also come under scrutiny and has been reexamined. Some have called the father of the present era the "nurturant father" (Lamb 1986) or the "post-modern father" (Pleck 1986)— that is, one who continues to be the primary breadwinner but also participates extensively in family life and offers more direct affection, counsel, and discipline to children than fathers in the past. Two of the many examples of such increased involvement are fathers' presence in the delivery room (Parke and Beitel 1986) and their greater likelihood of obtaining custody of their children after divorce (Santrock and Warshak 1986).

Child Development Research

Although greater father involvement during the 1970s an 1980s cannot be denied, we also caution that this is not universally true in U.S. society (Lamb 1986; Parke and Tinsley 1984). Nevertheless, accompanying the cultural shift in expectations for fathers' roles has been a significant change in scientific fields related to child development. In 1975, Lamb published an article entitled "Fathers: Forgotten Contributors to Child Development" (Lamb 1975). Since that time researchers in child development have moved beyond an exclusive focus on the mother-child relationship as the central way of conceptualizing child development.

Father-child relationships have been increasingly studied over the past ten years, and more importantly, theoretical development has occurred, so that now children are studied within a family context (Belsky 1981; Chase-Lansdale and Owen 1987; Pedersen 1981). In other words, there is growing impetus within scientific inquiry that the whole family should be taken into account and viewed as an organized system, comprised of several interdependent relationships, or subsystems (Hetherington and Camara 1984; Parke and Tinsley 1984; Reiss 1981; Sroufe et al. 1985). In order to predict child development, it is necessary to understand the quality of all the subsystems, or relationships, within the family (e.g., mother/child, father/child, and mother/father relationships).

The body of literature on the influence of the father on child development is still underdeveloped. However, a number of findings can be summarized. To date, there have been two major ways of conceptualizing the father's impact on the child: (1) direct effects and (2) indirect effects (mediated through the mother). In addition, findings from the father-absence literature have contributed to an understanding of the father's influence.

Direct Effects

Regarding direct effects, a broad conclusion to be drawn is that fathers can be instrumental in their children's emotional development, psychological adjustment, and cognitive growth. We will briefly review the following areas: emotional ties, peer relations, sex typing, and cognitive development.

Emotional Ties. Children develop very strong emotional ties to their fathers. Contrary to the prevailing view of the 1960s and 1970s (e.g., Bowlby 1969), the mother is not the sole, monolithic attachment figure for the child. Fathers too are attachment figures, and infants' attachment relationships to fathers emerge at the same time as attachment to mothers, around seven months of age (Lamb 1977), and continue into adulthood (Main, Kaplan, and Cassidy 1985). As with infant/mother attachment, there is variability in the quality of infant/father attachment, with two-thirds of infants developing secure attachment relationships, and one-third with insecure attachments, to mothers and fathers (Main and Weston 1981).

Mothers and fathers treat children in different ways, and most of the research focuses on infants and preschoolers. Mothers are more likely to be responsible for caretaking activities, while fathers tend to be affiliative playmates, engaging in far more physical, arousing play than mothers, who are usually more verbally communicative (Belsky, Gilstrap, and Rovine 1984; Lamb 1976; Parke and Tinsley 1984).

While infants and young children prefer their mothers over their fathers in time of stress (illness, fatigue, injury), this should not diminish conclusions regarding the emotional salience of fathers. For example, the majority of children, especially those under age six, are highly upset when they learn of their parents' plans to divorce and in particular show intense separation anxiety (fearfulness, distress, infantile behaviors, anger) when the father departs the household (Chase-Lansdale and Hetherington 1990). Regular, frequent visitation by the noncustodial father is an important factor in soothing children's separation fears and emotional distress. Furthermore, children who show the best psychological adjustment after parental divorce are those who have healthy close relationships with *both* parents (Camara and Resnick 1988; Hetherington, Cox, and Cox 1982; Peterson and Zill 1986).

Sex Typing. A second important area of fathers' influence is sex-role development. Fathers' sex-typing behavior toward boys and girls is more extreme than that of mothers (Fagot 1974). Fathers serve as examples of masculinity for boys and girls, and if fathers are affectionate and authoritative toward their sons and daughters, the children's sex-role behavior is promoted (Radin 1982; Sears, Maccoby, and Levin 1957). Fathers are particularly influential in the development of daughters' femininity; appropriate, close father/daughter relationships teach girls about femininity in the context of male responses (Hetherington 1972; Johnson 1963). Available data suggest that when young girls lose their fathers due to divorce or death, they experience disturbances in female identity and show inappropriate sexual behavior in adolescence (Chase-Lansdale and Hetherington 1990).

Other areas of direct effects of fathers include emotional development, peer relations, and cognitive development. These areas are particularly understudied. New work by Parke and his associates (e.g., MacDonald and Parke 1984) suggests that fathers' physical play and emotional arousal with children not only contributes to children's own experience of a range of affect, but also enables them to distinguish and regulate emotions appropriately, a skill that facilitates the children's peer relations. In terms of cognitive development and achievement, the little available evidence suggests that paternal involvement and warmth are related to improved cognitive development and achievement in sons. Fathers' influence on girls in this domain is not as clear (Radin 1982).

Indirect Effects

There are two major mechanisms by which fathers indirectly affect their children: (1) economic support, and (2) emotional support to the mother. We have discussed economic support in previous sections. We would like to reiterate here that adequate economic support is related to healthy child development. Children growing up in poverty are at risk for problems in cognitive development, psychological adjustment, and educational attainment (Brooks-Gunn 1989; Furstenberg, Brooks-Gunn, and Morgan 1987; Lee, Brooks-Gunn, and Schnur 1988). In addition, whether in poverty or not, single mothers experience great stress due to economic uncertainty, and this in turn negatively affects the child.

With regard to emotional support of the mother, the father influences his children indirectly in a number of ways. The first is via a harmonious marital relationship. A harmonious marriage promotes healthy child development, presumably by providing a positive context for family life and a positive model of human interaction (Cowan and Cowan 1988; Peterson and Zill 1986). A second form of emotional support to the mother is the father's encouragement and praise for her efficacy as a mother. When fathers are supportive to mothers in this way, the mother's own parenting (i.e., responsiveness toward younger children, effective discipline toward older children) is positively affected, as is child outcome (Gjerde, Block, and Block 1986; Parke and Tinsley 1984).

Finally, fathers also provide emotional support to mothers by directly assisting in parenting themselves, thus alleviating, at times, mothers' responsibility and burden for full-time child care. There have been very few studies of the effects of fathers' assistance in coparenting, but the divorce literature indicates that single mothers are highly stressed by the overload of sole parenting combined with household and job responsibilities. Divorced mothers who receive some parenting assistance from their ex-husbands adjust more readily to their single-parent status and experience fewer problems in parenting (Hetherington, Cox, and Cox 1982).

To summarize, the father can play a very important role in the psychological development of his children. He offers special attributes to family life and is not interchangeable with the mother. His role in the family affects his children's economic well-being, their attachment to him, their sex-role and cognitive development, and their emotional adjustment. Father absence due to divorce has serious consequences for children, as mediated not only by the separation from him, his unavailability, but also by stressors associated with motherhood and any pre-existing or continuing conflict between mother and father. We stress, however, that fathers are a heterogeneous group, and in all our syntheses, the quality of his relationship with his children is a significant factor in child development.

IMPLICATIONS FOR TEENAGE-MOTHER FAMILIES

In our final section, we will draw implications for fathers in teenage-mother families from our preceding analyses of adolescent pregnancy, the U.S. child support system, and research findings on the role of the father in child development. As is evident from this essay, policymakers and researchers alike have regarded adolescent parenthood as what Parke and Neville (1987) have called a "female issue." As a result, there is exceedingly little research on fathers in teenage-mother families, and only within the past decade has there been an interest on the part of federal and state governments in such fathers or service programs specifically devoted to fathers.

In general, the predominant viewpoint toward fathers of children born to teen mothers has been very negative: Such fathers are typically seen as incapable of being good husbands, good providers for their families, or competent parents for their children. In point of fact, we believe that the available research suggest much greater *potential* on the part of these young men than is popularly believed.

Potential of Young Fathers

There are three areas of potential that we will touch upon: marriage, educational and occupational attainment, and parenting.

Marriage. There are higher rates of marriage among young fathers than is often believed. Lerman (1986) found in his large sample from the National Longitudinal Survey of Youth that a significant proportion of young men who had fathered children out-of-wedlock eventually married the mother or lived with the children. There are large differences by race. Almost two-thirds of white unwed fathers married the mothers of their children, compared to less than one-quarter of black unwed fathers.

In addition, teenage marriages are more resilient than is commonly assumed. Although the rate of marital stability is lower among teens than among older adults, we believe that the evidence for stability of teen marriages has not received sufficient attention. In a recent study by O'Connell and Rogers (1984), using Current Population Survey data from 1976 and 1982, 76 percent of women who married at age eighteen or nineteen were still married five years later. Additional studies by McLaughlin and his associates (1986), using the 1982 National Survey of Family Growth, found evidence for substantial stability of teenage marriages over a ten-year period, for both white and black adolescents.

Educational and Economic Attainment. Although young unwed fathers have higher rates of unemployment and lower levels of education than young men who are not unwed fathers, there is evidence for greater income potential than previously believed. Lerman's (1986) analyses reveal that in 1985 the median income for young absent fathers was $10,700, slightly above the poverty level for a family of three. Among twenty-five- to twenty-nine-year-old unwed fathers, the median income was $12,500 for whites and $9,500 for blacks. Although these income levels are low, they would contribute to the children's economic well-being. Furthermore, these fathers' economic status does improve over time. Perhaps one of Lerman's most compelling findings is that county unemployment rates did not relate significantly to rates of unwed fatherhood, contrary to an argument that is used extensively to explain unwed fatherhood (Wilson 1987). Yet despite young fathers' economic potential, very few provide child support to their children.

Parenting. There is very little evidence regarding young fathers' ability to parent. The tendency to focus on mothers and children in the child development literature is even more pronounced among studies of teenage-mother families (Parke and Neville 1987). More observational studies including young fathers are particularly needed. To date, there has been only one such observational study (Lamb and Elster 1985), and its findings indicate that the behavior of young fathers toward their infants is similar to that of older fathers. A number of self-selected samples of young fathers who participate in special service programs targeted at this group also suggest that a subset of young fathers are very interested in and involved with their children (Klinman et al. 1986) .

POLICY RECOMMENDATIONS

The following policy recommendations emerge from the evidence we have marshaled that indicates that young fathers have the potential to be adequate providers, husbands, and parents. This essay has been devoted to issues surrounding father involvement once adolescent parenthood has occurred. We would like to underscore that our priority is the prevention of teenage pregnancy in the first place. New initiatives to address the problem of teenage pregnancy should emphasize preventive approaches. Specifically, youngsters and teenagers should be encouraged to postpone sexual involvement, but if they become sexually active, they should be taught how to be effective contraceptors. Prevention programs would also benefit enormously from the application of existing theoretical and empirical work documenting adolescents' cognitive and emotional development, so that efforts to change adolescent sexual behavior can be informed by the broader context of how adolescents behave (Paikoff and Brooks-Gunn n.d.).

With regard to young men who have already fathered children, we propose two major recommendations: (1) improvement of the child support enforcement system for adolescent mothers; and (2) encouragement of marriage as a life-course option.

Child Support Enforcement and Adolescent Mothers

Although the passage of the Family Support Act has the potential of strengthening child support enforcement for impoverished, never-married mothers, the extent to which adolescent mothers will benefit remains to be seen. Most teenage mothers are unaware of their rights or their children's rights to paternity and economic support under existing law. Whereas divorcing mothers have the opportunity to learn about the child support system in the course of contact with the legal system during divorce proceedings, teenage mothers do not have this source of information. Theoretically, teenage mothers learn about their rights to child support when they apply for AFDC, but often it is a parent of the teenage mother who applies for AFDC. In addition, caseworkers are overworked and may fail to inform the teenage mother of her rights. Extensive outreach efforts are needed to educate teen mothers about paternity and child support. Many young mothers may not understand the long-term consequences of the absence of child support over eighteen years; nor are they considering their children's rights to paternity establishment. Currently, approximately 25 percent of adolescent mothers have had paternity established, and of those who did, followed by court orders for support in 1985, 75 percent received some child support (Danziger 1987). Given previous patterns, it appears that levels of paternity establishment for adolescent mothers can be significantly improved (Garfinkel and McLanahan 1989)

In addition, policymakers need to orient toward the long-term outcomes of bringing young, unwed fathers into the child support enforcement system, and steps in this direction are evident in the Family Support Act. Although they may not be able to make large payments in the beginning, these fathers tend to continue their education and training and thus over time to earn higher incomes (Lerman 1986; Marsiglio 1988). Thus, we commend the automatic withholding of wages of absent fathers, and in cases where paternal income is negligible, we recommend that a token child support payment system be implemented for such young fathers. Although garnishing of wages may not be practical for fathers with extremely low incomes from unstable jobs, a token payment system in the early years will demonstrate to young fathers that they are responsible for their children. It is not clear at this time under the Family Support Act if token payments by young fathers are envisioned. If not, they should be.

Marriage as a Life-course Option

As out-of-wedlock births have reached unprecedented levels in the 1980s, it is necessary that we reexamine our policies and societal norms that may inadvertently promote single motherhood. Government and private programs are needed that help young couples stay together rather than focus exclusively on the single young mother. Although intervention and research programs are under way to assist older married couples in managing the transition to parenthood and maintaining or strengthening their marriage over time (Cowan and Cowan 1987), such interventions are very rare for teenage couples. Rather than assume that teenage mothers are better off living with their parents, programs should be available that support teenage mothers who wish to undertake a long-term marital commitment to the father of their child.

CONCLUSION

Although policies related to adolescent parenthood and child support enforcement have been highly disparate in the past, they have become increasingly interrelated in recent years.

The common links between these two areas of policy are the children who are at risk for a lifetime of poverty. Children of teenage mothers are very likely to live in impoverished conditions for years, and one central reason for this outcome is the high rate of nonmarital childbearing in the United States today. Although mandated economic support of children by absent fathers would seem to be a logical policy response to this situation, this has been very slow in coming.

Recent efforts over the past fifteen years, and especially the passage of the Family Support Act in 1988, may well succeed in ensuring that absent fathers contribute more to their children's economic well-being. However, obstacles remain to fathers' support to children of adolescent mothers. These include societal tolerance for weak links between the young father and his teenage-mother family, the belief that such fathers have little economic value, difficulties in establishing paternity, and the lack of knowledge on the part of adolescent mothers regarding their rights and their children's rights to paternity establishment and child support enforcement. We have argued in this essay that these obstacles can be overcome, and indeed, benefits to children are not only economic, but psychological as well.

REFERENCES

Alan Guttmacher Institute. 1976. *Eleven million teenagers: What can be done about the epidemic of adolescent pregnancies in the United States.* New York: Planned Parenthood Federation of America.

Bane, M. J., and D. Ellwood. 1983. *The dynamics of dependence: The routes to self-sufficiency.* Cambridge, Mass.: Urban Systems Search.

Bell, W. 1965. *Aid to dependent children.* New York: Columbia University Press.

Belsky, J. 1981. Early human experience: A family perspective. *Developmental Psychology* 17 (1): 3-23.

Belsky, J., B. Gilstrap, and M. Rovine. 1984. The Pennsylvania infant and family development project. 1. Stability and change in mother-infant and father-infant interaction in a family setting. *Child Development* 55 (3): 692-705.

Bloom-Feshbach, J. 1981. Historical perspectives on the father's role. In *The role of the father in child development*, ed. M. E. Lamb, 2d ed. New York: Wiley.

Bowlby, J. 1969. *Attachment and loss. Vol. 1, Attachment.* Middlesex, England: Penguin Books.

Brooks-Gunn, J. 1989. *Opportunities for change: Effects of intervention programs on mothers and children.* Paper presented at the National Forum on children and the Family Support Act, sponsored by the Foundation for Child Development, November, Washington, D.C.

Burt, M. A. 1986. Estimating the public costs to teenage childbearing. *Family Planning Perspectives* 18 (5): 221-26.

Camara, K., and I. Resnick. 1988. Interparental conflict and cooperation: Factors moderating children's post-divorce adjustment. In *Impact of divorce, single parenting, and steparenting on children,* ed. E. Hetherington and J. Arasteh. Hillsdale, N.J.: Erlbaum.

Chase-Lansdale, P. L., and E. M. Hetherington. 1990. The impact of divorce on life-span development: Short and long term effects. In *Life-span development behavior,* ed. P. Baltes, D. Featherman, and R. Lerner, vol. 10, 105-49. Hillsdale, N.J.: Erlbaum.

Chase-Lansdale, P. L., and M. Owen. 1987. Maternal employment in a family context: Effects on infant-mother and infant-father attachments. *Child Development* 58:1505-12.

Chase-Lansdale, P. L., and M. A. Vinovskis. 1989. Whose responsibility? An historical analysis of the changing roles of mothers, fathers, and society in assuming responsibility for U. S. children. Paper presented at the National Forum on Children and the Family Support Act, sponsored by the Foundation for Child Development, November, Washington, D.C.

Cherlin, A. J. 1981. *Marriage, divorce, remarriage.* Cambridge: Harvard University Press.

———. 1989. The weakening link between marriage and the care of children. *Family Planning Perspectives* 20:302-6.

Cowan, C. P., and P. A. Cowan. 1987. A preventative intervention for couples becoming parents. In *Research on support for parents and infants in the postnatal period,* ed. C. F. Z. Boukydis. Hillsdale, N.J.: Ablex.

———. 1988. Who does what when partners become parents: Implications for men, women, and marriage. *Marriage and Family Review* 12 (3-4): 105-31.

Danziger, S. 1987. *The status of children in Wisconsin: Recent trends in family resources and child well-being.* Madison: Bureau for Children, Youth, and Families, Division of Community Services, Wisconsin Department of Health and Social Services.

Degler, C. J. 1980. *At odds: Women and the family in America from the revolution to the present.* New York: Oxford University Press.

Demos, J. 1982. The changing faces of fatherhood: A new exploration in American family history. In *Father and child: Developmental and clinical perspectives,* ed. S. H. Cath, A. R. Gurwitt, and J. Minder, 425-45. Boston: Little, Brown.

Duncan, G. J., and W. Rodgers. 1987. Single-parent families: Are their economic problems transitory or persistent? *Family Planning Perspectives* 19:171-78.

Emery, R. E. and M. M. Wyer. 1987. Child custody mediation and litigation: An experimental evaluation of the experience of parents. *Journal of Consulting and Clinical Psychology,* 55:1979-86.

Fagot, B. 1974. Sex differences in toddlers' behavior and parental reaction. *Developmental Psychology* 10:554-58.

Furstenberg, F. F., Jr., J. Brooks-Gunn, and P. L. Chase-Lansdale. 1989. Teenage pregnancy and childbearing. *American Psychologist* 44:313-20.

Furstenberg, F. F., Jr., J. Brooks-Gunn, and S. P. Morgan. 1987. *Adolescent mothers in later life.* Cambridge: Cambridge University Press.

Garfinkel, I. 1988. Child support assurance: A new tool for achieving social security. In *Child support: From debt collection to social policy,* eds. A. J. Kahn and S. B. Kamerman, 328-42. Newberry Park, Calif.: Sage.

Garfinkel, I., and S. McLanahan. 1986. *Single mothers and their children: A new American dilemma.* Washington, D.C.: Urban Institute Press.

——— . 1989. *The effects of the child support provision on child well-being.* Paper presented at the National Forum on Children and the Family Support Act, sponsored by the Foundation for Child Development, November, Washington, D.C.

P. F. Gjerde, J. H. Block, and J. Block. 1986. Egocentrism and ego resiliency: Personality characteristics associated with perspective-taking from early childhood through adolescence. *Journal of Personality and Social Psychology* 51:423-34.

Grigg, S. 1984. *The dependent poor of Newburyport: Studies in social history, 1800-1830.* Ann Arbor, MI: Research Press.

Griswold, R. L. 1982. *Family and divorce in California, 1850-1890: Victorian illusions and everyday realities.* Albany, N.Y.: State University of New York Press.

Hartley, S. F. 1975. *Illegitimacy.* Berkeley, Calif.: University of California.

Hayes, C. D., ed. 1987. *Risking the future: Adolescent sexuality, pregnancy, and childbearing,* vol. 1. Washington, D.C.: National Academy Press.

Hetherington, E. M. 1972. Effects of father-absence on personality development in adolescent daughters. *Developmental Psychology* 7:313-28.

Hetherington, E. M., and K. Camara. 1984. Families in transition: The process of dissolution and reconstitution. In *Review of Child Development Research.* Vol. 7, *The Family,* ed. R. D. Parke, 398-439. Chicago: University of Chicago Press.

Hetherington, E. M., M. Cox, and R. Cox. 1982. Effects of divorce on parents and children. In *Nontraditional families: Parenting and child-development,* ed. M. E. Lamb, 233-88. Hillsdale, N.J.: Erlbaum.

Hofferth, S. I., and C. D. Hayes, eds. 1987. *Risking the future: Adolescent sexuality, pregnancy, and childbearing. Working papers and statistical appendixes,* vol. 2. Washington, D.C.: National Academy Press.

Johnson, M. 1963. Sex role learning in the nuclear family. *Child Development* 34:319-33.

Kahn, A. J., and S. B. Kamerman. 1988. Child support in the United States: The problem." In *Child support: From debt collection to social policy,* ed. A. J. Kahn and S. B. Kamerman, 10-19. Newbury Park, Calif.: Sage.

Karlsen, C. F. 1987. *The devil in the shape of a woman: Witchcraft in colonial New England.* New York: Norton.

Katz, M. B. 1986. *In the shadow of the poorhouse: A history of welfare in America.* New York: Basic Books.

Katz, S. N. 1983. A historical perspective on child support laws in the United States. In *The parental child support obligations: Research, practice, and social policy,* ed. J. Cassetty, 17-33. Lexington, Mass.: Lexington Books.

Klinman, D. G., J. H. Sander, J. L. Rosen, and K. R. Longo. 1986. The teenage father collaboration: A demonstration and research model. In *Adolescent fatherhood,* ed. A. B. Elster and M. E. Lamb, 155-70. Hillsdale, N.J.: Erlbaum.

Kulikoff, A. 1986. *Tobacco and slaves: The development of southern cul-*

tures in the Chesapeake, 1680-1800. Chapel Hill: University of North Carolina Press.

Lamb, M. E. 1975. Fathers: Forgotten contributors to child development. *Human Development* 18 (4): 245-66.

———. 1976. Effects of stress and cohort on mother-and father-infant interaction. *Developmental Psychology* 12:435-43.

———. 1977. The development of mother-infant and father-infant attachments in the second year of life. *Developmental Psychology* 13:637-48.

———. 1986. The changing role of fathers. In *The father's role: Applied perspectives,* ed. M. E. Lamb. New York: Wiley.

Lamb, M. E., and A. Elster. 1985. Adolescent mother-infant-father relationships. *Developmental Psychology* 21:768-73.

Lebsock, S. 1984. *The free women of Petersburg: Status and culture in a southern town, 1784-1860.* New York: Norton.

Lee, V., J. Brooks-Gunn, and E. Schnur. 1988. Does Head Start work? A one-year follow-up comparison of disadvantaged children attending Head Start, no preschool, and other preschool programs. *Developmental Psychology* 24:210-22.

Lehrer, S. 1987. *Origins of protective labor legislation for women, 1905-1925.* Albany, N.Y.: State University of New York Press.

Lerman, R. I. 1986. Who are the absent young fathers? *Youth and Society* 18 (1): 3-27.

Lima, L. H., and R. C. Harris. 1988. The child support enforcement program in the United States. In *Child support: From debt collection to social policy,* ed. A. J. Kahn and S. B. Kamerman, 20-44. Newbury Park, Calif.: Sage.

Lockridge, K. A. 1974. *Literacy in colonial New England: An enquiry into the social context of literacy in the early modern West.* New York: Norton.

Lopata, H. Z., and H. P. Brehm. 1986. *Widows and dependent wives: From social problem to federal program.* New York: Praeger.

MacDonald, K. and R. Parke. 1984. Bridging the gap: Parent-child play interaction and peer interactive competence. *Child Development* 55:1265-77.

Main, M., N. Kaplan, and J. Cassidy. 1985. Security in infancy, childhood, and adulthood: A move to the level of representation. In

Growing pains of attachment theory and research, ed. I. Bretherton and E. Waters. Monograph of the Society for Research in Child Development, vol. 50, nos. 1-2, serial #209. Chicago: University of Chicago Press.

Main, M., and D. Weston. 1981. The quality of the toddler's relationship to mother and to father: Related to conflict behavior and the readiness to establish new relationships. *Child Development* 53:932-40.

Marsiglio, W. 1988. Commitment to social fatherhood—predicting adolescent males' intentions to live with their child and partner. *Journal of Marriage and the Family* 50:427-41.

Mason, K., M. A. Vinovskis, and T. K. Hareven. 1978. Women's work and the life course in Essex County, Massachusetts, 1880. In *Transitions: The family and the life course in historical perspective,* ed. T. K. Hareven, 187-216. New York: Academic Press.

May, D., and M. A. Vinovskis. 1977. A ray of millenial light: Early education and social reform in the infant school movement in Massachusetts, 1826-1840. In *Family and kin in American urban communities, 1800-1940,* ed. T. K. Hareven, 62-99. New York: Watts.

May, E. G. 1980. *Great expectations: Marriage and divorce in post-Victorian America.* Chicago: University of Chicago Press.

McLaughlin, S. 1986. The effect of marital status at first birth on marital dissolution among adolescent mothers. *Demography* 23 (3): 329-49.

Moore, K. A. 1987. *Facts at a glance, 1987.* Washington, D.C.: Child Trends.

Moore, K. A., and M. R. Burt. 1982. *Private crisis, public cost: Policy perspectives on teenage childbearing.* Washington, D.C.: Urban Institute Press.

Moran, G. F. 1980. Sisters in Christ: Women and the church in seventeenth-century New England. In *Women in American religion,* ed. J. W. James, 47-65. Philadelphia: University of Pennsylvania Press.

Moran, G. F., and M. A. Vinovskis. 1986. The great care of godly parents: Early childhood in Puritan New England. In *History and research in child development,* ed. A. B. Smuts and J. W. Hagen. Monographs of the Society for Research in Child Development, vol. 50, no. 4-5, serial no. 211, 24-37. Chicago: University of Chicago Press.

National Center for Health Statistics. 1987. Advanced report of final natality statistics, 1985. *Monthly vital statistics report*, 36, no. 4, Supp. DHHS, Publication no. (PHS) 87-1120. Hyattsville, Md.: Public Health Service.

O'Connell, M., and C. Rogers. 1984. Out-of-wedlock births, premarital pregnancies, and their effect on family formation and dissolution. *Family Planning Perspectives* 16 (4): 157-62.

Oellerich, D., and I. Garfinkel. 1983. Distributions: Impacts of existing and alternative child support systems. *Policy Studies Journal* 12:119-29.

Orloff, A. S. 1988. The political origins of America's belated welfare state. In *The politics of social policy in the United States*, ed. M. Weir, A. S. Orloff, and T. Skocpol, 37-80. Princeton, N.J.: Princeton University Press.

Paikoff, R., and J. Brooks-Gunn. n.d. Taking fewer chances: Teenage pregnancy prevention programs. *American Psychologist*. Forthcoming.

Parke, R. P., and A. Beitel. 1986. Hospital-based interventions for fathers. In *The father's role: Applied perspectives*, ed. M. Lamb. New York: Wiley.

Parke, R. P., and B. Neville. 1987. In *Risking the future: Adolescent sexuality, pregnancy, and childbearing*, ed. S. L. Hofferth and C. D. Hayes, 145-73. Washington, D.C.: National Academy Press.

Parke, R. P., and B. J. Tinsley. 1984. Fatherhood: Historical and contemporary perspectives. In *Life span developmental psychology: Historical and generational effects*, ed. K. A. McClusky and A. W. Reese, 203-47. New York: Academic Press.

Pedersen, F. 1981. Father influences viewed in a family context. In *The role of the father in child development*, ed. M. Lamb, 2d ed, 295-317. New York: Wiley.

Peterson, J. L., and N. Zill. 1986. Marital disruption, parent-child relationships, and behavior problems in children. *Journal of Marriage and the Family* 48:103-11.

Pleck, J. H. 1986. Employment and fatherhood: Issues and innovative policies. In *The father's role: Applied perspectives*, ed. M. E. Lamb. New York: Wiley.

Radin, N. 1982. Primary caregiving and role-sharing fathers. In *Nontraditional families: Parenting and child development*, ed. M. Lamb, 175-204. Hillsdale, N.J.: Erlbaum.

Reiss, D. 1981. *The family's construction of reality.* Cambridge: Harvard University Press.

Rodgers, H. R., Jr. 1986. *Poor women, poor families: The economic plight of America's female-headed households.* Armonk, N.Y.: M. E. Sharpe.

Rothman, E. K. 1984. *Hands and hearts: A history of courtship in America.* New York: Basic Books.

Rutman, D. B., and A. H. Rutman. 1984. *A place in time: Middlesex, Virginia, 1650-1750.* New York: Norton.

Santrock, J. W., and R. A. Warshak. 1986. Development of father-custody relationships and legal clinical considerations in father-custody families. In *The father's role: Applied perspectives*, ed. M. E. Lamb, 135-66. New York: Wiley.

Sears, R. R., E. E. Maccoby, and H. Levin. 1957. *Patterns of child rearing.* Evanston, IL: Row and Peterson.

Shorter, E. 1975. *The making of the modern family.* New York: Basic Books.

Sroufe, L. A., D. Jacobvitz, S. Mangelsdorf, E. L. DeAngelo, and M. J. Ward. 1985. Generational boundary dissolution between mothers and their preschool children: A relationship systems approach. *Child Development* 56:317-25.

Stone, L. 1977. *The family, sex, and marriage in England, 1500-1800.* New York: Harper & Row.

Trattner, W. I. 1989. *From poor law to welfare state: A history of social welfare in America*, 4th ed. New York: Free Press.

Uhlenberg, P. 1980. Death and the family. *Journal of Family History* 5:313-320.

U.S. Bureau of the Census. 1989. *Statistical abstract of the United States: 1989*, 109th ed. Washington, D.C.: U.S. Government Printing Office.

U.S. Congress, House Select Committee on Population. 1978. *Fertility and contraception in the United States.* 95th Congress, 2d sess., ser. B. Washington, D.C.: Government Printing Office.

Vinovskis, M. A. 1976. Angels heads and weeping willows: Death in early America. *Proceedings of the American Antiquarian Society* 86:273-302.

———. 1986. "Teenage Pregnancy." *Social Sciences: An Interdisciplinary Digest of Research*, 71, Nos. 2/3 (Fall), 158-164.

———. 1988a. *An "epidemic" of adolescent pregnancy? Some historical and policy considerations.* New York: Oxford University Press.

———. 1988b. The unraveling of the family wage since World War II: Some demographic, economic, and cultural considerations. In *The family wage: Work, gender, and children in the modern economy,* ed. B. J. Christensen, 33-58. Rockford, IL: Rockford Institute.

Walsh, L. S. 1979. Till death us do part: Marriage and family in seventeenth-century Maryland. In *The Chesapeake in the seventeenth century: Essays on Anglo-American society and politics,* ed. T. W. Tate and D. L. Ammerman, 126-52. Chapel Hill: University of North Carolina Press.

Weitzman, L. J. 1985. *The divorce revolution: The unexpected special consequences for women and children in America.* New York: Free Press.

Wilson, W. J. 1987. *The truly disadvantaged: The inner city, the underclass and public policy.* Chicago: University of Chicago Press.

10

Reversing the Poverty Cycle with Job-Based Education

INTRODUCTION

Real growth in personal incomes should reduce poverty, at least as measured by the absolute standard used in the United States. Between 1960 and 1974, poverty rates were cut in half (falling from 22 to 11 percent) in line with increases in disposable income. But during the 1974 to 1988 period, the share of the population in poverty actually increased from 10.5 to 11.6 percent, in spite of 31 percent growth in real disposable income per person.[1]

The divergence between trends in poverty and income per person took place partly because of changes in family patterns. The share of families with children headed by two parents declined dramatically.

In 1970, 90 percent of white and 58 percent of black children lived in two-parent families; by 1988, the proportions dropped to 79 percent among whites and 39 percent among blacks. During the same period, the poverty rate among children increased from 15 to over 20 percent.

The figures on the newly formed families with children are even more disturbing. Between 1970 and 1986, births to unmarried women as a percent of all births jumped from 5.7 to 15.7 percent among whites and from 37.6 to 61.2 percent among blacks. Table 1 shows the extremely high rates of female headship and poverty among families headed by fifteen- to twenty-four-year-olds.

Table 1
Poverty and Female Headship by Race and Spanish Origin, 1984

Age of Family Head	Percentage of Families with Chidren in Poverty		
	White	Black	Hispanic
15-24	33.5	67.5	48.7
25-34	13.2	37.3	28.3
35-44	7.1	23.4	23.6
45-64	7.2	26.2	20.4
Age of Family Head	Percentage of Families with Children Headed by Women		
	White	Black	Hispanic
15-24	31.5	73.2	30.0
25-34	16.9	55.4	26.1
35-44	14.1	46.3	25.7
45-64	13.7	42.6	23.6

Source: U.S. Bureau of the Census, *Current Population Reports*, Series P-60, No. 166, *Money Income and Poverty Status in the United States: 1988* (Washington, D.C.: Government Printing Office, 1989), 136, 142.

The rising out-of-wedlock-births ratios resulted partly from delays in marriage and partly from declining birthrates among married young people. In 1960, nearly half (47 percent) of twenty- to twenty-four-year-old men were already married. However, by 1988, men who married by their mid twenties were the exception; the married proportion of twenty- to twenty-four-year-olds had dropped to about 22 percent. Generally, delays in marriage went together with declining birthrates and delays in having children. Births per 1,000 women, ages twenty to twenty-four, fell dramatically from 258 in 1960 to 108 in 1983, where the birthrate remained through 1986.[2] However, not enough young men and women delayed childbearing to avoid raising the proportion of children born into one-parent families.

Viewing the rise in out-of-wedlock-births ratios as part of broad social trends offers little consolation to those concerned about child poverty. The large inflow into poverty of young unmarried mothers and their children virtually guarantees a large pool of chronically poor families for the foreseeable future.

The president, the Congress, governors, and state legislatures have tried to change the welfare system in ways that help mothers earn their way off welfare and that improve the collection of child support payments. The 1988 Family Support Act strengthened work requirements, increased funds for state-run training programs, and mandated rules to make it easier to collect child support. Other policies have widened access to educational and medical services, especially for preschool students and teenage mothers. The key goal of these interventions is to insure that the 20 percent of children who are poor, and the nearly 60 percent of black children born to unwed mothers, develop normally in the critical years before elementary school begins.

Many fear that the problems are already so solidly rooted in the inner-city minority areas as to be virtually intractable. The recent widespread use of the term *urban underclass* captures concerns about the chronic and intergenerational component of poverty. A stylized description of the process would run as follows:

- Black young men experience (or expect) high unemployment, low wages, and few serious career options; thus,
- black women find (or expect to find) few employable black men;
- as neither sees any cost in preventing pregnancy, the result is high rates of out-of-wedlock births;
- young unmarried mothers heading families have little ability to escape poverty or welfare:
- growing up in a poor mother-headed family increases the chances that children will fail in school, engage in crime, become involved in the abuse and sale of drugs, and be unable to obtain a good job;
- large concentrations of such families disrupt entire commu-

nities, putting at risk the children in working class, two-parent families;

• although many escape this harsh pattern, enough young people repeat the cycle to reproduce the underclass.

While young black and other minority males are central to this process, the thrust of welfare reform policies has been to help unmarried or divorced mothers gain self-sufficiency. But as Robert Moffitt[3] has shown, any foreseeable welfare reform policy is unlikely to have enough impact on women's earnings to raise large numbers out of poverty. Reducing the number of children at risk will require major improvements in the career expectations and outcomes of black and other low-income young men and women. Moving these youth into mainstream careers would reduce poverty directly through their increased earnings and indirectly by encouraging young people to delay childbearing until they can afford to support the children financially. This paper argues that a specific approach—*youth apprenticeship*—is the most promising policy for realizing these goals. Before making the case for a youth apprenticeship system, I examine recent trends in employment and earnings as well as past efforts to reduce youth unemployment and prevent long-term poverty.

Reviewing the current job market and past policies makes clear the need for a new approach. The last sections develop the rationale for establishing formal apprenticeships in the late high school years and discuss strategies for implementing this new system of linking high school students to occupational training and actual careers.

JOB MARKET TRENDS AMONG BLACK AND OTHER NONCOLLEGE YOUTH

The 40 percent unemployment rates faced by black teenagers in the late 1970s and early 1980s dramatized the disastrous job market situation of low-income and black youth. Their extreme joblessness developed after the full-employment period of the late 1960s.[4] It was ironic and troubling that the job options for black youth were worsening just as civil rights and the War on Poverty were becoming institutionalized.[5]

Employment patterns vary substantially within cohorts of black youth. Most black youth work and do not experience any unemployment over the year. On the other hand, a rising share report no paid work at all over the entire previous year. Between 1967 and 1977, the share of black twenty- to twenty-four-year-olds employed during the typical week declined from 62 to 52 percent. Nearly all of this decline resulted from the fact that the proportion with no job during the entire year jumped from 14 to 26 percent. Meanwhile, among black youth with work experience, wages relative to whites were actually increasing.

The employment picture worsened with the recession of 1982, but overall the market improved for black youth between 1981 and 1988. The proportion of black twenty- to twenty-four-year-old men holding jobs rose from 56.7 percent in the first quarter of 1981 to 61.3 percent in the first quarter of 1988; unemployment rates fell from 25.3 to 22.1 percent.

The diverging trends within the black population are most noticeable by education level. Black college graduates (ages twenty to twenty-four) increased their real annual earnings between 1973 and 1984 by 16 percent, while black high school dropouts and high school graduates suffered reductions of over 50 percent.[6] At the highest education levels, the racial gap in earnings has been disappearing. In 1984, black male college graduates in their late twenties earned more than white college graduates.[7]

Despite these gains, the situation deteriorated for noncollege black men. An extraordinary share of black male dropouts (40 percent of twenty- to twenty-four-year-olds) did not work at all in 1986.[8] This rate was nearly triple the comparable figure (15 percent) for 1974. The decline for young black high school graduates was less dramatic but nevertheless real. The proportion employed dropped from 75 to 65 percent (for sixteen- to twenty-four-year-olds), while the share of twenty- to twenty-four-year-olds not working the whole year rose from 9 to almost 16 percent.

Gordon Berlin and Andrew Sum have argued that the earnings losses of noncollege youth, but especially black youth, helped cause the declining rates of marriage. The proportion of black men, ages twenty to twenty-four, who were married and living with their spouses declined dramatically from nearly 40 percent to under 10 percent between 1964 and 1984. To quote Berlin and Sum:

> The wage stagnation of the 1970s and the recession-induced unemployment and underemployment of the 1980s severely affected the earning capacity of young men, espe-

cially those with limited education and skills. These changes dealt a devastating blow to family formation patterns, which in turn helped to increase the number of children living in poverty.[9]

William J. Wilson[10] also links the rising proportion of black mother-headed families to the scarcity of employable black men.

While inner-city black youth with a high school education or less have experienced the worst job market outcomes, other noncollege youth have also done poorly. Between 1973 and 1984, the real earnings of white twenty- to twenty-four-year-old men declined by 39 percent among high school dropouts, 26 percent among high school graduates, but only 11 percent among college graduates.[11] Occupations and industries that traditionally provided moderate wages to low-skill workers are accounting for a declining share of employment.

The rise in the premium for college education was unexpected. Only a decade ago, Richard Freeman argued that substantial increases in college attendance were raising the supply of college-educated workers and thereby lowering the rate of return to college.[12] Apparently, the shifting job structure generated a large enough demand for college-educated workers that it more than offset the increased supplies of college graduates.

In a sense, the economy's rising demand for skill represents an opportunity, not a problem. The education and training system need only produce the skilled young workers, and employers will be ready to absorb them. On the other hand, failure to upgrade the skills of large numbers of young workers will increase inequality by widening further the earnings gaps between skilled and unskilled workers. Thus, the central question is, How can the country increase the academic and occupational skills of noncollege youth and especially of young black men? What kinds of education and training reforms are most likely to succeed? So far, most reforms have stressed purely academic skills, using mechanisms like teacher testing, merit pay for teachers, parent involvement in the schools, school-based management, and mandatory testing of students.

While these and other school reforms may be necessary, I believe they will not prove sufficient to the task, that an *academic only* approach will do little to reduce dropouts or to raise the job prospects of most noncollege youth. Before considering the role for apprenticeship approaches that complement the education reforms, let us briefly review current and past approaches to raising the earning capacities of disadvantaged youth.

LEARNING FROM PAST POLICIES

Segmentation in Education and Employment Policies

The federal government has been undertaking programs to improve the career opportunities of disadvantaged youth since the mid 1960s. The Neighborhood Youth Corps (NYC) and the Job Corps—two key components of the War on Poverty—tried to prevent poverty by providing education and training to prepare low-income youth for jobs. These and subsequent federal employment and training initiatives operated largely outside local school systems. Separate federal education programs provided school districts with money to develop remedial education programs and other methods for improving the educational attainment of minority and low-income youth.

As supplements to an ongoing educational system, jobs programs spent limited amounts on participants in comparison to the school system. This was one reason policymakers restricted eligibility to only youth from low-income families. Ironically, this meant that the federal government was sponsoring segregated training programs at the same time that federal courts were pressing local governments to desegregate their schools.

Federally sponsored youth employment programs faced close scrutiny. In contrast, local schools rarely had to prove cost-effectiveness in educating students and preparing them for jobs, especially youth from low-income families. Despite their mediocre performance, federal youth programs continued to receive substantial funding through the early 1980s. Faced with the severity of the youth unemployment and school dropout problems, Congress often reorganized programs but continued to spend on separate federal youth employment programs.

Congress recognized the important role of the school system and provided financial incentives for local operators and school officials to collaborate. Some of these initiatives bore fruit, but the usual result was only marginal changes in the way young people prepared for jobs and careers. Federal officials whose primary mission is to foster a healthy labor market exerted little influence over schools.

In large part, federal, state, and local policies have been segmented by departmental interests. Education officials view their role as providing young people with a strong general education. Test scores, school retention, high school graduation, and college attendance are their primary measures of success. Few if any school departments even collect information about the postschooling job status of their students. To most school officials the education mission is difficult enough, especially when supplemented by such noneducational concerns as school desegregation, bilingual education, appropriate placements for the handicapped, crime and drugs, and child care for teenage mothers.

To Department of Labor officials and their local program operators, what happens within the school system is outside their control. Yet when schools are unable to provide basic education, labor programs must come to the rescue. Students who leave school without an adequate basic education tend to do worst in the labor market and then become the target group for second-chance employment, training, and job placement programs.

If all but a few students learned enough in school to cope effectively in the job market, the labor programs would have an achievable mission to educate and train the remaining youth. But when a large percentage of minority twenty-one-year-olds are functionally illiterate, labor programs are forced to become a second educational system as well as a training and job placement program.

It is difficult to start over with the education of any twenty-one-year-old and then retain the person long enough to train him or her with a salable skill. It is nearly impossible when supplemental programs must repeat the performance for a large share of the youth cohort.

The weak link between schools and jobs is one reason that noncollege youth see no incentive to do well in high school. High school counselors typically focus on helping students choose an appropriate college; they do little to advise students on career preparations or to place graduates in full-time jobs. Employers have little connection with high schools and rarely know anything about the high school performance of prospective employees. John Bishop makes a strong case that more educated workers are more productive but that the wage advantage does not catch up with productivity differences until several years after workers leave high school. Students rarely perceive these long-term gains from working harder in high school. The lack of positive incentives, together with frequent peer pressure against working hard in school, leaves most American high school students (except those going to selective colleges) with little motivation to achieve academic success.[13]

In other advanced countries, grades are crucial in determining entry-level positions in large companies and, in Germany, the type of apprenticeship a youth can attain. Students have access to career-oriented jobs directly out of secondary school. Given the commitment companies are making, it is not surprising that they select potential long-term employees using grades, teacher recommendations, scores on national tests and other indicators of achievement and trainability.

Student alienation from academic modes of learning is another barrier that limits educational achievement. Lauren Resnick points out that schools use learning methods that differ enormously from the way people learn at work and in other life contexts. For example, schools stress individual, rather than team, approaches; schools manipulate symbols and abstract thoughts, while outside of school people use tools and deal with specific situations. Not surprisingly, many students do better when learning in a contextual environment.[14]

The experience of the armed forces offers solid evidence that some students, particularly recruits with limited abilities, succeed better in courses taught under the *functional context* approach than through standard methods. For example, many students learn electronics most effectively in the context of how equipment functions and how to maintain the equipment. Overemphasis on the academic approach does little to recognize the *school-weary* youth phenomenon. Unlike earlier periods, when students left school to help support their families, today's dropouts leave because they do not like, or feel they are doing poorly with, the academic approach to learning.[15]

For middle-class and most working-class youth, social and family influences are generally strong enough to cause students to learn something and to stay in school until graduation. These young people lose long-term earnings and occupational possibilities, and the nation loses productivity. But the damage from an absence of incentives is much greater for poor youth. Often they drop out of high school entirely and pay little attention to the school's educational content. Worse, many turn to illicit occupations, to drug use and drug sales, and/or to despair, while others become parents well before they can support their children financially. Even when inner-city youth complete high school, their job chances are limited by the scarcity of informal job contacts; the increasing concentration of the poor makes it less likely that young men will connect to jobs through relatives and friends.

To summarize, federal policies to help disadvantaged youth succeed in the labor market at best have played only a modest secondary role, because they have operated outside the main action—the high schools. The disastrous outcomes in inner-city ghettos result partly from the same ill that harms overall performance in high schools—the disassociation between the education and job systems for noncollege youth. The silver lining in this story is that restructuring the mainstream education and job entry systems for all noncollege youth will be especially beneficial for disadvantaged youth.

Perhaps because of differences in learning styles, many students choose vocational over academic education programs. Students go to these programs because they like work over school and because they prefer practical applications over theory. The vocational education option is appealing enough to prevent some students from dropping out of high school.

But what is the record of the vocational education system? Could the expansion of vocational education make a meaningful dent in the employment and earnings problems of disadvantaged youth? Or does the vocational education system require a major reorientation?

Vocational Education in High Schools

The world of vocational education is diverse, ranging from specialized high schools, area technical institutes, and postsecondary schools to vocational components of comprehensive high schools and even to typing courses in academic programs. Nearly all high school students take at least one vocational course, and 25 percent take seven or more.[16]

The national assessment divides courses into three categories: (1) consumer and homemaking education, (2) general labor market preparation, and (3) specific labor market preparation. Typing and career exploration are part of general preparation. The major programs included in specific preparation are agriculture, business, marketing, health, occupational home economics, trades (including construction, mechanics, precision production, and transportation), and technical and communications.

Of all students in the high school class of 1982 not planning to complete college, nearly half took seven or more vocational courses. However, only 22 percent specialized to the point of taking at least four courses in a specific labor market field.

Many researchers have attempted the difficult job of measuring the impacts of vocational education on earnings and employment of graduates. Despite analytical difficulties, the following findings have emerged from a vast array of studies:

- Male graduates of vocational education achieve no higher employment and earnings than do similar male graduates of a general curriculum.
- Black students are more likely to complete high school if enrolled in vocational education.
- For females, vocational education raises employment and earnings.
- Vocational education has a positive impact on school enrollment and school completion.[17]
- Vocational education raises earnings, hours worked, and employment among groups specializing in selected fields, such as trade and industry.[18]

Most importantly for the apprenticeship approach, researchers have found that vocational education helps raise the earnings of young men and women students who are able to work in jobs where they can utilize their school training. Vocational graduates in training-related jobs spent 11 to 12 percent more time in the labor force, about 14 to 15 percent more time in jobs, and earned 11 to 12 percent more per hour, implying earnings gains of about 25 percent. Added productivity was at least partly responsible for the earnings gains. Vocational education graduates in training-related jobs required less training time and achieved higher productivity than other workers. Finally, job-related vocational education virtually eliminated the gap between black and white youth in employment and earnings gaps.[19]

The ability of vocational education to help young workers, including minority and disadvantaged youth, depends on the ability of graduates to obtain jobs using their newly acquired skills. Unfortunately, most vocational education graduates who seek jobs after high school do not work in jobs related to their education. Figures on the match between training and jobs vary with how detailed the occupational definitions are. By a restrictive definition, about one in five had a job using the skills within two years of leaving school. On a broader definition, about 40 percent use their training in some way in their final job. The percentage using their training in jobs rises very little beyond two years.

What accounts for this mismatch? The main reason is the absence of mechanisms to link students receiving training with jobs. This, in turn, may be largely due to the fact that financing for vocational education programs has no relationship to the performance of schools in placing students in training-related jobs. In any event, high schools are not sensitive enough to the market to relate their mix of training to the demands of employers.

Some vocational schools have developed excellent reputations for training and placing students. Teachers in these schools maintain close contact with employers and can provide credible references for their students. Their programs even include supervised work experience related to their school vocational programs.

Unfortunately, however, these schools are the exception, not the rule. Still, given the partial success of vocational education, it makes sense to ask: (1) what approaches can best build on the lessons of the country's experience with vocational education? and (2) Can such initiatives exert an especially large impact on disadvantaged youth?

THE INTERNSHIP STRATEGY

The Economic Context

Occupational and educational systems are closely interdependent. Where an educational system produces a range of potential workers who differ in their academic abilities, employers will develop jobs that mirror this hierarchy of knowledge. The most capable will enter at the high levels, while the least capable will begin at the low rungs of the job ladder. Mobility within the job system will be limited, except perhaps for promotions through seniority. Those filling the top positions will have little or no experience working at the lower or middle ranges of jobs. Wage differentials will be relatively large, partly because high-level workers will receive most of the specific training. Demands for upward mobility among disadvantaged students will be directed at expanding higher education.

Where students achieve academic competence together with skills provided on jobs in a wide range of occupations, job ladders will become more pervasive in the employment system. A large share of workers will start at relatively low positions but have access to training and mobility within their occupations. Workers in blue-collar and semiskilled white-collar jobs will be more likely to earn a certification through job-based training. Many who ultimately attain managerial positions will know from experience how entry-level work takes place. Finally, wage differentials associated with differences in formal education will be low. In this economic setting, policymakers can expand mobility for the disadvantaged either through improving their chances for college positions or by increasing their ability to obtain desirable occupational placements.

This picture of alternative education/job streams has a basis in fact. The education and employment systems in France have operated largely as we have described the school-based system. In contrast, the job structure in (the former) West Germany developed the type of mobility, training, and low wage differentials that seems to occur when close linkages exist between job-based training and the educational system.[20]

The fear that jobs-education approaches train students in obsolete skills makes it important to shift from traditional vocational education to the internship approach. The evidence is clear that employer-based training is much more likely to have an existing and continuing use than is school-based vocational training. Further, there is no reason to believe that job-related occupational training becomes obsolete faster than knowledge learned in academic subjects. John Bishop points out that skills and knowledge deteriorate from nonuse at least as fast as from obsolescence. He notes that new occupational skills tend to build on, rather than replace, old skills.[21] The experience in several European countries is that apprenticeships teach generalizable skills that can be adapted as new types of job openings occur. For example, young people trained in electronics apprenticeships can take advantage of telecommunications openings. The best evidence for the adaptive ability of skill training is that today the German apprenticeship system continues to thrive. A recent *New York Times* article[22] reported that German executives attribute much of their success to their sophisticated work force, trained largely under their apprenticeship program. Currently, German companies spend about $20 billion per year on the program.

For job-based education to work effectively, the internship fields must offer genuine opportunities for occupational mobility. Interning at a service station will be unappealing unless students are persuaded that, through training in related mechanical, computer, and business subjects, they have the chance to reach the level of high-paid mechanical specialist or owner-operator. Similarly, a banking internship will achieve little if it is simply a way for banks to attract students who can read well enough to perform a teller's job. Students will have to be shown the relationship between their education and the chance to sell financial services and ultimately manage a branch of the bank.

Success in the development of internships might alarm those who have witnessed the restrictiveness of existing U.S. apprenticeships in the construction trades. Might graduate interns restrict entry into jobs and training in the occupation in order to obtain market power? This could exclude disadvantaged workers from many new jobs. This danger can be averted. So long as employers and employer associations play a strong role in the programs, the problem of restrictive worker practices is unlikely.

The experiences in Germany and Switzerland suggest that such monopoly power need not develop. The supply of apprenticeships in those countries is limited only by the number of job positions employers expect to fill. Employers have no incentive to restrict entry. Indeed, a frequent complaint is that employers offer too many apprenticeships in order to obtain low-wage, entry-level workers. Even with Germany's unemployment rate over 8 percent, employers there are able to provide enough apprenticeships to meet the demand.

The U.S. Education Context

The role of job-based education in U.S. high schools has been hotly debated for nearly a hundred years. Manufacturers have long argued that to become as efficient as Germany, the secondary education system needs to provide students with the theoretical knowledge and practical training required by industry. As long ago as 1905, the National Association of Manufacturers stated:

> The German technical and trade schools are at once the admiration and fear of all countries. In the world's race for commercial supremacy, we must copy and improve upon the German system of education. Germany relies chiefly upon her [high school] trained workers for her commercial success and prosperity. She puts no limit on the money to be expended in trade and technical education.[23]

While vocational education has developed in U.S. high schools, educators have continued to favor an academic, liberal approach to education. They favor upgrading academic content as the best counter to the general decline in educational quality and to the poor performance of black students. Their reforms involve increasing academic requirements of students; replacing frill courses with serious mathematics, literature, writing, and history; and establishing a single curriculum for all students. There is an aversion to tracking the less able students into the vocational and general curriculum. Reformers want teachers to have confidence that all students can learn, albeit at different speeds and with different techniques. Diane Ravitch expresses this view often, as, for example, in this statement:

> Tracking is wasteful of children's minds; it unnecessarily narrows their educational experiences. . . . I strongly believe that all children who are capable of learning should receive a broad liberal education during their years of school. All should study literature, history, science, mathematics, a foreign language, and the arts. In the ideal school, there would be no curricular tracking. All children would be expected to learn the major disciplines of knowledge; some would learn faster, some slower, but all would share in the riches of our cultural and scientific heritage.[24]

The case for academic reforms is compelling, but ignoring job-based education would have serious limitations, especially for disadvantaged and other students who will not attend college. A purely academic approach will leave noncollege youth with few incentives to do well in high school, fail to recognize the importance of linking theory with activities of immediate relevance to students, and promote a single route to successful careers.

Even if principals and teachers could make literature and mathematics more exciting to students, academic-only reforms will lead to a unidimensional focus on educational abilities and thus on differences in educational achievement. Young people who leave school with only a high school education will find themselves lacking any occupational direction, part of an undifferentiated pool of moderately educated, but unskilled, workers. Occupational positions and careers will depend mostly on mobility within the educational system. As prior education matters more, mobility within industry will decline or will take place only through seniority.

Internships and Apprenticeships in High Schools

An internship or apprenticeship system that adapts elements of successful European approaches can help avoid a new educational stratification in the United States. In an internship system, employers would agree to provide training, education, a job experience that would teach the student enough competencies for her or him to become certified in a particular occupational field. The internships would not substitute for schooling, but rather would operate in combination with classroom education.

Internships can reinforce good school performance with immediate rewards that compete with the alternatives (including those available on the street). Black high school students will come to recognize that there are avenues to occupational success that they can realistically achieve without going to college. Spending part of the day at a job site will reduce the amount of time black students are exposed to negative peer pressure.

The internship strategy would mean the creation of complementary systems of education and training delivered jointly by schools and employers. Under internships, employers would agree to provide training, education, and job experience that would teach the student enough competencies for him or her to become certified in a particular occupational field. After receiving extensive vocational counseling, including visits to work sites, students would be able to enter internships beginning tenth or eleventh grade.

They would sign a contract with employers, under which the employer provides training and the student meets school and work-site performance standards. Upon completion of the internship stage, students would have a chance to become certified in a skill area that was broad enough to make them qualified for a range of jobs.

The internships would be similar to apprenticeships in their use of industry-based training, contractual agreements between workers and employers, the linking of theoretical and practical knowledge, and certification in an occupational field. However, unlike in existing U.S. apprenticeships, the interns would be high school students who are taking academic as well as job-related courses; the fields would cover a broad range of occupations; and entry would be open as long as employer slots were available.

High school students choosing the internship stream would still have to complete courses in literature, writing, mathematics, and science. However, their school schedules would be less extensive than those of most students expecting to attend college. Internship students would split their weeks or days between the job site and the school. As the students move closer to high school graduation, they would increase their time spent on the job. Where the internship involved a substantial time commitment, the student would continue to take high school courses beyond the twelfth year of schooling. Course work relevant to the student's occupational area might be learned at the work site, either formally through talks by instructors or employers or informally through on-the-job experience. In either case, the content would have to meet substantive standards, and students would take tests on the content learned on their internships. Students expecting to stay with employers providing internships will have a particularly strong incentive to perform well in their general and occupational courses. Employers will certainly keep track of the progress of their interns.

The internships would cover a broad range of occupational and industrial areas, such as financial services, nursery education, landscaping, auto or truck repair services, computer repair, computer software, food services, health services, and medical testing and equipment. In each area, state education and labor departments, employer associations, and perhaps unions and schools would establish competencies that could be taught and tested. The students would work with an employer while obtaining training and instruction in the relevant areas.

Internships could develop by widening the school-based vocational programs education system. Existing state and federal vocational funds could pay for this training after employers specified the course content and testing procedures. Savings from the shorter amounts of total school hours of interns could support certification counseling, and continuing review of the quality of training provided by employers.

Extensive involvement of employers in the jobs-education program would reduce the mismatch between training and job positions and would avoid the problem of outdated equipment and unqualified instructors. Studies have demonstrated that employer-controlled training leads to significantly higher utilization than does vocational school training. Basing training positions on employer demands will build a feedback mechanism into the process that will minimize, though not eliminate, the mismatch between training and jobs.

In choosing among student candidates for internships, employers would have access to school records and student performance. Schools would have to devote guidance time to the matching of students with internships. For ninth- or tenth-graders, schools would bring employer representatives to the school to describe their internships as well as the career ladders and long-term occupational possibilities associated with the internship area. Students performing well in school, in both courses and conduct, would no doubt have the widest choices of internship fields.

To succeed, the jobs-education approach would have to appeal to a wide range of students and employers. The program cannot work if it becomes a dumping ground for academic failures taking dead-end jobs. At the same time, the range of occupational areas must be broad enough to encompass various types and levels of talents.

The internship approach is a short-run and long-run strategy. In the short-run, internships extend the employer linkages and complementary work and schooling already implemented in the best high school vocational programs. Another short-run task would be to improve the process of certifying occupational competencies and to widen its scope. In the long term, the internship approach would reorient the normal transition from school to work. Students would come to recognize the relevance of high school performance and the desirability of a range of middle-skill careers. Employers would adjust to the new group of skilled young workers by building job ladders. Wage differentials would narrow between college graduates and noncollege youth in response to the improved productivity of graduate interns. No longer would college education be perceived as the only route to a successful career.

The internship approach could yield particularly important gains for black youth for several reasons:

- Since performance through grade nine or ten would affect a student's choice of internship and probable career, students would have a meaningful and early incentive to work hard in school.
- Once students are in internships, they will see that their long-term mobility depends on their ability to read, write, and have competence in mathematics.
- Linking educational content to job experience might permit students to learn with examples of immediate relevance to their careers.
- Spending time in internships with working adults who have experience in careers will offer black young men constructive role models and make them familiar with work environments and realistic ways to achieve occupational success.
- The availability of internships will reduce entry barriers to jobs faced by young blacks, who typically lack the informal networks that help other young people into entry-level jobs.
- Employers will have the ability to exert an early influence on the education of their potential workers and to develop experience with potential workers before they become difficult to fire.

Implementation of the Internship Approach

Can these efforts be implemented? What role can the federal government play in stimulating local internship programs? As is the case in nearly all domestic programs, the internship and job placement approaches must become a reality through action at a local level. However, the federal government can play an important role by rechanneling money for Job Training Partnership Act, the Vocational Education program, and other educational grants. Matching grants could be made available for local school districts that implement new internship and placement programs.

Secretaries of labor and education can assist local schools, employers, and labor organizations to develop certification programs for apprenticeships as well as for somewhat less formal internship programs. More importantly, the secretary of education might encourage state and local administrators to grant students in internship programs time away from school at instructional on-the-job sites. Those students also need curriculum adjustments that allow them to meet curriculum standards through courses that impart basic skills in applied settings. In addition, federal administrators might help local school districts pick up added insurance and transportation costs.

The Pittsburgh school system has already begun implementing programs that move closely toward the internship approach. Today, high school students can only enroll as either precollege or vocational students. That is, Pittsburgh became the first urban public school system to eliminate its "general education" track. Typically, 35 percent of the city's students had not been able to meet academic or vocational graduation requirements and became general education graduates by default. The city's academic students were graduating with a marketable diploma, and its vocational students benefitted from a series of innovative programs that made their diplomas highly marketable as well. Now the city has gone a step further and essentially forced its vocational and academic programs to shake hands with the city's most disadvantaged students and graduate them with marketable diplomas.

Students who do well in the city's internship programs not only graduate with marketable diplomas, they graduate with assured, professionalized careers in the fields in which they trained. This is precisely the kind of signaling that lets students know that there is a correlation between academic performance and good, professional-quality jobs.

To achieve these goals, the school system decentralized itself around a well-defined core academic program in which every student must meet basic skill requirements but can then reach any vocational or academic goal they choose with step-by-step assistance from the school system.

For noncollege youth, the system has a dense array of programs, classes, and remedial exercises for students of all backgrounds, including these:

• An intensive complementary internship program for motivated students who have had no economic or educational dis-

advantages, or who overcome them. This contains the main professional, complementary training features important for internship programs.
- Survey courses that outline the system's vocational and academic opportunities for nonmotivated, at-risk students. Included are special internships that expose students to professional jobs in ways that present such jobs as realistic choices for high school graduates; counseling, financial support, and others services these students need are also provided.
- Special programs for nonmotivated youth who do not have educational or economic disadvantages.

These kinds of systems offer something for all students regardless of socioeconomic background and academic level. Although Pittsburgh has been hard hit by industrial setbacks, 70 to 80 percent of its co-op graduates remain in the jobs for which they were trained.

The central administrative unit in systems like this fulfill monitoring, coordination, and integration roles. For example, all jobs located by the school system are routed to an overarching student placement section that increases the city's ability to leverage funds from federal, state, and local sources.

Pittsburgh's approach solves several problems with creating professionalized programs for noncollege youth. It operates on a large scale; it offers its benefits to all students regardless of background; and it does so at a cost of about $3,000 per at-risk student above regular school costs. The key element of its implementation scheme is that schooling performance—the system's performance—is linked in part to the outcomes of professionalized training. In historical context, this means that perhaps for the first time, jobs and rewards for administrators of large American school systems will be based not only on how well athletic programs perform, how well students place in college and score on SAT tests, but also on how well everyone else in the system does in the job market.

School systems can also build on the lessons of the in-school apprenticeship pilot projects sponsored by the U.S. Department of Labor, which began in 1977. As Robert Glover reports, pilot projects operated in eight areas with a variety of sponsors, including local school districts, state education agencies, community colleges, and nonprofit corporations.[25] The projects clearly demonstrated the feasibility of the approach. By July 1981, nearly fifteen hundred apprenticeship programs were operational, and over three thousand youth had become apprentices. In four of the eight pilot sites, the projects continued after federal monies ran out.

The costs were extremely low, averaging only $1,384 per apprentice, including money spent to subsidize employers. Moreover, the low-cost projects worked nearly as well as more expensive alternatives. On the other hand, local projects often utilized, but did not compensate, apprenticeship field staff and cooperative education coordinators. In a national or statewide program, these positions would have to expand significantly.

Not everything ran smoothly in the projects. It took a few years to develop the close working collaboration among schools, apprenticeship agencies, and employers. It became clear that participation by small employers was most effective if they joined employer associations to sponsor the apprenticeship. The occupations covered a somewhat narrow range, with half in metalworking, auto mechanics, or small-engine repair.

The results were highly positive. Nearly all (95 percent) of student apprentices expressed satisfaction with the experience. Most employers also approved, as indicated by the fact that 63 percent had already recommended the program to other employers. No net-benefit estimates are available.

Expanding from pilot projects to a statewide and nationwide effort can be gradual but should be steady. To help the program reach the largest number of disadvantaged youth, federal and state funds should give most encouragement to inner-city high schools in large cities. This is where the most concentrated, long-term poverty is.

However, federal and state agencies should avoid limiting the program to inner-city schools. Otherwise, the programs will be viewed as another effort to channel black youth into marginal or dead-end careers. One possibility is to vary the matching amounts so as to make the program least costly in the target areas.

Broadening internships and apprenticeships in American high schools should increase the productivity and earnings of all noncollege youth, including disadvantaged youth. If internships covered a wide range of occupations, the program will appeal to students from all income groups who prefer not to attend college. After all, college is an expensive and risky alternative in terms of years of lost earnings, high tuition, and uncertainty about the ability to translate coursework into occupational success. In countries where apprenticeships play a central role in youth education and training, many students from upper-middle-class families and able to attend college choose to take apprenticeships. Many apprenticeship programs lead to as much occupational prestige as do college programs. Moreover, some internships such as in drafting and technical testing, might subsequently lead to college for successful completers. A student who wanted to become an architect might first take an apprenticeship in carpentry and then move to the university for the architectural program.

The evidence from foreign countries is highly persuasive, concerning the feasibility and durability of broad-based internship/apprenticeship programs. Germany's economy has gained substantially, not lost, from their system of intensive early training in specific career streams. Apparently, the common criticism that skills training becomes obsolete within a few years has little validity in Germany, Austria, and Switzerland.

Beatrice Reubens reports that other European countries are learning to shift toward industry-based training. She points out the "growing unanimity on the need for a large part of the school-based training to occur in actual workplaces."[26]

Some might regard the development of internships as creating a second-class education system. In fact, it would greatly improve career options for noncollege youth in general. The new system would be especially beneficial to black and economically disadvantaged students who do not attend college. They are less likely than other youth to have confidence that their school performance will influence their job opportunities. The availability of internships will encourage them that their behavior and academic abilities can have an immediate impact on their career chances. Unlike white noncollege youth, blacks lack the informal channels and credible references that lead to good jobs. Black young men face a special stigma of belonging to a group with high crime rates and low basic skills. The formal mechanisms associated with internships will connect black youth with jobs as well as help employers know about the background of the young men they are hiring and training. Finally, going to a work site will draw ghetto youth away from the often-destructive peer pressure and toward the peer group of the people working at the company.

Although there are few internship projects with detailed information on the special gains for minorities and disadvantaged, there is evidence that programs using work-site education and training are appealing. Consider the St. Louis Off-Campus Work-Study program, which provides on-the-job training to high school seniors (mostly minorities) in coordination with school activity. Students take general courses in the morning and go to training stations in companies in the afternoon. Supervisors from the businesses monitor closely the work and training components. The overall results in terms of job placement and continuing education have been excellent. Rich's Academy in Atlanta, Georgia, is another example of work-site training and education that has worked effectively for low-income and minority students.

While the program is likely to benefit disadvantaged and other noncollege youth, employers must benefit for the program to succeed. There are several reasons for expecting benefits for individual employers.

- Improved recruiting and screening. The school's increased attention to guidance, and to providing firms with reliable information about individuals, would improve the match between workers and firms at little added cost to employers.
- Extensive control over training. Giving employers resources and control over training will give them a better chance to develop a well-qualified work force than will accepting what other institutions deliver.
- Building up a work force that has knowledge and experience with a large number of tasks. Evidence from Germany suggests that firms achieve high productivity partly because many of their senior workers have a broad understanding of all of the production processes.

Employers as a group would gain from the system's ability to increase the number of productive workers, including the supply of employees with occupational skills and experience. This advantage could prompt employer associations to encourage internship programs.

While the internship strategy can benefit students and employers, it is important to recognize the potential tension between the interests of each party. Employers may be especially interested in providing highly specific training well-tailored to their firm. This may be most helpful to the firm in the short run as well as limit the graduate's options once she or he completes the program. Concerns about worker mobility may prompt schools to insist on highly general training. Such an approach may drive away even employer associations, may limit training slots, and may give graduates too little of a salable skill. Thus, programs should be strike the appropriate balance between current relevance and breadth.

CONCLUDING COMMENTS

The development of internship programs in high schools offers the potential for exerting a major positive impact on the earnings and career options of disadvantaged youth. And success in achieving these goals is likely to yield important social effects, including the reduction of crime, drug use, and high rates of out-of-wedlock childbearing. At the same time, the internship approach is a broad-based program that can command wide public support, both for spreading benefits across a large group and for doing so largely by improving productivity. Unlike marginal, highly targeted programs, the internship approach will help disadvantaged youth succeed within the regular school system.

The emphasis on hands-on training as well as decentralized training away from youth peer pressure is likely to encourage disadvantaged youth to stay in school. Even school-based vocational education has a positive impact on school retention of minority students. A more formalized program that has close connections with employers and attractive careers is almost certain to do better.

The shortcomings of the approach have most to do with implementation and potential misperceptions about tracking. As the pilot projects indicate, effective implementation takes time and local initiative. No large federal allocation can quickly produce action. Employers must become convinced of the efficacy of the approach, small firms must utilize employer associations, and agencies, schools, and employers must work to specify competencies that are worthwhile and testable. Actors must be able to widen the range of occupations beyond the traditional mechanical skill and construction fields into financial services, food services, and health occupations.

Some advocates might view the internship approach as another effort to channel black and low-income students into marginal, dead-end jobs. Allaying concerns of this kind is another reason for making the internships reach middle-class noncollege youth as well as disadvantaged youth and for having internships in a wide range of occupations.

Another potential shortcoming is that internships pressure young people into making career decisions at too young an age. This is a legitimate concern, that can be partly overcome by making sure that interns take enough academic studies to graduate high school and by developing internships that encompass a broad area. However, in part, internships are intended to give students a greater sense of responsibility. Perhaps more important, delaying entry into career training is likely to make it too late for many disadvantaged youth. They will have already dropped out of school and perhaps other social institutions as well.

Ultimately, the most important barrier to success is the availability of internship slots. Even in Germany, where the apprenticeship system is deeply rooted, a high unemployment period generated some shortages of slots and fears of large-scale shortfalls. In the event, German employers came through with adequate numbers of apprenticeships, and the system has maintained broad support.

It is unclear whether an internship/apprenticeship approach can generate enough enthusiasm for U.S. employers to develop and maintain large numbers of positions in a wide range of occupations. But if they do, the new policy is likely to have the rare distinction of both making our economy more efficient and helping low-income families.

NOTES

This paper draws on joint research conducted with Hillard Pouncy. Partial funding came from the Council of State Planning Agencies (CSPA) and Office of the Assistant Secretary for Planning and Evaluation (ASPE), Department of Health and Human Services. The author thanks these agencies for their support. Of course, the opinions expressed in this paper are those of the author and do not necessarily represent those of ASPE or CSPA.

1. The 1974-88 numbers are from newly tabulated poverty counts in which the Census Bureau uses an improved adjustment for infla-

tion. See U.S. Bureau of the Census, Current Population Reports, P-60, No. 166, *Money Income and Poverty Status in the United States: 1988*, U.S. Government Printing Office, Washington, D.C., 1989, Appendix F, 129.

2. It is interesting that while the declines in births took place in the turbulent '60s and early '70s, most of the decline in marriage did not occur until the 1975-84 period.

3. See Robert Moffitt, "Incentive Effects of the U.S. Welfare System: A Review," *Journal of Economic Literature*, forthcoming.

4. In the 1965-69 period, about 80 percent of both white and black 20- to 24-year-old men had jobs. Black male 16- to 19-year-olds had already fallen behind by 1960.

5. Charles Murray argues that Great Society social policies actually were the root cause of the rising joblessness of black youth. See Charles Murray, *Losing Ground* (New York: Basic Books, 1984). Many take issue with Murray's analysis and argue that the chronic recessionary conditions of the 1970s bore primary responsibility.

6. See Gordon Berlin and Andrew Sum, *Toward A More Perfect Union* (New York: Ford Foundation, 1988).

7. Robert Lerman and Hillard Pouncy, *Effective Transitions: A Job-Based Strategy for Raising the Earnings of Black Young Men*, unpublished manuscript, Brandeis University, 1989.

8. The figures in this paragraph come from John Markey, "The Labor Market Problems of Today's High School Dropouts," *Monthly Labor Review* June 1988, 36-43.

9. Berlin and Sum, *Toward a More Perfect Union*, 19.

10. See William J. Wilson. *The Truly Disadvantaged: The Inner City, the Underclass, and Public Policy* (Chicago: University of Chicago Press, 1987).

11. Berlin and Sum, *Toward a More Perfect Union*.

12. Richard Freeman, *The Overeducated American* (New York: Academic Press, 1976).

13. John Bishop, "Occupational Training in High School: When Does It Pay Off," *Economics of Education Review* 8 (no. 1, 1989), 1-15.

14. Lauren Resnick, "Learning in School and Out," *Educational Researcher*, December 1987. In a more recent article, Resnick argues that even basic literacy should be viewed in terms of the link between abstract reading and writing skills and their applications related to the

immediate goals of the student. See "Literacy In School and Out," *Daedalus*, Spring 1990.

15. Markey, "Labor Market Problems," reports data from the High School and Beyond survey in which about 35 percent of male dropouts gave "school not for me" and 36 percent gave "had poor grades" as the reasons for dropping out. In New York City, a dropout prevention program providing special guidance services and other training failed to improve grades, attendance, or graduation rates. See Joseph Berger, "Dropout Plans Not Working, Study Finds," *The New York Times*, 16 May 1990, B1-B2.

16. The numbers in this and the following paragraphs come from the *First Interim National Assessment of Vocational Education*, U.S. Department of Education, Washington, D.C., January 1988.

17. One study found that taking one vocational course during ninth, tenth, and eleventh grade lowered dropout rates from 20 percent to 14 percent. Among dropout prone youth, taking two vocational courses per year for four years could increase graduation levels from 64 to 76 percent. See Bishop, "Occupational Training in High School."

18. See, for example, Alan Gustman and Thomas Steinmeier, *The Relationship Between Vocational Training in High School and Economic Outcomes*, National Bureau of Economic Research, Cambridge, Massachusetts, July 1981.

19. See Paul Campbell, Karen Basinger, Mary Beth Dauner, and Marie Parks, "Dynamics of Vocational Education Effects on Labor Market Outcomes," National Center for Research in Vocational Education, Columbus, Ohio, 1987. Campbell et al. found that in comparing blacks and whites who took similar educational programs and had similar personal characteristics, race no longer exerted an independent effect on employment rates and hourly earnings.

20. In a recent book, a group of French sociologists have documented the impacts of the these alternative educational and employment systems. See Marc Maurice, Francois Sellier, and Jean-Jacques Silvestre. *The Social Foundations of Industrial Power: A Comparison of France and Germany* (Cambridge: MIT Press, 1986).

21. See Bishop. "The Productivity Consequences of What Is Learned in High School," *Journal of Curricular Studies* 22 (no. 2), 101-126.

22. See Steven Greenhouse, "An Unstoppable Export Machine," *The New York Times*, 6 October 1988, D1-D7.

23. See David Nasaw, *Schooled to Order: A Social History of Public Schooling in the United States* (New York: Oxford University Press, 1979), 123.

Contemporary Public Discourse

24. Diane Ravitch, *The Schools We Deserve* (New York: Basic Books, 1985), 15-16.

25. Robert Glover, "Collaboration in Apprenticeship Programs: Experience with In-School Apprenticeship," in *Collaboration: Vocational Education and the Private Sector, 1984 Yearbook of the American Vocational Association* (Arlington, VA: American Vocational Association, 1985).

26. Beatrice Reubens, "Vocational Education in Other Countries," in *Education and Work, Eighty-first Yearbook of the National Society for the Study of Education, Part 2*, Harry Silberman, ed. (Chicago: University of Chicago Press, 1982).

JUDITH D. AUERBACH

11

Public Policy and Child Care: The Question of Quality

While child-care has become an increasingly salient issue with the rise in mothers' labor-force participation during the past two decades, only in the last few years has it been significantly addressed in public legislation.

Since President Nixon's veto of the Comprehensive Child Development Act in 1971—a bill that by most accounts would have provided a national system of child-care services—child-care has been treated as a private, family concern. Indeed, during the years of the Reagan administration, which reflected the most rapid rise in the labor force rates of mothers of very young children as well as in the number of single-parent households headed by women, federal child-care policy was characterized by cutbacks, decentralization, deregulation, and privatization (Kahn and Kamerman 1987). The most significant change was the 1981 conversion of Title XX funds—the chief source of child-care spending—into social service block grants administered by the states at their discretion, which resulted in tremendous variation among states in child-care delivery and funding. As a result of this conversion, proposed minimum standards for federally subsidized programs were eliminated.[1] Consequently, states implemented a wide range of regulatory policies, in many cases cutting the monitoring and enforcement of standards they previously performed. In total, Title XX funding was cut by 21 percent between 1981 and 1983, eliminating most money earmarked for child-care (Blank 1984).

Privatization of child-care during the eighties was furthermore encouraged by the institution of the Child Care Tax Credit and by incentives for employers to provide child-care benefits to their employees. While providing some financial and informational assistance to many parents, neither of these approaches did much to enhance the total supply and quality of child-care programs in the country (Auerbach 1988b). Overall, this policy approach exacerbated the child-care problems of most families, especially those earning low or moderate incomes and working for less than benevolent employers.

The general failure of privatized arrangements to address the real needs of working families has led us finally to begin reconsidering the role of government in providing child-care services to all in need. Beginning in the One-hundredth Congress, a number of significant child-care bills emerged—the first concerted effort toward comprehensive national child-care since 1971. Although it is tempting to think that this new interest is inspired by a growing concern for the well-being of children, I argue in this paper that something else is going on. An examination of recent policy debates reveals that beneath the current urgency about child-care lies a greater concern about the nation's economic future. In particular, the focus on *quality* care reflects the belief that early childhood experiences are essential in shaping future adult performance and that children subjected to less than adequate care are at risk of becoming poor economic actors when they grow up. Consequently, the persuasive argument for policymakers is that ignoring the need for good-quality child-care in the current period will place the nation's economic future at risk.

Although this formulation has strategic significance for child-care advocates—in that national economic self-interest sells a bill better than compassion—it is a distortion of what child-care policy ought to be about; that is, ensuring a sufficient supply of good-quality, affordable arrangements that have at their core the immediate, as well as long-term, health and developmental needs of children.

Over the past few years, the debate about appropriate child-care policy has revolved around two seemingly opposed perspectives. The first, usually identified with Democrats, may be called a "grants-based" approach. Proponents argue that the federal government should take a direct role in enhancing the supply, affordability, and quality of child-care services across the nation by granting money to the states to expand and improve their existing programs and to develop new ones. Furthermore, it is generally argued, in order to eliminate the wide diversity in quality of care among the states, the federal government ought to introduce a set of national standards of care with which all recipients of funds should comply.

The other approach, more popular among Republicans, is the "tax credit" or "voucher" approach. Proponents argue that the only appropriate role of the federal government is to give money directly to parents—through a tax credit or a voucher— and let them spend it on child-care however they wish. They argue further that the federal government has no right to impose one set of standards on the different states and to determine who should be caring for children: the choice should in all cases be left to parents.

Different versions of these two positions appear in all the significant child-care bills introduced during the last congressional sessions of the 1980s and reflect opposing ideologies and definitions of quality care.

One of the first significant child-care bills of the One-hundredth Congress was the Child Care Act of 1987, introduced by Representative Nancy Johnson (R-Connecticut). This bill allocated $300 million in federal funds to set up a system of child-care certificates. Families with incomes below 200 percent of the poverty level would be eligible for these certificates, which could be applied to child-care in licensed centers or registered or licensed family day-care homes. Family day-care providers would be required to *register* with the state immediately but would be given three years to meet *licensing* standards. In addition to providing certificates, the bill required state or local agencies to conduct outreach programs to all providers by offering training assistance and support services. Furthermore, any parent who applied for a certificate would be provided with information about state standards, parental support groups, how to select quality care, and where to file a complaint.

According to Johnson's staff, the aim of the Child Care Act, as evidenced in these provisions, was threefold: The act was intended to "(1) help poor working families find and afford child-care; (2) encourage unregulated family day care providers to emerge from underground and upgrade their services; and (3) assist parents in choosing the best care for their children" (Ceja 1987, 4-6).

While Johnson's bill aimed at the bottom-line issue of supply, it was harshly criticized for its leniency with regard to licensing requirements. Its most outspoken critic was the Children's Defense Fund (CDF), represented by Marian Wright Edelman, president, and Helen Blank, director of the child-care division, who argued that allowing family day-care providers to receive public funding for three years without meeting their states' licensing standards "trades off one essential feature of child-care (basic safety standards) for another (increased supply)"; furthermore, they argued, "by sanctioning unlicensed child-care, this bill actually undermines state and local protections for children" (Edelman and Blank 1987, 5-6).

Implicit in the CDF critique of Johnson's Child Care Act is the notion that licensed care equals quality care and unlicensed care equals nonquality care. Licensing requires meeting certain standards relating to group size, staff/child ratios, staff training, physical space, nutrition, health, and safety. If these standards are met, child-care is considered to be of quality; if they are not, child-care is considered not to be of quality. According to Edelman and Blank, the implication of funding unregulated child-care during the three years allowed under Johnson's bill is that it "would create the possibility that tens of thousands of low-income children will be warehoused in potentially harmful child-care situations" (Edelman and Blank 1987, 5-6). As it is, they argued, the range in licensing standards among the states is so broad that, in some states, one child-care worker could be responsible for as many as eight infants at a time. This puts children at great risk of insufficient care and attention and makes evident the need for a set of model federal standards.

This concern about quality care, coupled with a general, long-standing commitment to protecting the interests of children, prompted the CDF, along with about two hundred other organizations, to sponsor an alternative bill, which became known as the Act for Better Child Care Services, or "ABC." The bill, introduced in the Senate in November 1987 by Christopher Dodd (D-Connecticut) and in the House by Dale Kildee (D-Michigan), authorized $2.5 billion in federal money in the first year, with a 20 percent match by states, to help states make child-care more affordable for low-income families, to make child-care standards more uniform across states, to increase the status of the child-care profession by providing money for expanded training and higher wages, and to enhance the supply of different child-care services. Seventy-five percent of the funding would be available only to families earning up to 115 percent of a state's median income (adjusted for family size).

All providers of child-care services who applied for funding under the act would have to be licensed or meet specific regulatory standards established by the state. States' standards would have to comply with minimal federal standards that would be established by the act. Indeed, one of the more significant aspects of the original ABC legislation was its provisions for enhancing the states' licensing and regulatory procedures. Funds would be used to ensure that licensing staff received training in child development, health and safety, and relevant law enforcement. These staff members would have responsibility for inspecting child-care facilities on a regular basis.

This provision, coupled with enhanced training and compensation of child-care staffs, was intended to ensure quality of care in programs receiving federal and state assistance. Quality is implicitly defined in the bill as meeting certain licensing standards and having staffs with particular training who receive reasonable compensation. Indeed, the argument was made that improved salary and compensation for child-care workers would attract "better" people into the child-care field, thereby improving the quality of care provided.

While the ABC bill had widespread support, one of its strongest critics was Utah Republican Senator Orrin Hatch (who, ironically, later became a chief cosponsor of the legislation). He argued that the ABC legislation was too expensive, gave too much control to the federal government, and did not directly enhance the supply of child-care. In reaction, Hatch introduced his own bill into Congress, called the "Child Care Services Improvement Act." This bill provided much less federal money ($375 million in the first year), emphasized community-controlled child-care, and encouraged an increase in the absolute supply of services. It authorized $250 million to be used as seed money by states to fund a variety of child-care programs in neighborhoods and communities, provided $100 million for states to establish liability insurance pools for licensed providers, and allocated $25 million to assist states in developing a revolving loan fund for child-care providers to make improvements required to meet licensing standards.

In addition, the Child Care Services Improvement Act encouraged expanding employers' involvement by providing a tax credit for those that establish on-site child-care programs and that include a child-care benefit as an option in cafeteria benefit plans. Finally, it provided an additional personal exemption for mothers who stay home with a newborn at least six months.

In all these ways, the bill was seen by Hatch to take a "supply-side" and "bottom-up" approach: "It is designed to *increase* the number of child-care slots in a variety of settings which will not only help reduce costs, but also will provide parents with greater options. It is an attempt to get at the root causes of child-care shortages: lack of capital financing, liability, and tax burden" (How S.1678 . . . differs 1987, unpaginated).

Unlike the ABC or Johnson's Child Care Act, Hatch's bill did not have an income test—all families were eligible for financial assistance—although it did include a sliding fee schedule to accommodate income differences. And unlike the ABC bill, which would require the federal government to establish standards for child-care providers, Hatch's bill gave responsibility to the states, arguing that "federal standards cannot possibly account for regional differences in the supply and variety of child-care. Federally determined quality standards may have adverse impacts in many states or might fail to reflect cultural or economic factors" (How S.1678 . . . differs 1987, unpaginated).

These three bills, then, all were concerned about the quality of child-care services but differed in their interpretations of what that means. Johnson's Child Care Act implies that quality is not entirely separable from quantity, that providing more child-care services is as important to children's well-being as ensuring that programs meet certain standards. In fact, Johnson pointed out, ensuring compliance with licensing standards does not ensure quality. If safety is one measure of quality, then there are plenty of instances of licensed child-care programs that are not of quality, as evidenced by claims and lawsuits against them alleging physical, sexual, and psychological harm to children.

A different approach to quality is presented in the Hatch bill, which suggests that quality might be a function of ethnic, class, religious, and community *values*, which cannot be reflected in a set of uniform standards. What one parent thinks is quality may not be what another parent thinks is quality. The issue is, who is to say which parent's notion is the appropriate one—the federal government, states, local communities, or individual families?

The proponents of the ABC bill would argue that there are fundamental notions of quality about which most people agree, regardless of their backgrounds—notions especially about health and safety. Beyond these, there are aspects of quality care that have been determined by years of scholarly, scientific research in child development and care. These aspects include consistency of caregiver, individualized attention, and social and educational stimulation—all of which are believed to be necessary for fostering the social, emotional, and cognitive development of the child. Supporters of ABC would argue that child-care legislation should aim to ensure the existence of these aspects in all child-care services and that we should not be supporting with federal dollars services in which these are absent.[2]

Through the normal course of the political process, the three bills discussed here underwent a tremendous amount of change and compromise—none was passed in its original form. By the middle of the 101st Congress, ABC had become the chief legislative vehicle for child-care in the Senate, and Orrin Hatch had become one of its chief cosponsors. The compromise version of the bill, which passed in the Senate in June 1989, no longer contained federal standards or incentive grants to states to improve their own licensing standards. It did contain a provision that required the states to give parents the option to take their assistance in the form of vouchers rather than channeling all funding into program grants.

In the House, major provisions of ABC were incorporated into a more comprehensive bill, introduced by Gus Hawkins (D-California), chair of the Education and Labor Committee, which included additional provisions for expanding the Head Start program and school-based child-care. Eventual compromise legislation, passed in March 1990, provided for additional Title XX block-grant funding earmarked for child-care (instead of establishing a new grant program, as ABC would do) and included expansion of the Earned Income Tax Credit for low-income families. It also required states to give families the option of receiving child-care vouchers that could be used in church-based care; and it authorized funds to encourage employer-supported child-care.

The compromise bills carved out in both houses of Congress illustrate the strength of ideological differences about definitions of quality child-care and the role of the government in general. Debate during the 100th and 101st Congress shifted back and forth from a focus on the appropriateness of setting federal standards, to a focus on the separation of church and state (the question of whether any federal funds could be applied to church-based child-care), to a focus on the notion of parental choice (i.e., whether parents should be given vouchers to apply to the program or individual caregiver of choice, regardless of licensing, church-state issues, etc.).[3]

This divergence in attitude about the nature of publicly supported child-care—including the question of quality—reflects ambivalence about its goals. For over a century, policy debates have centered around the question of whether the goal of child-care programs is to enable more mothers to work outside the home or to provide enriching experiences to children; whether child-care is "for women" or "for children." These goals are usually viewed as separate, and sometimes in conflict, and have resulted in the advocacy and implementation of different types of programs for different populations.

Child-care "for women" (which is often really child-care "for the state") has predominated government-supported programs since the mid nineteenth century (Auerbach 1988a). The day nurseries of that era, WPA nurseries during the depression, on- and off-site defense-industry centers during World War II, Kennedy's welfare assistance program of the early 1960s, and contemporary workfare programs in some states all have as their primary aim control over the employment of mothers and a reduction in the welfare rolls. With the exception of the defense-industry centers, they have been geared toward low-income, poor, and single mothers for whom employment is a compelling economic necessity. They have been primarily concerned with supervising, not necessarily educating, the children of these women; and their clients have been stigmatized for being in need of public assistance.

The only government-supported child-care program that is

evidently "for children" is Head Start, although, even with its clear educational emphasis, its association with the disadvantaged is strong. Aside from Head Start, most child-care programs with an explicit educational-enrichment component have been the domain of the private sector—particularly the system of nursery schools and preschools. On the whole, these programs are considered to be of high quality and are aimed at providing a supplementary educational experience to children from middle-class families in which the mother is not employed. Most nursery schools (and, until 1991, Head Start) are only part-day programs.

In sum, as one child-care analyst puts it, "our long term tradition of day care in America is one of supervision for the children of working mothers and 'enrichment' for the children of non-working parents who can afford it" (Gerald 1972).

This stratification of goals and services is precisely what is at the center of contemporary child-care policy debates. For years it has been taken for granted that quality child-care (as defined by the CDF and child development experts) is an expensive luxury, available only to those who can afford it and not possible to achieve in public programs. Providing a sufficient quantity of services to assist in the employment of parents rather than ensuring quality of services to assist in the development of children has been the primary concern of public child-care policy to date.

But this appeared to have changed by the late 1980s as the debate about comprehensive child-care legislation was renewed. As noted above, the bills introduced by Nancy Johnson, Orrin Hatch, Christopher Dodd, and Gus Hawkins all addressed the issue of quality head-on. Hearing testimony was garnered from child-care advocates and child development experts who cited studies attesting to the need to establish uniform standards for staff/child ratios and basic nutrition, health, and safety measures, as well as developmentally appropriate curricula. Horror stories were told about dangers posed to children in unlicensed programs, such as the toddler Jessica McClure's falling down the well in the yard of an unlicensed family day-care home.

Nevertheless, by 1990, the tenacity of child development experts and child-care advocates could not withstand the political pressure to compromise on the issue of federal standards, the chief measure of quality in the debate, in order to ensure that at least some comprehensive bill would pass. Consequently, most of the language relating to quality controls in programs with federal financing—whether grants, vouchers, or tax credits—was softened. For example, the ABC provision for federally mandated minimum standards for licensing was whittled down to federal incentives to states to develop their own standards and to improve the overall quality of their programs. Then these incentive grants were eliminated from the Senate's bill. The definition of quality was left to the states, as it has been all along.

What is significant throughout this process is that virtually no one was claiming that the federal government had no role in child-care, as had been argued vehemently in the past. Rather, the debate was about what the *appropriate* role of government was, and arguments over quality and standards reflected ideological differences about federalism more than a dispute about the need for quality care.[4]

Why, after so many years of declining federal activity on child-care in favor of privatized solutions, did the push for public programs reemerge when it did? For years, as the number of employed and single mothers increased precipitously, advocates had been calling for more government child-care services, but their calls had been unheeded. What changed in the late 1980s? I believe the main catalyst was a growing fear that appropriate childhood socialization is not being experienced in an increasing number of families, and that this has implications for the future of the nation. This fear in turn stems from the changing social position of mothers.

In the American past, employed, poor, and single mothers were the exception to the "normal," nuclear family structure and were therefore viewed as deviant, even pathological. Providing child-care services to these women was a necessary evil, a way of protecting society from problems of child neglect and delinquency.[5] The essential goal of early public assistance was providing custodial care where mothers were unable to provide it themselves, as it was assumed in the "normal" situation they would.[6] So long as *most* mothers were not employed and were at home, child-care, for all but the deviant mothers, was a private matter; it was assumed that most mothers were "doing their job."

But now that a majority of mothers with preschool-age children are employed, coupled with the tremendous growth in single-parent families and poverty among women and children, we no longer make this assumption. Indeed, the very nature of the "job" is being reconceptualized. Responsibility for child-care is shifting from the private to the public sphere as mothers themselves are moving from the private to the public sphere (and fathers are not, on the whole, taking on any more child-care responsibility). In other words, as women become redefined as public persons (through work, political participation, homelessness, etc.), so do their children.[7] Consequently, how children should be cared for becomes appropriate for public debate.

For years, the dominant sociological paradigm of the family argued that in modern industrial society, the family's primary function is the socialization of children (Parsons and Bales 1955). This is accomplished by a division of labor by gender, in which the father works outside the home, connecting family to the public world through his role as breadwinner, and the mother works inside the home, providing emotional support and nurturance as well as performing necessary domestic tasks. The childrearing role of the mother provides the most fundamental context of socialization, as it is in their relationship to their mother as a primary object that children begin to develop socially appropriate personalities and identities. This entire arrangement is considered (by functionalist sociologists) to be essential for the maintenance of social order. Thus, when it is altered, as is now the case with the employment of mothers and the absence of fathers in many families, the question of how the socialization function will be fulfilled becomes a public concern.

The contemporary emphasis on quality as a necessary component of public-supported child-care represents an attempt to ensure that certain aspects of the mother-child relationship that sociologists and child development experts have determined to be essential for the proper individual and social development of children are reproduced in alternative child-care arrangements. In the absence of good-quality care, children are considered at risk of improper social, emotional, and cognitive development.

But rather than having the immediate well-being and healthy development of children for children's own sake as its central concern, the contemporary child-care policy debate is really about children's future adult roles. Specifically, children are viewed not so much in the present moment, but as the workforce of tomorrow.

This orientation has resulted from the popularization of demographic and labor force projections, such as those published in the widely disseminated *Workforce 2000* (Hudson Insti-

tute 1987), which assert that current trends in birthrates, marriage and divorce rates, and migration mean that new entrants
into the work force by the year 2000 will primarily be women,
racial/ethnic minorities, and immigrants. Low birthrates among
native-born Americans, combined with increased immigration
among non-English-speaking people, point to a shrinking labor
pool in absolute numbers and especially of skilled workers. As
we shift further toward a service economy, language, communication, and technical skills—skills that are predicted to be lacking among future recruits in the absence of interventions—will
become increasingly important in jobs. If we wish to remain
competitive as a nation in the world economy, this argument
goes, then we will have to invest a great deal in the better training of this future work force. Good-quality child-care then
becomes an important first step in this preparation; and the
rationale for federal child-care support is the buzzword *competi-
tiveness.*

This formulation has been adopted by virtually everyone
lobbying for federal child-care legislation in the latter years of
the twentieth century, including members of Congress and children's-issues advocates. Noting the change in interest since she
had unsuccessfully introduced child-care legislation ten years
earlier, Representative Cardiss Collins testified in the floor
debate for H.R. 3:

> Today, however, everybody understands that the care of
> our children is the most important thing that we can do
> for our Nation as a whole. Additionally, we find that this is
> not just a children's issue, but it is a national economic
> issue. It is one that is necessary so that our economy can
> begin to grow stronger and so that the parents of children
> can work with the satisfaction of knowing that their chil-
> dren are going to be well provided for.[8]

Her comments were typical of those made by many others in
support of H.R. 3.

Perhaps more surprising is the wholehearted endorsement
of this argument by Marian Wright Edelman, president of the
Children's Defense Fund, a woman considered to be the nation's
leading advocate for children. For years, Edelman and other
advocates had been trying to sell child-care policy as "the right
thing to do" for children. But this proved ineffective. Only as

the nation's economic self-interest and "doing the right thing" converged did child-care become more marketable; for the sake of action, Edelman was willing to appropriate the sales pitch. In an article discussing the link between social policy and economic policy (Edelman 1989), she argued:

> The child of today is the worker of tomorrow. We say and hear this phrase over and over again—so often that we barely consider its implications. The opportunities available to a child help determine not only his or her eventual self-sufficiency or lack thereof, but also the degree to which that child becomes a productive adult who contributes to building the nation's economy. (324)

Good-quality child-care and early childhood education are important, Edelman said, because "too many of our children are growing up ill-equipped to succeed in the world economy, let alone to generate the level of income supports that will soon be needed by aging parents and grandparents" (342). Furthermore, she asserted, our demographic destiny makes support for these programs a necessity:

> As the 1980s draw to a close, we are struggling to increase productivity and restore our competitiveness in world markets. We are experiencing the pain that comes from being bested by nations that have placed a higher priority on preparing all of their children for productive roles in the national economy. We must act now to reverse the effects of the trends that are crippling our future work force at an early age. A commitment to providing early childhood education is more than a logical extension of the commitment we already make to children from five to eighteen, and to college students. It is a national imperative. As the population of youth declines, every one of our children becomes more precious to us, not just to our families but to our economy (349).

It is easy to understand why this formulation has been endorsed by child-care advocates: national economic self-interest sells better than compassion, especially in the world of politics and business. Advocates for employer-supported child-care have used this approach since the 1970s, arguing to individual employers that providing a child-care benefit to employees would reduce the costs of attrition, absenteeism, and tardiness due to unstable child-care arrangements, and ultimately it would improve their profits. Advocates knew that this was the only way to convince employers that they ought to get "in the business of child-care" (Auerbach 1988a). Now, the argument for enlightened self-interest is extended to the whole nation.

But equating support for child-care with the nation's economic future is a dangerous approach, because, to my mind, it distorts what child-care policy ought to be about: children. Casting the importance of support services to children primarily in terms of their future contribution as adults suggests we don't imbue any immediate value to children. It also sets us up to ignore their real needs and capacities. In this age of the "hurried child," we ought to be wary of imposing adult expectations on children too young to live up to them. We should celebrate, rather than rush, childhood, and we should work to make that experience as good as it can be for all children. As a nation, we have already begun to see the implications of not doing so, in drug addiction, homelessness, poverty, poor educational performance, and physical and mental abuse among children. These social problems attest to our lack of commitment to protecting and caring for our children.

Political pragmatism requires both rhetorical and substantive concessions, but we must be mindful in the case of child-care policy not to make them at the expense of the very people we wish to help. Whether or not we agree that federally mandated minimum standards are the essential ingredient for ensuring quality in publicly funded child-care throughout the states, we must put the immediate health, safety, and developmental needs of children foremost, simply because it *is* the right thing to do. We must express love and concern for children for what they are, not for what they will become.

NOTES

1. In 1968, a committee of policymakers and child development experts, under the auspices of the Department of Health, Education, and Welfare, developed a set of standards, called the Federal Interagency Day Care Requirements (FIDCR), which were to be incorporated into national child-care policy, but were abandoned with the conversion of Title XX funds into social service block grants.

2. One of the strongest proponents of federal child-care standards, the National Association for the Education of Young Children (NAEYC), has lobbied hard for its own criteria of quality care. These include age-specific criteria in areas such as staff qualifications and development, administration, staffing, curriculum, physical environment, health and safety, nutrition and food, interactions among the staff and children, and interactions among staff and parents. For details see NAEYC, *Accreditation Criteria and Procedures* (Washington, D.C.: NAEYC, 1984).

3. See the *Congressional Record* of June 21-23 (Senate) and 29 March 1990 (House).

4. See, for example, the debate over H.R.3 in the *Congressional Record*, 29 March 1990, H1257-H1339.

5. Some have argued that this was the main motivation for the infant schools of the nineteenth century. See, for example, Pence 1986.

6. The assumption that poor women and families fail to properly care for their children, which has dominated public policy approaches, is deemed patronizing by Carol Stack (1980).

7. The notion that definitions of motherhood and childhood are socially constructed and change over time is advanced in a number of works by social scientists and historians, including Badinter 1980, Kessen 1979, Liljestrom 1983, Schutze 1987, and Kaestle and Vinovskis 1978.

8. *Congressional Record*, 29 March 1990: H1274.

REFERENCES

Auerbach, Judith D. 1988a. *In the business of child care: Employer initiatives and working women.* New York: Praeger.

Auerbach, Judith D. 1988b. The privatization of child care: The limits of employer support. Paper presented at the annual meeting of the American Sociological Association, Atlanta, Georgia.

Badinter, Elisabeth. 1980. *Mother love: Myth and reality.* New York: Macmillan.

Blank, Helen. 1984. *Child care: The states' response. A survey of state child care policies 1983-1984.* Washington, D.C.: Children's Defense Fund.

Ceja, Kathryn Stern. 1987. A good solution. *American Family* 10:4-6.

Edelman, Marian Wright, 1989. Economic issues related to child care and early childhood education. *Teachers College Record* 90 (3): 342-51.

Edelman, Marian Wright, and Helen Blank. 1987. Not the answer. *American Family* 10:5-6.

Gerald, Patricia. 1972. The three faces of day care. In *The future of the family*, ed. Louis Kapp Howe, 268-82. New York: Simon & Schuster.

How S.1678, the "Child Care Services Improvement Act," differs from S.1885, the "Act for Better Child Care (ABC)." 1987. Washington, D.C.: Office of Senator Orrin Hatch.

Hudson Institute. 1987. *Workforce 2000: Work and workers for the twenty-first century.* Indianapolis: Hudson Institute.

Kaestle, Carl F., and Maris A. Vinovskis. 1978. From apron strings to ABCs. In *Turning points: Historical and sociological essays on the family*, ed. John Demos and Sarane S. Boocock. Chicago: University of Chicago Press.

Kahn, Alfred J., and Sheila B. Kamerman. 1987. *Child care: Facing the hard choices.* Dover, Mass.: Auburn House.

Kessen, William. 1979 The American child and other cultural inventions. *American Psychologist* 34:815-20.

Liljestrom, Rita. 1983. The public child, the commercial child, and our child. In *The child and other cultural inventions*, ed. Frank S. Kessel and Alexander W. Siegel. New York: Praeger.

Parsons, Talcott, and Robert F. Bales. 1955. *Family, socialization, and interaction process.* Glencoe, IL: Free Press.

Pence, Alan R. 1986. Infant schools in North America. In *Advances in early education and day care*, ed. Sally Kilmer, vol. 4. Greenwich, Conn.: JAI Press.

Schutze, Yvonne. 1987. The good mother: The history of the normative model, 'mother-love.' *In Sociological studies of child development*, ed. Patricia A. Adler and Peter Adler, vol. 2. Greenwich, Conn.: JAI Press.

Stack, Carol. 1980. Comments on Caldwell's paper. In *Care and education of young children in America: Policy, politics, and social science*, ed. Ron Haskins and James J. Gallagher. Norwood, N.J.; ABLEX.

JAMES GARBARINO
KATHLEEN KOSTELNY

12

Public Policy and Child Protection

INTRODUCTION

When we talk about policy, we are talking about what we think is desirable and attainable, somehow in the same breath. We're talking about a statement of will, a statement of goals, and the social maps that we see giving us the route to attain these goals. Or as someone else once put it: "Policy is what you preach; practice is what you do."

What are the central social policy issues when it comes to children? Some of us, sometimes, take the easy way out and more or less say that our social policy ought to be to end poverty, racism, violence, and sexism, period. But sometimes when people talk about social policy, they have in mind something much more specific. In the first years of the Reagan administration, issues of child and family services and support had become very politicized, in the sense of becoming very much a partisan political issue. At a seminar in which he spoke about his research on the impact of early nutrition on child development, a researcher who had worked for many years in Latin America presented a sophisticated, technical exposition of the results of his work on the impact of early nutritional supplement programs and their effects on birth weight and brain growth. At the end of this very technical presentation, in the question period, someone asked him the major public policy implication of his work. He thought for a moment and said, "Vote Democratic."

POLICY MODELS FOR UNDERSTANDING CHILD PROTECTIVE SERVICES

What about policy in the United States with regard to child protection? Just how child-centered is it? We can address this question by discussing a series of issues we face in making social policy about children, youth, and families. The first reflects our conception of how the problem of troubled families fits into the broader society.

We often hear voiced the view that the child abuse and neglect we see is simply the tip of the iceberg and the problem deep into our society and is somehow tied to problems of race (and racism), gender (and sexism), and social class (and classism).

But there is another view. Its adherents argue that child abuse and neglect are really the result of specific and identifiable individual families' being in trouble, families that exist within a basically justifiable, basically good society—mere "ice cubes" of trouble floating in a buoyant society. Incidentally, although this view developed as a way to look at child abuse and neglect, we can apply it to a whole range of problems—teenage parents, low-birth-weight infants, and child mortality, for example.

Is child maltreatment simply the result of problem people? Or do the experiences and behaviors of these people reflect something wrong in the social structures of the community? The answer we give to that question has many implications for the policy and practice of child protection, particularly when it comes to prevention.

One approach to preventing child maltreatment says that there is no programmatic approach that makes any sense whatsoever. The only way to think about preventing child maltreatment is to think about total social reform. From this view one might argue, we aren't going anywhere unless we end poverty, racism, and sexism, and do it by uprooting those problems right from the heart of the society.

The other view says that we need not engage in total social reform to prevent child maltreatment, but can do something that might be called "patchwork prevention." Following this metaphor, on a cold night, a stack of small patches of cloth won't keep us warm; but if we somehow stitch them together into a quilt, then we can put that over us and stay warm. Patchwork prevention implies that we can find a set of programs, no one of which independently produces total social reform but that when put together in a coherent package will prevent child maltreatment. When the community stitches together all of the elements of a comprehensive program, the result is sufficient social influence to achieve prevention.

Having to choose between a total social reform orientation and a patchwork prevention approach presents a troublesome and challenging dichotomy for us because there are many pressures—political pressures, pressures in our culture—that make us *want* to believe in a patchwork prevention approach. It doesn't rock the big boat of social class. It doesn't put us in conflict with powerful, entrenched economic interests. It makes it possible for corporations to support child abuse prevention efforts because they do good but don't threaten the fundamental status quo. That has a lot of appeal.

In fact, there's some evidence that this kind of approach to preventive services *can* make a real difference. For example, recent evidence from Western Europe tells us that big preventive effects on infant mortality are to be had through a patchwork approach. There, governments have set standards for prenatal care and postnatal support that have both preserved the current socioeconomic and political order and resulted in declining infant mortality rates.

On the other hand, we can't lose sight of the fact that total social reform may be what it takes to change some of the big problems. That dichotomy puts a lot of pressure on us, as people interested in child protection, because it forces us to live in a kind of schizophrenic state. Indeed, years ago a colleague remarked that "to get along in the twentieth century, you really must manage as an ambulatory schizophrenic." By that he meant that we're constantly faced with the fact that some of the things that need doing are awesome, if we really think about them. We have to get up every morning knowing that there are enough nuclear weapons in the world to target every community of fifteen hundred people or more with its own thermonuclear weapon. We have to know that the ozone layer is eroding. We have to know that the ice caps may be melting. We have to know that massive economic inequality continues and racism persists. We have to know all of this and yet get up in the morning, brush our teeth, give our kids breakfast, send them off to school, do the laundry, and go to our jobs—perhaps in the field of child protection.

We have to live as ambulatory schizophrenics if we are to wrestle with the problem of preventing child maltreatment. That's the way the world comes to us. We must neither forget the impulse to total social reform while we do small good works nor simply sit back saying, "I'll wait to do my program until reform comes." Children can't wait.

METAPHORS FOR PROTECTIVE SERVICES

Assuming we see our way clear to proceed with a patchwork approach to child protection, how do we decide how specifically to target our programs? A group of Canadian government policymakers couched this issue as one of "pudding" versus "salad." They explained that the pudding approach meant mixing together all of your child protection efforts into one approach. The salad model meant that you kept all the programmatic elements distinct, although they might operate under the umbrella of some large agency. A pudding approach makes a lot of sense for preventing child maltreatment, where you want a few powerful homogeneous prevention programs that reach broadly, that will do a lot of things at once. Home health visitors, for example, can do good on many fronts all at once—including child protection (cf. Olds et al., 1986).

But for treating problems once they come about, you should recognize a need to be specialized, as in the case of intrafamilial and extrafamilial sexual abuse. A policy issue that we have to face is to find the best balance of generic preventions and specialized prevention.

INCORPORATING THE ROLE OF HUMAN BIOLOGY

Another issue we have to face is the role of biological investment in shaping the dimensions of the child protection problem. Daly and Wilson (1984) have computed the risk to children of various kinds of harm as a function of how close they are to a family with two biologically related parents, (that is, biologically related to the child). Moving across a continuum in which there is less and less biological connection between the adults who care for children, the level of risk increases, ultimately by a factor of forty to one. Many of us recognize that one of the situations associated with jeopardy for children and accounting disproportionately for child protection problems is the young mother caring for a child in the presence of a biologically unrelated male.

Why is that biologically unrelated male such a threat to the child? Perhaps one reason is that there isn't the same biological investment in the child (Trivers 1972). That child represents for that man something very different from what that child represents to a biological father—not continuity but sexual discontinuity (i.e., that the mother has had a previous sexual life). Of course, the genius of human society lies partly in overcoming such biological probabilities. However, when we seek to do so as a matter of personal practices, we should make it a matter of well-supported policy and take precautions to minimize the harm when we fall short of our goals. We haven't quite found a way to work recognition of this biological investment factor into our child protection policy.

HOW FAR INTO THE POPULATION AT RISK DO PROGRAMS REACH?

Another issue in child protection policy is the issue of "skimming" versus "program reach." We have known for many years that when we offer a program, particularly a prevention program, the easiest people to reach are the people who have an edge already. Twenty years ago, the early Head Start intervention programs demonstrated the principle that "those who have the most, gain the most." This becomes important when thinking about policy for child protection, because it is very tempting to simply lay out the program and skim off the cream of the crop, even the cream of the high-risk crop.

Thus, one set of measures for evaluating the soundness of our prevention programs has to be whether they reach down and out to the down and out in the society. How far do they reach now? How far could they reach? What does it take to participate in a program? How does policy motivate and reward program reach and discourage skimming?

A related question is whether our program activities really involve prevention of child abuse or only family enhancement. Enhancing already adequate functioning families can certainly be a route to prevention, and it is a worthwhile endeavor. However, in the child abuse field we have a real risk that programs will present themselves as prevention programs but may in fact only be enhancement programs. Such programs reach only people who are *not* at significant risk for child abuse and neglect, but they do succeed in enhancing their functioning by making them better parents. This is a laudable goal, but we shouldn't confuse it with preventing child abuse and neglect. If we know that the vast proportion of child abuse and neglect occurs among 10 to 20 percent of our population, and if our programs don't reach that 10 to 20 percent, then we aren't significantly preventing child abuse. If we only reach the people marginally at risk, enhance their functioning, make them better parents, and make their children develop better, we are improving the social environment, whatever we *aren't* doing.

WHAT IS THE COST OF DECREASING RISK FOR CHILDREN?

The problem of enhancement versus prevention is an issue in sexual abuse prevention programs aimed at young children. There is some evidence that programs that try to reach children, reach most effectively the same children who learn how to read well, who learn how to do arithmetic well, who do well in everything in school. Thus, rather than preventing sexual abuse (in the sense of decreasing incidence), we may simply be concentrating the likelihood of victimization in that group of kids who do not learn very well in school or may not be in school.

This problem with enhancement and skimming is a particular concern in the United States, because our strategy of choice is often volunteerism. We ask, Who would like to be part of this prevention program? We should be asking, How do we make sure that everyone who needs this prevention program gets it?

Another policy issue we face is the question of how to allocate the costs of child protection efforts. One of our persistent problems is that we attempt to allocate the costs of prevention too narrowly, on a categorical basis. Going back to the pudding and salad metaphor, if we indeed adopt a pudding approach to prevention, it means that we think a few key preventive interventions will succeed with respect to a wide range of problems. Therefore, we must insist that the costs of those programs be understood in terms of all the various things they might prevent. This produces a lower "cost per success" than does conventional categorical accounting.

A good example comes from the Home Health Visitor Program, conducted by David Olds and his colleagues in Elmira, New York (Olds et al. 1986). Olds's project is cited often because it is one of the few that combines both a strong intervention with a strong piece of research. Home health visitors (registered nurses) in the primary experimental condition began visiting high-risk young parents prenatally and continued for as long as two or three years after the birth of a child. That intervention was contrasted with three other conditions: home health visitors whose visits began after the child was born; families who didn't get a home health visitor at all but simply had access and transportation to a regular clinic; and still others whose only extra service was routine developmental screening of the children.

Olds found that the poor, teenage, unmarried mothers who were in the home health visitor program starting prenatally evidenced dramatic and significant preventive effects, in contrast to the other groups. What were the effects of the home health visitor program, which costs about $2,500 per family?

One effect was reduced child abuse in the first two years of life. Among this high-risk group of mothers, about 4 percent ended up being reported for abuse and neglect in the first two years of life, as compared to about 19 percent of the group that did not get the home health visitor prenatally. If the only justification for the program's cost were its prevention of child abuse, however it looks like an expensive program to run.

Of course, every prevention of serious physical abuse may mean a great deal financially (let alone morally). If we prevent the permanent placement of a child or the permanent hospitalization of a child, hundreds of thousands of dollars are saved.

Indeed, the home health visitor program conducted in Denver in the 1970s offered just such a cost-effectiveness rationale. They were able to prevent five cases of serious hospitalization (out of one hundred families served), one of which called for lifelong nursing care. Even at two thousand dollars a family, preventing one bill for two hundred thousand dollars is doing a lot of good and doing it cost-effectively.

However, the key to Olds' study, and the beauty of it, lies in the fact that it didn't simply stop with cost-effectiveness in terms of preventing cases of child abuse. The home health visitor program reduced prematurity rates, increased birth weight, decreased smoking during pregnancy, decreased accidental ingestions of poison in the first years of life, and improved the mother's attitude and her perception of the child. One of the most important findings was the dramatic reduction of the likelihood of a second pregnancy within thirteen months of the first birth: from approximately 60 percent in the comparison group to about 20 percent in the group who got the home health visitor starting prenatally.

These results permit us to draw some powerful inferences: If we allocate the cost of the home health visitor across all of those areas—and probably even delinquency, teenage years, illiteracy, and school failure—we see an intervention that more than pays for itself. So the policy question becomes, From whose budget do we fund prevention programs?

PAYING FOR PREVENTION PROGRAMS

One of our advocacy efforts has to be to insist that key prevention programs like prenatal home health visitors ought to be paid for by many different budgets, because they have their effects across the board, not just in child protection. We recognize, and we have to point out to policymakers, that the families that "produce" child maltreatment are also linked to delinquency, infant mortality, and illiteracy.

If one works in a small community, one often knows the families by name. Case workers in big cities often lose that connection, due to agency specialization and sampling from a much bigger pool of families. Agencies may deal exclusively with runaways, abused teenagers, infant mortality, or child abuse. And yet, these are often the same people, if not concurrently, then at least sequentially (and across generations).

THE ROLE OF COMMUNITY DIFFERENCES

We have to recognize the policy issues that arise from community variations. A colleague of ours used to say, "No one lives in the United States. People live in Omaha, or Louisville, or the South Side of Chicago." Of course, what he meant was that while there are some national effects, the actual experience of families comes from the communities they live in. Some effects come from the state, some even come from the neighborhood.

Consider an example of how dramatic those community effects can be. It is often reported that identical twins grow up with very similar IQ scores. What often isn't reported is that identical twins growing up in very dissimilar communities end up much less similar than identical twins growing up in similar communities—with the correlation between their IQ scores being more like .2 or .3 (not a strong relationship) than .8 or .9 (a very strong relationship). Even something as fundamental as the expression of genetic heritage in IQ can differ in twins who grow up in different communities.

In a sense we live in one world. In a sense we live in one society. In a sense we live in fifty states. But really we live in over three thousand counties in the United States. And those variations are important, particularly in the area of child protection, where county-based systems dominate the scene (even when formal authority lies with a statewide system).

THE ROLE OF THE COMMUNITY IN SETTING
MINIMAL STANDARDS FOR THE CARE OF CHILDREN

Where shall we set the minimum standard of care for children? The process of setting that standard is a negotiation between professional expertise and scientific knowledge, on one hand, and community standards, values, or culture, on the other, and we are constantly renegotiating. For example, thirty years ago, if you drove a car with an infant sitting on your lap or a two-year-old standing on the front seat, and you unintentionally hit a lamp post and the child went through the windshield, the injuries to your child would have been considered an "accident," much as it would be if you had your child sitting with you in a theater and a chandelier fell on his head.

But over the last thirty years, there has been an effort to build up a knowledge base about automotive safety. We know now that children's riding unrestrained is high-risk behavior. There is a relatively simple technology for preventing harm to children in automobiles—60 percent of the injuries and 90 percent of the fatalities.

Eventually, what was previously considered an accident came to be redefined as a "preventable accident"—that is, the most progressive, informed parents who have the most resources will do something to take preventive measures against such injuries.

Twenty-five years ago, there were few people who were taking steps. By the 1970s, however, there was widespread recognition that this clearly was a preventable accident, even though only 25 percent of American parents were doing something about it.

This set the stage for the next step in moving the process forward. Advocates maintained that it was not enough to classify these injuries as results of preventable accidents. They argued that we knew enough to call these events "negligence." Having made that decision, they set out to change the minimal standard of care: it is an act of negligence to drive a car containing a child who is not protected against injury. Making this declaration does not mean full compliance, of course. For example, in Illinois, after the law went into effect, only 50 percent of the parents were meeting their obligation. But progress is made by implementing the policy changes that result from progressively upgrading the minimum standard.

INFANT MORTALITY

We have seen minimal standards change most clearly in the area of infant mortality rates, of course, which have dropped dramatically in the last fifty years. Building a knowledge base about what it takes to produce a healthy infant permitted dramatic declines in mortality rates for infants and mothers in this century. Now maternal and infant deaths are rare in most parts of most communities. So the question becomes, Where do we set that minimum standard of caring? How do we make it higher, and how do we come up with the resources to make sure people meet it?

HOW BIG A ROLE FOR SOCIAL CLASS?

The second policy question is related to the first. Will we allow social class (or, more precisely, poverty or low incomes) to determine basic life prospects for children? The power of low income in predicting infant and child morbidity, child abuse, and other forms of developmental pathology is not established. In some communities and societies, it is a much more powerful predictor than in others. In most European countries now, low income is a much less powerful predictor of child outcome than it is in the United States. In our research of child abuse rates, for example, we found that social class/low income is a very powerful predictor of the amount of child abuse and neglect in neighborhoods within American cities (Garbarino and Sherman 1980; Garbarino and Kostelny 1990).

Why? One key is whether or not having a low income means lack of access to, or lack of utilization of, basic prenatal and postnatal health care. Many observers have reported that the link between low income and access to services is much stronger here than it is in other modern industrial societies. Thus, the question of policy becomes, Will we *allow* low income to be a powerful predictor of child mortality, morbidity, and pathology? It is one thing to say that social class is a powerful predictor of lifestyle—whether you drink white wine, whether you watch PBS, whether you eat brie. In most moral systems those kinds of cultural differences linked to socioeconomic differences are acceptable. But the policy question we have to face is this, in addition to liking white wine, watching PBS, and eating brie, should you also have a very small chance of having a child die in the first year of life, having a child be born with disabilities or fail in school, becoming involved in child maltreatment? Are those equivalent things?

For our society, it is a genuine question. In Chicago's seventy-seven community areas the rate of infant mortality varies from about four per thousand to about thirty per thousand. Virtually all of the difference is attributable to the presence of low-income and minority families.

Some people worry that the gap is growing still wider in recent years and will continue to grow wider as our economy becomes more dichotomous between rich and poor and, for children, protected and unprotected.

BALANCING PRIVACY AND CHILD PROTECTION

The third policy question is, Are we willing to "compromise" privacy and autonomy to prevent child maltreatment? Or

do we view a high level of child maltreatment (with its attendant mortality, morbidity, and pathology) as the cost of doing
business in a free society? In Chicago, a task force empowered to
look at deaths of children whose families enter the protective
services system has highlighted a situation that illuminates this
issue.

Many times the task force is confronted with situations of
repeated child maltreatment. A family brings a child with serious physical injury to the hospital. The child is removed from
the home. The mother disappears. A year later, the mother
brings her new injured child into the hospital. The child dies.
Where was that mother? Is there not some way that we could
have known that she had a baby? Some say no, she has a right to
her privacy and freedom of movement, to be presumed innocent and competent until proved otherwise in regard to each
individual child. Some say that these deaths are the price we
must pay for a free society.

What follows is the policy statement developed by this task
force in an attempt to protect children from harm by binding
high-risk parents to the community:

> The Department of Children and Family Services (DCFS)
> will assure that its own risk assessment system is used to
> allocate priority ratings for follow-up unit use in allocating
> resources. Thus, DCFS supervisors will ensure timely and
> effective transition from investigation to follow-up units in
> cases where risk assessment indicates high probability of
> serious harm to a child. As efforts proceed to develop special
> assessment procedures for determining high risk for child
> fatality and other serious outcomes, these procedures will be
> incorporated into the ongoing risk assessment process.
> Where indicated cases involve serious injury or an assess-
> ment that serious injury is probable, a special tracking sys-
> tem will be begun. Where there is involvement of the courts
> in the case, DCFS will seek to include in all court orders a
> mandate for periodic follow-up to determine the family's
> status and composition. Where there is no involvement of
> the courts, DCFS will itself place a high priority on tracking
> such families, with one possible outcome being the filing
> of court orders to mandate contact with the family. This will
> include all cases in which children have been removed from
> the home. The maximum period between reviews will be

two months. The term of this special concern will extend through the family's child bearing years or until there is clear evidence that risk has been reduced to low levels.

If caseworkers are unable to verify the family's status as a result of the two month periodic review, they will initiate an immediate trace procedure for locating the family. This will include Department of Public Aid, Department of Public Health, schools, and any other agencies that may be of assistance in locating "missing" families. The process will also include the use of prior addresses and other personal contacts.

The purpose of the periodic review is first to provide a check on changes in family composition and status, and second to provide an occasion for revising the level of risk attributed to the family. Thus, the periodic review might lead to a new assessment of overall risk (either lower or higher). This in turn would lead to new recommendation for case management and perhaps the filing of court orders. Information resulting from such reviews will be made available to all relevant involved parties (e.g., the child's attorney, court personnel, other professionals involved in the case).

DCFS will employ a computer-assisted system for implementing these policies. This system will generate requests for verification of status and location for all families included in the "dangerous" category. This computer-assisted system will aid supervisors as they maintain quality control over the case management process. The system will generate reports for supervisors of its requests to caseworkers for verification of family status, and will document caseworker response.

WHAT KIND OF SOCIETY PERMITS CHILD ABUSE?

The DCFS statement (which has not been implemented fully) and the policy it represents may serve as a kind of litmus test for policymakers. Some say that they would like child abuse to be prevented, but that preventing all child abuse would require living in a prison-like society, which would be undesirable. Is the prison the model for a preventive society? Is it such an invasion of privacy to say that every pregnant person in America should have a home health visitor who comes in a supportive role and who represents the community? Is that fundamentally different from creating a system for "tracking" high-risk families? If we say that's compromising freedom, we're also saying that it is a person's right to drive around with a young child in the front seat of their car unprotected. And of course in many states there are attempts to repeal those car seat laws claiming that they are invasions of privacy.

WHAT ARE THE CULTURAL PRECONDITIONS FOR A FAMILY SUPPORT POLICY TO PREVENT CHILD MALTREATMENT?

This leads to the fourth policy question: Do we have the will to implement full-fledged family support systems to protect children from maltreatment? We must keep in mind that the concept of support systems derives from Gerald Caplan's formulation in the mental health movement thirty years ago. At the core of this formulation is the idea that a support system combines nurturance *and* feedback. Support is not simply the giving of resources, of strokes, of nurturance. It is also the coupling with feedback, guidance, and information.

In David Olds's study the same home health visitors who were providing nurturance and support were also providing feedback. In several cases, they persuaded young pregnant women that they were unable to care adequately for their impending children, and they negotiated a settlement that led to an adoptive placement at birth for some of those kids as a way of preventing later harm. These are real support systems, because they provide nurturance and feedback *in the same relationship.* The villain is isolation from prosocial support systems. Some of those support systems are the natural corrective mechanisms of day-to-day life that one has in relationship with people. Some of them require deliberate intervention to produce.

Underlying all of these issues is the question, Who is responsible for children? We don't ask who "owns" the children. We object to viewing children as property. So we respond that the question really is, Who is responsible for children? Who has custody for children? John Demos, the American historian, has looked back three centuries and found there was a very strong answer in Puritan New England. In the Puritans' view, children were God's children, and therefore the church had direct responsibility for them. Demos's documentation includes church councils and church elders making declarations along these lines: "Family Smith, you're not taking care of God's child. We demand that you do. We're God's representatives; take care of the child!" In the Soviet Union, families were viewed as taking care of children on behalf of the state; the child was first and foremost a citizen. Families have been delegated the responsibility of caring for young citizens.

Decades ago, people said the idea that the state could compel people to register children for school was an intrusion on family privacy. It was un-American, and it threatened the fabric of our society. (Of course some people still say that.) Some people argue, "Who are you to tell me that I should have my child inoculated against childhood diseases? If I want my child to have the measles, plague, and diphtheria, that's my right as an American citizen." In most communities, we have said, "No, I'm sorry, that isn't your right." It's interesting how the AIDS issue is bringing up some of those same questions again. Does an individual have the right to infect another person? Does being an American give one the right to do as one pleases? We are in a helpless, hopeless crunch until we develop an ideology that says the community is really responsible for children. Part of that responsibility means that the community ought to know where the children are. We not only don't know where the children are, we don't know how many they are, what their status is, or what's happening with them. We don't even know how many children are in foster care, let alone how many children are in the community.

Who has custody of children? One model says the family has custody—period. If that family really screws up, *then* we will take that right away, and the community will assume custody. That's not a healthy model for public policy to protect children.

Another model says the family has custody, but the community has visiting rights, the community has a basic right to know what's going on with *its* kids. That's a better model if the goal is child protection.

But even further, we might choose a model that says family and community have joint custody for children and decisions about their lives should be reached jointly. It's a joint responsibility to care for them and make sure they're being cared for. The evidence on joint custody arrangements in the microenvironment of two parent families gives us pause about this model, however. It appears that joint custody depends upon the parties having enough regard for the children and for each other to put aside whatever issues separate them in favor of the greater good of the child. It's not easy between former spouses. One danger is that the child will feel secure and stable with neither parent (rather than with both, as is the goal). It remains to be seen whether joint custody arrangements involving the parents and the community can be made to work.

CONCLUSION

We have to work to answer all of the many tough policy questions we face, from the position that these are *our* children and we all have a stake in how they turn out. Such a statement is the foundation for an effective policy of child protection. Once we make a commitment to such a policy, the problems that remain are those of implementation. We have not reached that point yet in American discussion of public policy and child protective services.

REFERENCES

Daly, M., and M. Wilson. 1984. Child abuse and other risks of not living with both parents. *Ethnology and Sociobiology* 6:197-210.

Garbarino, J., and K. Kostelny. 1990. A model for assessing child abuse and neglect. Erikson Institute, Chicago.

Garbarino, J., and D. Sherman. 1980. High risk neighborhoods and high risk families: The human ecology of child maltreatment. *Child Development* 51:188-98.

Olds, D., C. Henderson, R. Chamberlan, and R. Tatelbaum. 1986. Preventing child abuse and neglect. *Pediatrics* 78:65-78.

Trivers, R. L. 1972. Parental investment and sexual selection. In *Sexual selection and the descent of man*, ed. B. Campbell. Chicago: Aldine.

Contributors

Judith Auerbach, "Public Policy and Child Care: The Question of Quality"

Professor Auerbach is a lecturer at the University of California Los Angeles, Department of Sociology. Her M.A. and Ph.D. are both from the University of California at Berkeley, 1981 and 1986 respectively, in sociology. Professor Auerbach's expertise is in the sociology of the family, child care, and gender studies. Her most current publication is *In the Business of Child Care: Employer Initiatives and Working Women*, forthcoming.

P. Lindsay Chase-Lansdale with **Maris A. Vinovskis**, "Adolescent Pregnancy and Child Support"

Professor Chase-Lansdale is currently Fellow for Developmental and Family Research, the Chapin Hall Center for Children, and assistant professor, the Irving B. Harris Graduate School of Public Policy Studies, both at the University of Chicago. She received her Ph.D. in developmental psychology from the University of Michigan in 1981. Her expertise is in the areas of adolescent parenthood, maternal employment, poverty, and divorce, as well as the interface between research and social policy for children and families. Her most current publications are: "Research and programs for adolescent mothers: Missing links and future promises," *Family Relations*, Special Issue, "Adolescent Pregnancy and Parenting: Interventions, Evaluations, and Needs," (1991) with J. Brooks-Gunn and R. Paikoff; and "The Children of the NLSY: A unique research opportunity for developmentalists," *Developmental Psychology* (1991) with F. Mott, J. Brooks-Gunn and D. A. Phillips.

Hamilton Cravens, "Child Saving in Modern America 1870s-1990s"

Professor Cravens is professor of history at Iowa State University. He received his M.A. from the University of Washington in 1962, and his Ph.D. from the University of Iowa in 1969. Professor Cravens' expertise is in the area of history of children and history of science. He is the author of *The Triumph of Evolution: the Heredity-Environment Controversy, 1900-1941* (Baltimore: Johns Hopkins U. Press, 1988 [1978]), among other publications on the influence of evolutionary science in American culture, and "Child Saving in the Age of Professionalism, 1915-1930," in Hawes and Hiner, eds., *American Childhood* (Westport, CT: Greenwood Press, 1986). He has recently completed a book-length study of the Iowa Child Welfare Research Station. He wrote this essay while visiting scholar, Department of History and Davis Humanities Institute, University of California, Davis.

Michelle Fine, "Making Controversy: Who's at Risk?"
    Professor Fine is the Goldie Anna Charitable Trust Professor of Education at the University of Pennsylvania, and for the past three years has been the lead consultant for the Philadelphia Schools' Collaborative Restructuring Project. She received her M.A. and Ph.D. in psychology and social psychology from Teachers College, Columbia University in 1978 and 1980 respectively. Professor Fine's areas of expertise include adolescent dropouts, women with disabilities, and "at risk" youth. Her most current books include: *Framing Dropouts: Notes on the Politics of an Urban High School* (Albany: SUNY Press, 1991); and *Rethinking Silence and Privilege: Voices of Race, Class and Gender in U.S. Schools*, co-edited with Lois Weis (Albany: SUNY Press, 1992); and *Discriptive Voices: the Transgressive Possibilities of Feminist Research* (Ann Arbor: University of Michigan Press, 1992).

Patricia Gandara, "Language and Ethnicity as Factors in School Failure: The Case of Mexican-Americans"
    Professor Gandara is assistant professor of education, Division of Education, University of California at Davis. She has been program manager for education research for the California state legislature and a state commissioner for post secondary education. She received her M.S. at California State University, Los Angeles in 1972, and her Ph.D. at University of California at Los Angeles in educational psychology in 1979. Professor Gandara's expertise is in education policy, bilingual education and educational reform. Her most current publications are "The Politics of Self-Interest: Chicanos and Higher Education," *American Journal of Education*, vol. 95, no. 1, 1986, "Those Children are Ours: Moving Towards Community," *NEA*

Today, vol. 7, No. 6, and *Through the Eye of the Needle: Chicanos who pursue higher education,* forthcoming.

James Garbarino with **Kathleen Kostelny,** "Public Policy and Child Protection"

Professor Garbarino is president of the Erikson Institute for Advanced Study in Child Development. He received his M.A.T. and Ph.D. from Cornell University in 1970 and 1973 respectively in human development and family studies. Professor Garbarino's areas of expertise are in child and adolescent abuse and neglect, child abuse prevention, and children living amidst community violence. His most current in an extensive publishing record include, *What Children Can Tell Us* (San Francisco: Jossey-Bass, 1989), and *No Place To Be A Child: Growing Up in a War Zone* (New York: Lexington-Free Press, 1991).

Alan Gartner with **Dorothy Lipsky,** "Children at Risk: Students in Special Education"

Professor Gartner is professor in the Graduate School and University Center of City University of New York since 1976, and director of the Office of Sponsored Research and Project Planning also at the Graduate School and University Center, City University of New york. He received his M.A. in 1960 from Harvard University, and his Ph.D. from the Union Graduate School, Union for Experimenting Colleges and Universities in 1972. Professor Gartner's expertise is in education for the disabled. His most current publications include (coauthored) *Supporting Families with a Child with a Disability: An International Outlook* (Brookes Publishing, 1991); *Beyond Separate Education: Quality Education for All* (Brookes Publishing, 1989); *Caring for America's Children* (The American Academy of Political Science, 1989); and *Images of the Disabled/Disabling Images* (Praeger, 1987).

Michael Grossberg, "Children's Legal Rights? A Historical Look at a Legal Paradox"

Professor Grossberg is associate professor of history at Case Western Reserve University. He received his Ph.D. from Brandeis University in the history of American civilization in 1979. Professor Grossberg's areas of expertise are in the history of American law and social policy. He has published extensively on issues about families and the law, including *Governing the Hearth: Law and the Family in Nineteenth Century America* (Chapel Hill: North Carolina Press, 1985). He is presently working on a study of an

1840 child custody trial, *Motherhood on Trial: The d'Hauteville Case and Social Change in Antebellum America.*

Margo Horn, "Inventing the Problem Child: 'At Risk' Children in the Child Guidance Movement of the 1920s and 1930s"
Professor Horn is currently the director of academic courses and lecturer in history at Stanford University. She received her M.A. and Ph.D. from Tufts University in history in 1975 and 1980 respectively. Professor Horn's areas of expertise include the history of child guidance and mental health services to children. Her most recent publication is *Before It's Too Late: The Child Guidance Movement 1918-1945* (Philadelphia: Temple University Press, forthcoming).

Robert I. Lerman, "Reversing the Poverty Cycle with Job-Based Education"
Professor Lerman is chair of the Department of Economics at The American University. He received his Ph.D. in economics from Massachusetts Institute of Technology in 1970. Lerman's areas of expertise include poverty and welfare programs, youth employment programs and patterns, and family formation of young people. His most recent publications include: "The Compelling Case for Youth Apprenticeship," *The Public Interest,* Fall 1990, and "Income Inequality and Income Stratification," *Review of Income and Wealth,* September 1991. Professor Lerman is currently serving on a National Academy of Sciences panel examining the U.S. postsecondary education and training system for the work place.

Dorothy K. Lipsky with **Alan Gartner,** "Children at Risk: Students in Special Education"
Dr. Lipsky is superintendent for Riverhead (N.Y.) Central School District, and senior research scientist, the Graduate School and University Center, the City University of New York. She received her Ph.D. in educational psychology from Hofstra University in 1979. Dr. Lipsky's areas of expertise are in instructional strategies, restructuring schools to serve all students, and parental involvement in educational activities. She is co-author of *Supporting Families with a Child with a Disability* (Brookes Publishing, 1991); and author of "A Parental Perspective on Stress and Coping," *American Journal of Orthopsychiatry,* 55 (4) October 1985.

Steven Schlossman with **Susan Turner,** "Status Offenders, Criminal Offenders, and Children 'At Risk' in Early Twentieth Century Juvenile Court"
Professor Schlossman is director of the Center for History

and Policy and professor of history at Carnegie Mellon University. He received his M.A. degrees from the University of Wisconsin and Teachers College, and his Ph.D. in history from Columbia University in 1976. Professor Schlossman's areas of expertise include the history of criminal justice, public schooling, and professional education. Among his publications are: *Love and the American Delinquent: The Theory and Practice of "Progressive" Juvenile Justice, 1825-1920* (Chicago: University of Chicago Press, 1977), (with Susan Turner) *Race and Delinquency in Los Angeles Juvenile Court, 1950* (Bureau of Criminal Statistics, California State Department of Justice, 1990), and (with Mary Odem) "Guardians of Virtue: The Juvenile Court and Female Delinquency in Early 20th Century Los Angeles," *Crime and Delinquency* 37 (April 1991).

Joseph L. Tropea, "Structuring Risks: The Making of Urban School Order"

Professor Tropea is an associate professor of sociology at George Washington University. He received his M.A. in social sciences from Michigan State University in 1965, and Ph.D. in sociology from George Washington University in 1973. Professor Tropea's areas of expertise are the sociology of children and schooling, rational-legal order, and socio-economics. His most current publications include: "Bureaucratic Order and Special Children: Urban Schools 1950-1960s," *History of Education Quarterly*, vol. 27, no. 3, Fall 1987 and "Bureaucratic Order and Special Children: Urban Schools 1890-1940s," *History of Education Quarterly*, vol. 27, no. 1, Spring 1987; "Cocaine, Courts, and Constitutional Rights: Legal Reforms and State Power in the U.S.," in *Laws and Rights*, Vincenzo Ferrari (ed.), (Milan: Giuffri, 1991); and "Situationally Negotiated Transactions and Domination: From Tribe to Rational-Legal Order in the Anglo-American Legal Tradition," in *History of Criminal Justice: An International Annual* (forthcoming).

Susan Turner with **Steven Schlossman**, "Status Offenders, Criminal Offenders, and Children 'At Risk' in Early Twentieth Century Juvenile Court"

Dr. Turner is a member of the Criminal Justice Program at the Rand Corporation in Los Angeles. She received her M.A. and Ph.D. (1983) degrees from the University of North Carolina, where she served as research coordinator at the Institute of Government. Her areas of expertise include the evaluation of innovative programs in criminal justice, especially prison, probation, and intensive supervision programs. Her most recent publications include (with Stephen Klein and Joan Petersilia) "Race and Imprisonment Decisions in California," *Science 247* (February 1990), and (with Joan Petersilia) *Intensive Supervision Probation for High-Risk Offenders: Findings from Three California Experiments* (Santa Monica: Rand, December 1990, R-3936-NIJ/BJA).

Maris A. Vinovskis with **P. Lindsay Chase-Lansdale**, "Adolescent Pregnancy and Child Support"

Professor Vinovskis is professor of history and a research scientist at the Institute for Social Research, both at the University of Michigan. He received both his M.A. and Ph.D. from Harvard University in 1966 and 1975 respectively. Formerly, he was the deputy staff director of the U.S. House of Representatives Select Committee on Population and was a consultant to the Office of Adolescent Pregnancy Programs at the Department of Health and Human Services. Professor Vinovskis' most recent in an extensive publishing history are: *The "Epidemic" of Adolescent Pregnancy? Some Historical and Policy Considerations* (New York: Oxford University Press, 1988) and *Religion, Family, and the Life Course: Explorations in the Social History of Early America* (Ann Arbor, MI: University of Michigan Press, forthcoming) [with Gerald Moran].

Roberta Wollons, editor

Professor Wollons is currently a visiting professor at Doshisha University in Kyoto, Japan. She received her M.A. and Ph.D. from the University of Chicago in 1977 and 1983, respectively. Professor Wollons' areas of expertise are in the history of education and women's history. Her most recent publications are "Women Educating Women: The Child Study Association as Women's Culture," in Joyce Antler, ed. *Changing Education: Women as Radicals and Conservators* (Albany: SUNY Press, 1990), and *Educating Mothers: A Study in Voluntarism*, forthcoming.

Index

A

Abortion: legalization of, 203; teenage, 204

Absent fathers: and Aid to Dependent Children, 206-07; and child support, 202-03, 208-09, 210, 221; income, 218

Academic Training: versus vocational education, 244-45 (*see* Vocational Education)

Act for Better Child Care Services (1987), 263: and quality, 265; minimum standards, 268

Adaptive Learning Environments Model, 175

Adjustment: child guidance, 18; classes, 70, 72-73; and juvenile court, 39; progressive era, 4; and maladjustment, 18, 146

Adolescent Crime: and dropouts, 95 (*see* Status Offenses; Criminal Offenses)

Adolescent Health Services and Pregnancy Prevention Act (1978), 203

Adolescent Parenthood, 202-29: adverse impact of, 204; demographics, 203-04; and dropouts, 95; epidemic, 203; "female issue," 217; prevention of, 219; welfare costs, 202, 205; welfare system, 232 (*see* Out-of-Wedlock;

Teenage Parenting)

Aid to Dependent Children (1935), 206: discrimination in, 24, 206; in 1930s, 16; moral rehabilitation, 17; and father's death, 206

Aid to Families With Dependent Children (1950), 207: administrative costs, 208; alternatives, 209; and child support, 219; history of, 207-08; and teenage parenting, 205

Alimony: and divorce, 207

Apprenticeships, European, 245: Austria, 252; Germany, 238, 242, 243, 244, 252, 255; Switzerland, 243, 252

Apprenticeships, U.S.: colonial period, x, 205; disadvantaged youth, 243, 251-52; policy, 233 (*see also* Internships and Apprenticeships)

Apprenticeship Pilot Projects (1977): Department of Labor, 250-51

Assimilation: and education, 184-85; European immigrants, 191, 196; generational, 184; Mexican American, 185-87; model of, 193

Attendance: and child labor laws, 62; enforcement of, 78-79; and probation, 78; special schools, 79 (table 11)